# Across China on Foot

# Across China on Foot

Edwin John Dingle

ARC
**MANOR**
Rockville, Maryland
2007

ISBN: 978-0-9794154-5-6

Library of Congress Cataloging-in-Publication Data

Dingle, Edwin John.
  [Borderlands of eternity]
  Across China on foot / by Edwin John Dingle.
    p. cm.
  ISBN 978-0-9794154-5-6 (alk. paper)
  1. China--Description and travel. 2. Vietnam--Description and travel. I. Title.

  DS710.D62 2007
  915.104'35092--dc22
  [B]
                    2007022846

Published by Arc Manor
P. O. Box 10339
Rockville, MD 20849-0339
www.ArcManor.com

Printed in the United States of America

## In Grateful Esteem

During my travels in interior China I once lay at the point of death. For their unremitting kindness during a long illness, I now affectionately inscribe this volume to my friends, Mr. and Mrs. A. Evans, of Tong-Ch'uan-Fu, Yuen-Nan, South West China, to whose devoted nursing and untiring care I owe my life.

# Contents

# *Author's Note*

To travel in China is easy. To walk across China, over roads acknowledgedly worse than are met with in any civilized country in the two hemispheres, and having accommodation unequalled for crudeness and insanitation, is not easy. In deciding to travel in China, I determined to cross overland from the head of the Yangtze Gorges to British Burma on foot; and, although the strain nearly cost me my life, no conveyance was used in any part of my journey other than at two points described in the course of the narrative. For several days during my travels I lay at the point of death. The arduousness of constant mountaineering—for such is ordinary travel in most parts of Western China—laid the foundation of a long illness, rendering it impossible for me to continue my walking, and as a consequence I resided in the interior of China during a period of convalescence of several months duration, at the end of which I continued my cross-country tramp. Subsequently I returned into Yuen-nan from Burma, lived again in Tong-ch'uan-fu and Chao-t'ong-fu, and traveled in the wilds of the surrounding country. Whilst traveling I lived on Chinese food, and in the Miao country, where rice could not be got, subsisted for many days on maize only.

My sole object in going to China was a personal desire to see China from the inside. My trip was undertaken for no other purpose. I carried no instruments (with the exception of an aneroid), and did not even make a single survey of the untrodden country through which I occasionally passed. So far as I know, I am the only traveler, apart from members of the missionary community, who has ever resided far away in the interior of the Celestial Empire for so long a time.

Most of the manuscript for this book was written as I went along>—a good deal of it actually by the roadside in rural China. When my journey was completed, the following news paragraph in the North China Daily News (of Shanghai) was brought to my notice:—

"All the Legations (at Peking) have received anonymous letters from alleged revolutionaries in Shanghai, containing the warning that an extensive anti-dynastic uprising is imminent. If they do not assist the Manchus, foreigners will not be harmed; otherwise, they will be destroyed in a general massacre.

"The missives were delivered mysteriously, bearing obliterated postmarks.

"In view of the recent similar warnings received by the Consuls, uneasiness has been created."

The above appeared in the journal quoted on June 3rd, 1910. The reader, in perusing my previously written remarks on the spirit of reform and how far it has penetrated into the innermost corners of the empire, should bear this paragraph in mind, for there is more Boxerism and unrest in China than we know of. My account of the Hankow riots of January, 1911, through which I myself went, will, with my experience of rebellions in Yuen-nan, justify my assertion.

I should like to thank all those missionaries who entertained me as I proceeded through China, especially Mr. John Graham and Mr. C.A. Fleischmann, of the China Inland Mission, who transacted a good deal of business for me and took all trouble uncomplainingly. I am also indebted to Dr. Clark, of Tali-fu, and to the Revs. H. Parsons and S. Pollard, for several photographs[1] illustrating that section of this book dealing with the tribes of Yuen-nan.

---

1    The photographs were included in the original hardcover edition of the book but are not included in this edition —publisher

I wish to express my acknowledgments to several well-known writers on far Eastern topics, notably to Dr. G.E. Morrison, of Peking, the Rev. Sidney L. Hulick, M.A., D.D., and Mr. H.B. Morse, whose works are quoted. Much information was also gleaned from other sources.

My thanks are due also to Mr. W. Brayton Slater and to my brother, Mr. W.R. Dingle, for their kindness in having negotiated with my publishers in my absence in Inland China; and to the latter, for unfailing courtesy and patience, I am under considerable obligation. "Across China on Foot" would have appeared in the autumn of 1910 had the printers' proofs, which were several times sent to me to different addresses in China, but which dodged me repeatedly, come sooner to hand.

*Edwin Dingle*

HANKOW, HUPEH,
CHINA.

# BOOK I

# Introductory

*The scheme. Why I am walking across Interior China. Leaving Singapore. Ignorance of life and travel in China. The "China for the Chinese" cry. The New China and the determination of the Government. The voice of the people. The province of Yuen-nan and the forward movement. A prophecy. Impressions of Saigon. Comparison of French and English methods. At Hong-Kong. Cold sail up the Whang-poo. Disembarkation. Foreign population of Shanghai. Congestion in the city. Wonderful Shanghai.*

*T*hrough China from end to end. From Shanghai, 1,500 miles by river and 1,600 miles walking overland, from the greatest port of the Chinese Empire to the frontier of British Burma.

That is my scheme.

I am a journalist, one of the army of the hard-worked who go down early to the Valley. I state this because I would that the truth be told; for whilst engaged in the project with which this book has mainly to deal I was subjected to peculiar designations, such as "explorer" and other newspaper extravagances, and it were well, perhaps, for my reader to know once for all that the writer is merely a newspaper man, at the time on holiday.

The rather extreme idea of walking across this Flowery Land came to me early in the year 1909, although for many years I had cherished the hope of seeing Interior China ere modernity had robbed her and her wonderful people of their isolation and antediluvianism, and ever since childhood my interest in China has always been considerable. A little prior to the Chinese New Year, a friend of mine dined with me at my rooms in Singapore, in the Straits Settlements, and the conversation about China resulted in our decision then and there to travel through the Empire on holiday. He, because at the time he had little else to do; the author, because he thought that a few months' travel in mid-China would, from a journalistic standpoint, be passed profitably, the intention being to arrive home in dear old England late in the summer of the same year.

We agreed to cross China on foot, and accordingly on February 22, 1909, just as the sun was sinking over the beautiful harbor of Singapore—that most valuable strategic Gate of the Far East, where Crown Colonial administration, however, is allowed by a lethargic British Government to become more and more bungled every year—we settled down on board the French mail steamer *Nera*, bound for Shanghai. My friends, good fellows, in reluctantly speeding me on my way, prophesied that this would prove to be my last long voyage to a last long rest, that the Chinese would never allow me to come out of China alive. Such is the ignorance of the average man concerning the conditions of life and travel in the interior of this Land of Night.

Here, then, was I on my way to that land towards which all the world was straining its eyes, whose nation, above all nations of the earth, was altering for better things, and coming out of its historic shell. "Reform, reform, reform," was the echo, and I myself was on the way to hear it.

At the time I started for China the cry of "China for the Chinese" was heard in all countries, among all peoples. Statesmen were startled by it, editors wrote the phrase to death, magazines were filled with copy—good, bad and indifferent—mostly written, be it said, by men whose knowledge of the question was by no means complete: editorial opinion, and contradiction of that opinion, were printed side by side in journals having a good name. To one who endeavored actually to understand what was being done, and whither these broad tendencies and strange cravings of the Chinese were leading a people who formerly were so indifferent to progress, it seemed essential that he should go to the country, and there on the spot make a study of the problem.

Was the reform, if genuine at all, universal in China? Did it reach to the ends of the Empire?

That a New China had come into being, and was working astounding results in the enlightened provinces above the Yangtze and those connected with the capital by railway, was common knowledge; but one found it hard to believe that the west and the south-west of the empire were moved by the same spirit of Europeanism, and it will be seen that China in the west moves, if at all, but at a snail's pace: the second part of this volume deals with that portion of the subject.

And it may be that the New China, as we know it in the more forward spheres of activity, will only take her proper place in the family of nations after fresh upheavals. Rivers of blood may yet have to flow as a sickening libation to the gods who have guided the nation for forty centuries before she will be able to attain her ambition of standing line to line with the other powers of the eastern and western worlds. But it seems that no matter what the cost, no matter what she may have to suffer financially and nationally, no matter how great the obstinacy of the people towards the reform movement, the change is coming, has already come with alarming rapidity, and has come to stay. China is changing—let so much be granted; and although the movement may be hampered by a thousand general difficulties, presented by the ancient civilization of a people whose customs and manners and ideas have stood the test of time since the days contemporary with those of Solomon, and at one time bade fair to test eternity, the Government cry of "China for the Chinese" is going to win. Chinese civilization has for ages been allowed to get into a very bad state of repair, and official corruption and deceit have prevented the Government from making an effectual move towards present-day aims; but that she is now making an honest endeavor to rectify her faults in the face of tremendous odds must, so it appears to the writer, be apparent to all beholders. That is the Government view-point. It is important to note this.

In China, however, the Government is not the people. It never has been. It is not to be expected that great political and social reforms can be introduced into such an enormous country as China, and among her four hundred and thirty millions of people, merely by the issue of a few imperial edicts. The masses have to be convinced that any given thing is for the public good before they accept, despite the proclamations, and in thus convincing her own people China has yet to go through the fire of a terrible ordeal. Especially will this be seen in the second part of this volume, where in Yuennan there are huge areas absolutely untouched by the forward movement, and where the people are living the same life of disease, distress and dirt, of official, social, and moral degradation as they lived when the Westerner remained still in the primeval forest stage. But despite the scepticism and the cynicism of certain writers, whose pessimism is due to a lack of foresight, and despite the fact that she is being constantly accused of having in the past ignominiously failed at the crucial moment in endeavors towards minor reforms, I am one of those who believe that in China we shall see arising a Government whose power will be paramount in the East, and upon the integrity of whose people will depend the peace of Europe. It is much to say. We shall not see it, but our children will. The Government is going to conquer the people. She has done so already in certain provinces, and in a few years the reform—deep and real, not the make-believe we see in many parts of the Empire to-day—will be universal.

Between Singapore and Shanghai the opportunity occurred of calling at Saigon and Hong-Kong, two cities offering instructive contrasts of French and British administration in the Far East.

Saigon is not troubled much by the Britisher. The nationally-exacting Frenchman has brought it to represent fairly his loved Paris in the East. The approach to the city, through the dirty brown mud of the treacherous Mekong, which is swept down vigorously to the China sea between stretches of monotonous mangrove, with no habitation of man anywhere visible, is distinctly unpicturesque; but Saigon itself, apart from the exorbitance of the charges (especially so to the spendthrift Englishman), is worth the dreary journey of numberless twists and quick turns up-river, annoying to the most patient pilot.

In the daytime, Saigon is as hot as that last bourne whither all evil-doers wander—Englishmen and dogs alone are seen abroad between nine and one. But in the soothing cool of the soft tropical evening, gay-lit boulevards, a magnificent State-subsidized opera-house, alfresco cafes where dawdle the domino-playing absinthe drinkers, the fierce-moustached gendarmes, and innumerable features typically and picturesquely French, induced me easily to believe myself back in the bewildering whirl of the Boulevard des Capucines or des Italiennes. Whether the narrow streets of the native city are clean or dirty, whether garbage heaps lie festering in the broiling sun, sending their disgusting effluvia out to annoy the sense of smell at every turn, the municipality cares not a little bit. Indifference to the well-being of the native pervades it; there is present no progressive prosperity. Every second person I met was, or seemed to be, a Government official. He was dressed in immaculate white clothes of the typical ugly French cut, trimmed elaborately with an *ad libitum* decoration of gold braid and brass buttons. All was so different from Singapore and Hong-Kong, and one did not feel, in surroundings which made strongly for the *laissez-faire* of the Frenchman in the East, ashamed of the fact that he was an Englishman.

Three days north lies Hong-Kong, an all-important link in the armed chain of Britain's empire east of Suez, bone of the bone and flesh of the flesh of Great Britain beyond the seas. The history of this island, ceded to us in 1842 by the Treaty of Nanking, is known to everyone in Europe, or should be.

Four and a half days more, and we anchored at Woo-sung; and a few hours later, after a terribly cold run up the river in the teeth of a terrific wind, we arrived at Shanghai.

The average man in Europe and America does not know that this great metropolis of the Far East is far removed from salt water, and that it is the first point on entering the Yangtze-kiang at which a port could be established. It is twelve miles up the Whang-poo. Junks whirled past with curious tattered brown sails, resembling dilapidated verandah blinds, merchantmen were there flying the flags of the nations of the world, all churning up the yellow stream as they hurried to catch the flood-tide at the bar. Then came the din of disembarkation. Enthusiastic hotel-runners, hard-worked coolies, rickshaw men, professional Chinese beggars, and the inevitable hangers-on of a large eastern city crowded around me to turn an honest or dishonest penny. Some rude, rough-hewn lout, covered with grease and coal-dust, pushed bang against me and hurled me without ceremony from his path. My baggage, meantime, was thrown onto a two-wheeled van, drawn by four of those poor human beasts of burden—how horrible to have been born a Chinese coolie!—and I was whirled away to my hotel for tucker. The French mail had given us coffee and rolls at six, but the excitement of landing at a foreign port does not usually produce the net amount of satisfaction to or make for the sustenance of the inner man of the phlegmatic Englishman, as with the wilder-natured Frenchman. Therefore were our spirits ruffled.

However, my companion and I fed later.

Subsequently to this we agreed not to be drawn to the clubs or mix in the social life of Shanghai, but to consider ourselves as two beings entirely apart from the sixteen thousand and twenty-three Britishers, Americans, Frenchmen, Germans, Russians, Danes, Portuguese, and other sundry internationals at that moment at Shanghai. They lived there: we were soon to leave.

The city was suffering from the abnormal congestion common to the Orient, with a big dash of the West. Trams, motors, rickshaws, the peculiar Chinese wheelbarrow, horrid public shaky landaus in miniature, conveyances of all kinds, and the swarming masses of coolie humanity carrying or hauling merchandise amid incessant jabbering, yelling, and vociferating, made intense bewilderment before breakfast.

Wonderful Shanghai!

# First Journey: From Shanghai Up the Lower Yangtze to Ichang

## CHAPTER I

*To Ichang, an everyday trip. Start from Shanghai, and the city's appearance.*
*At Hankow. Meaning of the name. Trio of strategic and military points of*
*the empire. Han-yang and Wu-ch'ang. Commercial and industrial future*
*of Hankow. Getting our passports. Britishers in the city. The commercial*
*Chinaman. The native city: some impressions. Clothing of the people. Cot-*
*ton and wool. Indifference to comfort. Surprise at our daring project. At*
*Ichang. British gunboat and early morning routine. Our vain quest for aid.*
*Laying in stores and commissioning our boat. Ceremonies at starting gorges*
*trip. Raising anchor, and our departure.*

*L*et no one who has been so far as Ichang, a thousand miles from the sea,
imagine that he has been into the interior of China.

It is quite an everyday trip. Modern steamers, with every modern
convenience and luxury, probably as comfortable as any river steamers in
the world, ply regularly in their two services between Shanghai and this
port, at the foot of the Gorges.

The Whang-poo looked like the Thames, and the Shanghai Bund like
the Embankment, when I embarked on board a Jap boat *en route* for Hankow, and thence to Ichang by a smaller steamer, on a dark, bitterly cold
Saturday night, March 6th, 1909. I was to travel fifteen hundred miles up
that greatest artery of China. The Yangtze surpasses in importance to the
Celestial Empire what the Mississippi is to America, and yet even in China
there are thousands of resident foreigners who know no more about this
great river than the average Smithfield butcher. Ask ten men in Fleet Street

or in Wall Street where Ichang is, and nine will be unable to tell you. Yet it is a port of great importance, when one considers that the handling of China's vast river-borne trade has been opened to foreign trade and residence since the Chefoo Convention was signed in 1876, that Ichang is a city of forty thousand souls, and has a gross total of imports of nearly forty millions of taels.

Of Hankow, however, more is known. Here we landed after a four days' run, and, owing to the low water, had to wait five days before the shallower-bottomed steamer for the higher journey had come in. The city is made up of foreign concessions, as in other treaty ports, but away in the native quarter there is the real China, with her selfish rush, her squalidness and filth among the teeming thousands. There dwell together, literally side by side, but yet eternally apart, all the conflicting elements of the East and West which go to make up a city in the Far East, and particularly the China coast.

Hankow means literally Han Mouth, being situated at the juncture of the Han River and the Yangtze. Across the way, as I write, I can see Han-yang, with its iron works belching out black curls of smoke, where the arsenal turns out one hundred Mauser rifles daily. (This is but a fraction of the total work done.) It is, I believe, the only steel-rolling mill in China. Long before the foreigner set foot so far up the Yangtze, Hankow was a city of great importance—the Chinese used to call it the centre of the world. Ten years ago I should have been thirty days' hard travel from Peking; at the present moment I might pack my bag and be in Peking within thirty-six hours. Hankow, with Tientsin and Nanking, makes up the trio of principal strategic points of the Empire, the trio of centers also of greatest military activity. On the opposite bank of the river I can see Wu-ch'ang, the provincial capital, the seat of the Viceroyalty of two of the most turbulent and important provinces of the whole eighteen.

Hankow, Han-yang, and Wu-ch'ang have a population of something like two million people, and it is safe to prophesy that no other centre in the whole world has a greater commercial and industrial future than Hankow.

Here we registered as British subjects, and secured our Chinese passports, resembling naval ensigns more than anything else, for the four provinces of Hu-peh, Kwei-chow, Szech'wan, and Yuen-nan. The Consul-General and his assistants helped us in many ways, disillusioning us of the many distorted reports which have got into print regarding the indifference shown to British travelers by their own consuls at these ports. We found the brethren at the Hankow Club a happy band, with every luxury around them for which hand and heart could wish; so that it were perhaps ludicrous to look upon them as exiles, men out in the outposts of Britain beyond the seas, building up the trade of the Empire. Yet such they undoubtedly were, most of them having a much better time than they would at home. There is not the roughing required in Hankow which is necessary in other parts of the empire, as in British East Africa and in the jungles of the Federated Malay States, for instance. Building the Empire where there is an abundance of the straw wherewith to make the bricks, is a matter of no difficulty.

And then the Chinese is a good man to manage in trade, and in business dealings his word is his bond, generally speaking, although we do not forget that not long ago a branch in North China of the Hong-kong and Shanghai Bank was swindled seriously by a shroff who had done honest duty for a great number of years. It cannot, however, be said that such behavior is a common thing among the commercial class. My personal experience has been that John does what he says he will do, and for years he will go on doing that one thing; but it should not surprise you if one fine morning, with the infinite sagacity of his race, he ceases to do this when you are least expecting it—and he "does" you. Keep an eye on him, and the Chinese to be found in Hankow having dealings with Europeans in business is as good as the best of men.

We wended our way one morning into the native city, and agreed that few inconveniences of the Celestial Empire make upon the western mind a more speedy impression than the entire absence of sanitation. In Hankow we were in mental suspense as to which was the filthier native city—Hankow or Shanghai. But we are probably like other travelers, who find each city visited worse than the last. Should there arise in their midst a man anxious to confer an everlasting blessing upon his fellow Chinese, no better work could he do than to institute a system approaching what to our Western mind is sanitation. We arrived, of course, in the winter, and, having seen it at a time when the sun could do but little in increasing the stenches, we leave to the imagination what it would be in the summer, in a city which for heat is not excelled by Aden.[2] During the summer of 1908 no less than twenty-eight foreigners succumbed to cholera, and the native deaths were numberless.

The people were suffering very much from the cold, and it struck me as one of the unaccountable phenomena of their civilization that in their ingenuity in using the gifts of Nature they have never learned to weave wool, and to employ it in clothing—that is, in a general sense. There are a

---

2    This was written at the time I was in Hankow. When I revised my copy, after I had spent a year and a half rubbing along with the natives in the interior, I could not suppress a smile at my impressions of a great city like Hankow. Since then I have seen more native life, and—more native dirt!—E.J.D.

few exceptions in the empire. The nation is almost entirely dependent upon cotton for clothing, which in winter is padded with a cheap wadding to an abnormal thickness. The common people wear no underclothing whatever. When they sleep they strip to the skin, and wrap themselves in a single wadded blanket, sleeping the sleep of the tired people their excessive labor makes them. And, although their clothes might be the height of discomfort, they show their famous indifference to comfort by never complaining. These burdensome clothes hang around them like so many bags, with the wide gaps here and there where the wind whistles to the flesh. It is a national characteristic that they are immune to personal inconveniences, a philosophy which I found to be universal, from the highest to the lowest.

Everybody we met, from the British Consul-General downward, was surprised to know that my companion and I had no knowledge of the Chinese language, and seemed to look lightly upon our chances of ever getting through.

It was true. Neither my companion nor myself knew three words of the language, but went forward simply believing in the good faith of the Chinese people, with our passports alone to protect us. That we should encounter difficulties innumerable, that we should be called upon to put up with the greatest hardships of life, when viewed from the standard to which one had been accustomed, and that we should be put to great physical endurance, we could not doubt. But we believed in the Chinese, and believed that should any evil befall us it would be the outcome of our own lack of forbearance, or of our own direct seeking. We knew that to the Chinese we should at once be "foreign devils" and "barbarians," that if not holding us actually in contempt, they would feel some condescension in dealing and mixing with us; but I was personally of the opinion that it was easier for us to walk through China than it would be for two Chinese, dressed as Chinese, to walk through Great Britain or America. What would the canny Highlander or the rural English rustic think of two pig-tailed men tramping through his countryside?

We anchored at Ichang at 7:30 a.m. on March 19th. I fell up against a boatman who offered to take us ashore. An uglier fellow I had never seen in the East. The morning sunshine soon dried the decks of the gunboat *Kinsha* (then stationed in the river for the defense of the port) which English jack-tars were swabbing in a half-hearted sort of way, and all looked rosy enough.[3] But for the author, who with his companion was a literal "babe in the wood," the day was most eventful and trying to one's personal serenity. We had asked questions of all and sundry respecting our proposed tramp

---

3    The *Kinsha* was the first British gunboat on the Upper Yangtze.

and the way we should get to work in making preparations. Each individual person seemed vigorously to do his best to induce us to turn back and follow callings of respectable members of society. From Shanghai upwards we might have believed ourselves watched by a secret society, which had for its motto, "Return, oh, wanderer, return!" Hardly a person knew aught of the actual conditions of the interior of the country in which he lived and labored, and everyone tried to dissuade us from our project.

Coming ashore in good spirits, we called at the Consulate, at the back of the city graveyard, and were smoking his cigars and giving his boy an examination in elementary English, when the Consul came down. It was not possible, however, for us to get much more information than we had read up, and the Consul suggested that the most likely person to be of use to us would be the missionary at the China Inland Mission. Thither we repaired, following a sturdy employe of Britain, but we found that the C.I.M. representative was not to be found—despite our repairing. So off we trotted to the chief business house of the town, at the entrance to which we were met by a Chinese, who bowed gravely, asked whether we had eaten our rice, and told us, quietly but pointedly, that our passing up the rough stone steps would be of no use, as the manager was out. A few minutes later I stood reading the inscription on the gravestone near the church, whilst my brave companion, The Other Man, endeavored fruitlessly to pacify a fierce dog in the doorway of the Scottish Society's missionary premises—but that missionary, too, was out!

What, then, was the little game? Were all the foreigners resident in this town dodging us, afraid of us—or what?

"The latter, the blithering idiots!" yelled The Other Man. He was infuriated. "Two Englishmen with English tongues in their heads, and unable to direct their own movements. Preposterous!" And then, making an observation which I will not print, he suggested mildly that we might fix up all matters ourselves.

Within an hour an English-speaking "one piece cook" had secured the berth, which carried a salary of twenty-five dollars per month, we were well on the way with the engaging of our boat for the Gorges trip, and one by one our troubles vanished.

Laying in stores, however, was not the lightest of sundry perplexities. Curry and rice had been suggested as the staple diet for the river journey; and we ordered, with no thought to the contrary, a picul of best rice, various brands of curries, which were raked from behind the shelves of a dingy little store in a back street, and presented to us at alarming prices—enough to last a regiment of soldiers for pretty well the number of days we two were to travel; and, for luxuries, we laid in a few tinned meats. All was practically settled, when The Other Man, settling his eyes dead upon me, yelled—

"Dingle, you've forgotten the milk!" And then, after a moment, "Oh, well, we can surely do without milk; it's no use coming on a journey like this unless one can rough it a bit." And he ended up with a rude reference to the disgusting sticky condensed milk tins, and we wandered on.

Suddenly he stopped, did The Other Man. He looked at a small stone on the pavement for a long time, eventually cruelly blurting out, directly at me, as if it were all my misdoing: "The sugar, the sugar! We *must* have sugar, man." I said nothing, with the exception of a slight remark that we might do without sugar, as we were to do without milk. There was a pause. Then, raising his stick in the air, The Other Man perorated: "Now, I have no wish to quarrel" (and he put his nose nearer to mine), "you know that, of course. But to *think* we can do without sugar is quite unreasonable, and I had no idea you were such a cantankerous man. We have sugar, or—I go back."

We had sugar. It was brought on board in upwards of twenty small packets of that detestable thin Chinese paper, and The Other Man, with commendable meekness, withdrew several pleasantries he had unwittingly dropped anent deficiencies in my upbringing. Fifty pounds of this sugar were ordered, and sugar—that dirty, brown sticky stuff—got into everything on board—my fingers are sticky even as I write—and no less than exactly one-half went down to the bottom of the Yangtze. Travelers by houseboat on the Upper Yangtze should have some knowledge of commissariat.

Getting away was a tedious business.

Later, the fellows pressed us to spend a good deal of time in the small, dingy, ill-lighted apartment they are pleased to call their club; and the skipper had to recommission his boat, get in provisions for the voyage, engage his crew, pay off debts, and attend to a thousand and one minute details—all to be done after the contract to carry the madcap passengers had been signed and sealed, added to the more practical triviality of three-fourths of the charge being paid down. And then our captain, to add to the dilemma, vociferously yelled to us, in some unknown jargon which got on our nerves terribly, that he was waiting for a "lucky" day to raise anchor.

However, we did, as the reader will be able to imagine, eventually get away, amid the firing of countless deafening crackers, after having watched the sacrifice of a cock to the God of the River, with the invocation that we might be kept in safety. Poling and rowing through a maze of junks, our little floating caravan, with the two magnates on board, and their picul of rice, their curry and their sugar, and slenderest outfits, bowled along under plain sail, the fore-deck packed with a motley team of somewhat dirty and ill-fed trackers, who whistled and halloed the peculiar hallo of the Upper Yangtze for more wind.

The little township of Ichang was soon left astern, and we entered speedily to all intents and purposes into a new world, a world untrammelled by conventionalism and the spirit of the West.

# Second Journey: Ichang to Chung-King, Through the Yangtze Gorges

## CHAPTER II

*Gloom in Ichang Gorge. Lightning's effect. Travellers' fear. Impressive intro-
duction to the Gorges. Boat gets into Yangtze fashion. Storm and its weird
effects. Wu-pan: what it is. Heavenly electricity and its vagaries. Beautiful evening scene, despite heavy rain. Bedding soaked. Sleep in a Burberry.
Gorges and Niagara Falls compared. Bad descriptions of Yangtze. World of
eternity. Man's significant insignificance. Life on board briefly described.
Philosophy of travel. Houseboat life not luxurious. Lose our only wash-basin.
Remarks on the "boy." A change in the kitchen: questionable soup. Fairly low
temperature. Troubles in the larder. General arrangements on board. Crew's
sleeping-place. Sacking makes a curtain. Journalistic labors not easy. Rats
preponderate. Gorges described statistically.*

*D*eeper and deeper drooped the dull grey gloom, like a curtain falling
slowly and impenetrably over all things.

A vivid but broken flash of lightning, blazing in a flare of blue and
amber, poured livid reflections, and illuminated with dreadful distinctness,
if only for one ghastly moment, the stupendous cliffs of the Ichang Gorge,
whose wall-like steepness suddenly became darkened as black as ink.

Thus, with a grand impressiveness, this great gully in the mountains
assumed hugely gigantic proportions, stretching interminably from east to
west, up to heaven and down to earth, silhouetted to the north against
a small remaining patch of golden purple, whose weird glamour seemed
awesomely to herald the coming of a new world into being, lasting but for
a moment longer, until again the blue blaze quickly cut up the sky into a
thousand shreds and tiny silver bars. And then, suddenly, with a vast down
swoop, as if some colossal bird were taking the earth under her far-out-

stretching wings, dense darkness fell—impenetrable, sooty darkness, that in a moment shut out all light, all power of sight. Then from out the sombre heavens deep thunder boomed ominously as the reverberating roar of a pack of hunger-ridden lions, and the two men, aliens in an alien land, stood beneath the tattered matting awning with a peculiar fear and some foreboding. We were tied in fast to the darkened sides of the great Ichang Gorge—a magnificent sixteen-mile stretch, opening up the famous gorges on the fourth of the great rivers of the world, which had cleaved its course through a chain of hills, whose perpendicular cliffs form wonderful rock-bound banks, dispelling all thought of the monotony of the Lower Yangtze.

Upstream we had glided merrily upon a fresh breeze, which bore the warning of a storm. All on board was settling down into Yangtze fashion, and the barbaric human clamor of our trackers, which now mutteringly died away, was suddenly taken up, as above recorded, and all unexpectedly answered by a grander uproar—a deep threatening boom of far-off thunder. In circling tones and semitones of wrath it volleyed gradually through the dark ravines, and, startled by the sound, the two travelers, roused for the first time from their natural engrossment in the common doings of the *wu-pan*,[4] saw the reflection of the sun on the waters, now turned to a livid murkiness, deepening with a threatening ink-like aspect as the river rushed voluminously past our tiny floating haven. Strangely silenced were we by this weird terror, and watched and listened, chained to the deck by a thousand mingled fears and fascinations, which breathed upon our nerves like a chill wind. As we became accustomed then to the yellow darkness, we beheld about the landscape a spectral look, and the sepulchral sound of the moving thunder seemed the half-muffled clang of some great iron-tongued funeral bell. Then came the rain, introduced swiftly by the deafening clatter of another thunder crash that made one stagger like a ship in a wild sea, and we strained our eyes to gaze into a visionary chasm cleaved in twain by the furious lightning. Playing upon the face of the unruffled river, with a brilliancy at once awful and enchanting, this singular flitting and wavering of the heavenly electricity, as it flashed haphazardly around all things, threw about one an illumination quite indescribable.

For hours we sat upon a beam athwart the afterdeck, in silence drinking in the strange phenomenon. We watched, after a small feed of curry and rice, long into the dark hours, when the thunder had passed us by, and in the distant booming one could now imagine the lower notes stream-

---

4    A wu-pan (literally wu of five and pan of boards) is a small boat, the smallest used by travelers on the Upper Yangtze. They are of various shapes, made according to the nature of the part of the river on which they ply.—E.J.D.

ing forth from some great solemn organ symphony. The fierce lightning twitched, as it danced in and out the crevices—inwards, outwards, upwards, then finally lost in one downward swoop towards the river, tearing open the liquid blackness with its crystal blade of fire. The rain ceased not. But soon the moon, peeping out from the tops of a jagged wall above us, looking like a soiled, half-melted snowball, shone full down the far-stretching gorge, and now its broad lustre shed itself, like powdered silver, over the whole scene, so that one could have imagined oneself in the living splendor of some eternal sphere of ethereal sweetness. And so it might have been had the rain abated—a curious accompaniment to a moonlight night. Down it came, straight and determined and businesslike, in the windless silence, dancing like a shower of diamonds of purest brilliance on the background of the placid waters.

Very beautiful, reader, for a time. But would that the rain had been all moonshine!

Glorious was it to revel in for a time. But, during the weary night watches, in a bed long since soaked through, and one's safest nightclothes now the stolid Burberry, with face protected by a twelve-cent umbrella, even one's curry and rice saturated to sap with the constant drip, and everything around one rendered cold and uncomfortable enough through a perforation in its slenderest part of the worn-out bamboo matting—ah, it was then, *then* that one would have foregone with alacrity the dreams of the nomadic life of the *wu-pan*.

Our introduction, therefore, to the great Gorges of the Upper Yangtze—to China what the Niagara Falls are to America—was not remarkable for its placidity, albeit taken with as much complacency as the occasion allowed.

I do not, however, intend to weary or to entertain the reader, as may be, by a long description of the Yangtze gorges. Time and time again have they fallen to the imaginative pens of travelers—mostly bad or indifferent descriptions, few good; none better, perhaps, than Mrs. Bishop's. But at best they are imaginative—they lack reality. It has been said that the world of imagination is the world of eternity, and as of eternity, so of the Gorges—they cannot be adequately described. As I write now in the Ichang Gorge, I seem veritably to have reached eternity. I seem to have arrived at the bosom of an after-life, where one's body has ceased to vegetate, and where, in an infinite and eternal world of imagination, one's soul expands with fullest freedom. There seems to exist in this eternal world of unending rock and invulnerable precipice permanent realities which stand from eternity to eternity. As the oak dies and leaves its eternal image in the seed which never dies, so these grand river-forced ravines, abused and disabused as may be, go on for ever, despite the scribblers, and one finds the best in his imagination returning by some back-lane to contemplative thought. But as a casual traveler, may I say that the first experience I had of the gorges made me modest, patient, single-minded, conscious of man's significant insignificance, conscious of the unspeakable, wondrous grandeur of this unvisited corner of the world—a spot in which blustering, selfish, self-conceited persons will not fare well? Humility and patience are the first requisites in traveling on the Upper Yangtze.

Reader, for your sake I refrain from a description. But may I, for perhaps your sake too, if you would wander hither ere the charm of things as they were in the beginning is still unrobbed and unmolested, give you some few impressions of a little of the life—grave, gay, but never unhappy—which I spent with my excellent co-voyager, The Other Man.

It is a part of wisdom, when starting any journey, not to look forward to the end with too much eagerness: hear my gentle whisper that you may never get there, and if you do, congratulate yourself; interest yourself in the progress of the journey, for the present only is yours. Each day has its tasks, its rapids, its perils, its glories, its fascinations, its surprises, and—if you will live as we did, its *curry and rice*. Then, if you are traveling with a companion, remember that it is better to yield a little than to quarrel a great deal. Most disagreeable and undignified is it anywhere to get into the habit of standing up for what people are pleased to call their little rights, but nowhere more so than on the Upper Yangtze houseboat, under the gaze of a Yangtze crew. Life is really too short for continual bickering, and to my way of thinking it is far quieter, happier, more prudent and productive of more peace, if one could yield a little of those precious little rights than to incessantly squabble to maintain them. Therefore, from the beginning to the end of the trip, make the best of everything in every way, and I can assure you, if you are not ill-tempered and suffer not from your liver, Nature will open her bosom and lead you by these strange by-ways into her hidden charms and unadorned recesses of sublime beauty, uneclipsed for their kind anywhere in the world.

Think not that the life will be luxurious—houseboat life on the Upper Yangtze is decidedly not luxurious. Were it not for the magnificence of the scenery and ever-changing outdoor surroundings, as a matter of fact, the long river journey would probably become unbearably dull.

Our *wu-pan* was to get through the Gorges in as short a time as was possible, and for that reason we traveled in the discomfort of the smallest boat used to face the rapids.

People entertaining the smallest idea of doing things travel in nothing short of a *kwadze*, the orthodox houseboat, with several rooms and ordinary conveniences. Ours was a *wu-pan*—literally five boards. We had no conveniences whatever, and the second morning out we were left without even a wash-basin. As I was standing in the stern, I saw it swirling away from us, and inquiring through a peep-hole, heard the perplexing explanation of my boy. Gesticulating violently, he told us how, with the wash-basin in his hand, he had been pushed by one of the crew, and how, loosened from his grasp, my toilet ware had been gripped by the river—and now appeared far down the stream like a large bead. The Other Man was alarmed at the boy's discomfiture, ejaculated something about the loss being quite irreparable, and with a loud laugh and quite natural hilarity proceeded quietly to use a saucepan as a combined shaving-pot and wash-basin. It did quite well for this in the morning, and during the day resumed its duty as seat for me at the typewriter.

Our boy, apart from this small misfortune, comported himself pretty well. His English was understandable, and he could cook anything. He dished us up excellent soup in enamelled cups and, as we had no ingredients on board so far as we knew to make soup, and as The Other Man had that day lost an old Spanish tam-o'-shanter, we naturally concluded that he had used the old hat for the making of the soup, and at once christened it as "consomme a la maotsi"—and we can recommend it. After we had grown somewhat tired of the eternal curry and rice, we asked him quietly if he could not make us something else, fearing a rebuff. He stood hesitatingly before us, gazing into nothingness. His face was pallid, his lips hard set, and his stooping figure looking curiously stiff and lifeless on that frozen morning—the temperature below freezing point, and our noses were red, too!

"God bless the man, you no savee! I wantchee good chow. Why in the name of goodness can't you give us something decent! What on earth did you come for?"

"Alas!" he shouted, for we were at a rapid, "my savee makee good chow. No have got nothing!"

"No have got nothing! No have got nothing!" Mysterious words, what could they mean? Where, then, was our picul of rice, and our curry, and our sugar?

"The fellow's a swindler!" cried The Other Man in an angry semitone. But that's all very well. "No have got nothing!" Ah, there lay the secret. Presently The Other Man, head of the general commissariat, spoke again with touching eloquence. He gave the boy to understand that we were powerless to alter or soften the conditions of the larder, that we were victims of a horrible destiny, that we entertained no stinging malice towards him personally—but ... *could he do it?* Either a great wrath or a great sorrow overcame the boy; he skulked past, asked us to lie down on our shelves, where we had our beds, to give him room, and then set to work.

In twenty-five minutes we had a three-course meal (all out of the same pot, but no matter), and onwards to our destination we fed royally. In parting with the men after our safe arrival at Chung-king, we left with them about seven-eighths of the picul—and were not at all regretful.

I should not like to assert—because I am telling the truth here—that our boat was bewilderingly roomy. As a matter of fact, its length was some forty feet, its width seven feet, its depth much less, and it drew eight inches of water. Yet in it we had our bed-rooms, our dressing-rooms, our dining-rooms, our library, our occasional medicine-room, our cooking-room—and all else. If we stood bolt upright in the saloon amidships we bumped our heads on the bamboo matting which formed an arched roof. On the nose of the boat slept seven men—you may question it, reader, but they did; in the stern, on either side of a great rudder, slept our boy and a friend of his; and between them and us, laid out flat on the top of a cellar (used by the ship's cook for the storing of rice, cabbage, and other uneatables, and the breeding-cage of hundreds of rats, which swarm all around one) were the captain and commodore—a fat, fresh-complexioned, jocose creature, strenuous at opium smoking. Through the holes in the curtain—a piece of sacking, but one would not wish this to be known—dividing them from us, we could see him preparing his globules to smoke before turning in for the night, and despite our frequent raving objections, our words ringing with vibrating abuse, it continued all the way to Chung-king: he certainly gazed in disguised wonderment, but we could not get him to say anything bearing upon the matter. Temperature during the day stood at about 50 degrees, and at night went down to about 30 degrees above freezing point. Rains were frequent. Journalistic labors, seated upon the upturned saucepan aforesaid, without a cushion, went hard. At night the Chinese candle, much wick and little wax, stuck in the center of an empty "Three Castles" tin, which the boy had used for some days as a pudding dish, gave us light. We generally slept in our overcoats, and as many others as we happened to have. Rats crawled over our uncurtained bodies, and woke us a dozen times each night by either nibbling our ears or falling bodily from the roof on to our faces. Our joys came not to us—they were made on board.

The following are the Gorges, with a remark or two about each, to be passed through before one reaches Kweifu:—

| Name of Gorge | Length | Remarks |
|---|---|---|
| Ichang Gorge | 16 miles | First and probably one of the finest of the Gorges. |
| Niu Kan Ma Fee (or Ox Liver Gorge) | 4 miles | An hour's journey after coming out of the Ichang Gorge, if the breeze be favorable; an arduous day's journey during high river, with no wind. |
| Mi Tsang (or Rice Granary Gorge) | 2 miles | Finest view is obtained from western extremity; exceedingly precipitous. |
| Niu Kou (or Buffalo Mouth Reach) | — | Very quiet in low-water season; wild stretch during high river. At the head of this reach H.M.S. Woodlark came to grief on her maiden trip. |
| Urishan Hsia (or Gloomy Mountain Gorge) | — | Over thirty miles in length. Grandest and highest gorge en route to Chung-king. Half-way through is the boundary between Hu-peh and Szech'wan. |
| Fang Hsian Hsia (or Wind-box Gorge) | — | Last of the gorges; just beyond is the city of Kweifu. |

# Chapter III

## The Yangtze Rapids

*The following is a rough list of the principal rapids to be negotiated on the river upward from Ichang. One of the chief discomforts the traveler first experiences is due to a total ignorance of the vicinity of the main rapids, and often, therefore, when he is least expecting it perhaps, he is called upon by the laoban to go ashore. He has then to pack up the things he values, is dragged ashore himself, his gear follows, and one who has no knowledge of the language and does not know the ropes is, therefore, never quite happy for fear of some rapid turning up. By comparing the rapids with the Gorges the traveler would, however, from the lists given, be able easily to trace the whereabouts of the more dangerous rushes; which are distributed with alarming frequency on the river between Ichang and Kweifu.*

### Ta Tong T'an (Otter Cave Rapid)

Low water rapid. Swirling volume of coffee and milk color; round about a maze of rapids and races, in the Yao-cha Ho reach.

### Tong Ling Rapid

At the foot of the Ox Liver Gorge. An enormous black rock lies amid stream some forty feet below, or perhaps as much above the surface, but unless experienced at low water will not appeal to the traveler as a rapid; passage dangerous, dreaded during low-water season. On Dec. 28th, 1900, the German steamer, *Sui-Hsiang* was lost here. She foundered in twenty-five fathoms of water, with an immense hole ripped in her bottom by the black rock; all on board saved by the red boats, with the exception of the captain.

37

### HSIN T'AN RAPIDS (OR CHIN T'AN RAPIDS)

During winter quite formidable; the head, second and third rapids situated in close proximity, the head rapid being far the worst to negotiate. On a bright winter's day one of the finest spectacles on the Upper Yangtze. Wrecks frequent. Just at head of Ox Liver Gorge.

### YEH T'AN (OR WILD RAPID)

River reduced suddenly to half its width by an enormous detritus of boulders, taking the form of a huge jagged tongue, with curling on edges; commonly said to be high when the Hsin T'an is low. At its worst during early summer and autumn. Wrecks frequent, after Mi Tsang Gorge is passed, eight miles from Kwei-chow.

### NIU K'EO T'AN (BUFFALO MOUTH RAPID)

Situated at the head of Buffalo Mouth Reach, said to be more difficult to approach than even the Yeh T'an, because of the great swirls in the bay below. H.M.S. *Woodlark* came to grief here on her maiden trip up river.

### HSIN MA T'AN (OR DISMOUNT HORSE RAPID)

Encountered through the Urishan Hsia or Gloomy Mountain Gorge, particularly nasty during mid-river season. Just about here, in 1906, the French gunboat *Olry* came within an ace of destruction by losing her rudder. Immediately, like a riderless horse, she dashed off headlong for the rocky shore; but at the same instant her engines were working astern for all they were worth, and fortunately succeeded in taking the way off her just as her nose grazed the rocks, and she slid back undamaged into the swirly bay, only to be waltzed round and tossed to and fro by the violent whirlpools. However, by good luck and management she was kept from dashing her brains out on the reefs, and eventually brought in to a friendly sand patch and safely moored, whilst a wooden jury rudder was rigged, with which she eventually reached her destination.

### HEH SHIH T'AN (OR BLACK ROCK RAPID)

Almost at the end of the Wind Box Gorge.

### HSIN LONG T'AN (OR NEW DRAGON RAPID)

Twenty-five miles below Wan Hsien. Sometimes styled Glorious Dragon Rapid, it constitutes the last formidable stepping-stone during low river onward to Chung-king; was formed by a landslip as recently as 1896, when the whole side of a hill falling into the stream reduced its breadth to less than a fourth of what it was previously, and produced this roaring rapid.

This pent-up volume of water, always endeavoring to break away the rocky bonds which have harnessed it, rushes roaring as a huge, tongue-shaped, tumbling mass between its confines of rock and reef. Breaking into swift back-wash and swirls in the bay below, it lashes back in a white fury at its obstacles. Fortunately for the junk traffic, it improves rapidly with the advent of the early spring freshets, and at mid-level entirely disappears. The rapid is at its worst during the months of February and March, when it certainly merits the appellation of "Glorious Dragon Rapid," presenting a fine spectacle, though perhaps a somewhat fearsome one to the traveler, who is about to tackle it with his frail barque. A hundred or more wretched-looking trackers, mostly women and children, are tailed on to the three stout bamboo hawsers, and amid a mighty din of rushing water, beating drums, cries of pilots and boatmen, the boat is hauled slowly and painfully over. According to Chinese myths, the landslip which produced the rapid was caused by the following circumstance. The ova of a dragon being deposited in the bowels of the earth at this particular spot, in due course became hatched out in some mysterious manner. The baby dragon grew and grew, but remained in a dormant state until quite full grown, when, as is the habit of the dragon, it became active, and at the first awakening shook down the hill-side by a mighty effort, freed himself from the bowels of the earth, and made his way down river to the sea; hence the landslip, the rapid, and its name.

## FUH T'AN RAPID (OR TIGER RAPID)

Eight miles beyond Wan Hsien. Very savage during summer months, but does not exist during low-water season. Beyond this point river widens considerably. Twenty-five miles further on travelers should look out for Shih Pao Chai, or Precious Stone Castle, a remarkable cliff some 250 or 300 feet high. A curious eleven-storied pavilion, built up the face of the cliff, contains the stairway to the summit, on which stands a Buddhist temple. There is a legend attached to this remarkable rock that savors very much of the goose with the golden eggs.

Once upon a time, from a small natural aperture near the summit, a supply of rice sufficient for the needs of the priests flowed daily into a basin-shaped hole, just large enough to hold the day's supply.

The priests, however, thinking to get a larger daily supply, chiselled out the basin-shaped hole to twice its original size, since when the flow of rice ceased.

## KWAN IN T'AN (OR GODDESS OF MERCY RAPID)

Two miles beyond the town of Feng T'ou. Like the Fuh T'an, is an obstacle to navigation only during the summer months, when junks are often obliged to wait for several days for a favorable opportunity to cross the rapid.

# CHAPTER IV

*Scene at the Rapid. Dangers of the Yeh T'an. Gear taken ashore. Intense cold. Further preparation. Engaging the trackers. Fever of excitement. Her nose is put to it. Struggles for mastery. Author saves boatman. Fifteen-knot current. Terrific labor on shore. Man nearly falls overboard. Straining hawsers carry us over safely. The merriment among the men. The thundering cataract. Trackers' chanting. Their life. "Pioneer" at the Yeh T'an. The Buffalo Mouth Reach. Story of the "Woodlark." How she was saved. Arrival at Kweifu. Difficulty in landing. Laying in provisions. Author laid up with malaria. Survey of trade in Shanghai and Hong-Kong. Where and why the Britisher fails. Comparison with Germans. Three western provinces and pack-horse traffic. Advantages of new railway. Yangtze likely to be abandoned. East India Company. French and British interests. Hint to Hong-Kong Chamber of Commerce.*

*W*ild shrieking, frantic yelling, exhausted groaning, confusion and clamor,—one long, deafening din. A bewildering, maddening mob of reckless, terrified human beings rush hither and thither, unseeingly and distractedly. Will she go? Yes! No! Yes! Then comes the screeching, the scrunching, the straining, and then—a final snap! Back we go, sheering helplessly, swayed to and fro most dangerously by the foaming waters, and almost, but not quite, turn turtle. The red boat follows us anxiously, and watches our timid little craft bump against the rock-strewn coast. But we are safe, and raise unconsciously a cry of gratitude to the deity of the river.

We were at the Yeh T'an, or the Wild Rapid, some distance on from the Ichang Gorge, were almost over the growling monster, when the tow-line, straining to its utmost limit, snapped suddenly with little warning, and we

41

drifted in a moment or two away down to last night's anchorage, far below, where we were obliged to bring up the last of the long tier of boats of which we were this morning the first.

And now we are ready again to take our turn.

Our gear is all taken ashore. Seated on a stone on shore, watching operations, is The Other Man. The sun vainly tries to get through, and the intense cold is almost unendurable. No hitch is to occur this time. The toughest and stoutest bamboo hawsers are dexterously brought out, their inboard ends bound in a flash firmly round the mast close down to the deck, washed by the great waves of the rapid, just in front of the 'midships pole through which I breathlessly watch proceedings. I want to feel again the sensation. The captain, in essentially the Chinese way, is engaging a crew of demon-faced trackers to haul her over. Pouring towards the boat, in a fever of excitement that rises higher every moment, the natural elements of hunger and constant struggle against the great river swell their fury; they bellow like wild beasts, *they are like beasts*, for they have known nothing but struggle all their lives; they have always, since they were tiny children, been fighting this roaring water monster—they know none else. And now, as I say, they bellow like beasts, each man ravenously eager to be among the number chosen to earn a few cash.[5] The arrangement at last is made, and the discordant hubbub, instead of lessening, grows more and more deafening. It is a miserable, desperate, wholly panic-stricken crowd that then harnesses up with their great hooks joined to a rough waist-belt, with which they connect themselves to the straining tow-lines.

And now her nose is put into the teeth of this trough of treachery—a veritable boiling cauldron, stirring up all past mysteries. Waves rush furiously towards us, with the growl of a thousand demons, whose anger is only swelled by the thousands of miles of her course from far-away Tibet. It seems as if they must instantly devour her, and that we must now go under to swell the number of their victims. But they only beat her back, for she rides gracefully, faltering timidly with frightened creaks and groans, whilst the waters shiver her frail bulwarks with their cruel message of destruction, which might mean her very death-rattle. I get landed in the stomach with the end of a gigantic bamboo boat-hook, used by one of the men standing in the bows whose duty is to fend her off the rocks. He falls towards the river. I grab his single garment, give one swift pull, and he comes up again with a jerky little laugh and asks if he has hurt me—yelling through his hands in my ears, for the noise is terrible. To look out over the side makes me giddy,

---

5    Cash, a small brass coin with a hole through the middle. Nominally 1,000 cash to the dollar.

for the fifteen-knot current, blustering and bubbling and foaming and leaping, gives one the feeling that he is in an express train tearing through the sea. On shore, far ahead, I can see the trackers—struggling forms of men and women, touching each other, grasping each other, wrestling furiously and mightily, straining on all fours, now gripping a boulder to aid them forward, now to the right, now to the left, always fighting for one more inch, and engaged in a task which to one seeing it for the first time looks as if it were quite beyond human effort. Fagged and famished beings are these trackers, whose life day after day, week in week out, is harder than that of the average costermonger's donkey. They throw up their hands in a dumb frenzy of protest and futile appeal to the presiding deity; and here on the river, depending entirely upon those men on the shore, slowly, inch by inch, the little craft, feeling her own weakness, forges ahead against the leaping current in the gapway in the reef.

None come to offer assistance to our crowd, who are now turned facing us, and strain almost flat on their backs, giving the strength of every drop of blood and fibre of their being; and the scene, now lit up by a momentary glimmer of feeble sunlight, assumes a wonderful and terrible picturesqueness. I am chained to the spot by a horrible fascination, and I find myself unconsciously saying, "I fear she will not go. I fear—" But a man has fallen exhausted, he almost fell overboard, and now leans against the mast in utter weariness and fatigue, brought on by the morning's exertions. He is instantly relieved by a bull-dog fellow of enormous strength. Now comes the culminating point, a truly terrifying moment, the very anguish of which frightened me, as I looked around for the lifeboat, and I saw that even the commodore's cold and self-satisfied dignity was disturbed. The hawsers strain again. Creak, crack! creak, crack! The lifeboat watches and comes nearer to us. There is a mighty yell. We cannot go! Yes, we can! There is a mighty pull, and you feel the boat almost torn asunder. Another mighty pull, a tremendous quiver of the timbers, and you turn to see the angry water, which sounds as if a hundred hounds are beating under us for entry at the barred door. There is another deafening yell, the men tear away like frightened horses. Another mighty pull, and another, and another, and we slide over into smooth water.

Then I breathe freely, and yell myself.

The little boat seems to gasp for breath as a drowning man, saved in the nick of time, shudders in every limb with pain and fear.

As we tied up in smooth water, all the men, from the *laoban* to the meanest tracker, laughed and yelled and told each other how it was done. We baled the water out of the boat, and one was glad to pull away from the deafening hum of the thundering cataract. A faulty tow-line, a slippery hitch, one false step, one false maneuver, and the shore might have been by that time strewn with our corpses. As it was, we were safe and happy.

But the trackers are strange creatures. At times they are a quarter of a mile ahead. Soft echoes of their coarse chanting came down the confines of the gully, after the rapid had been passed, and in rounding a rocky promontory mid-stream, one would catch sight of them bending their bodies in pulling steadily against the current of the river. Occasionally one of these poor fellows slips; there is a shriek, his body is dashed unmercifully against the jagged cliffs in its last journey to the river, which carries the multilated corpse away. And yet these men, engaged in this terrific toil, with utmost danger to their lives, live almost exclusively on boiled rice and dirty cabbage, and receive the merest pittance in money at the journey's end.

Some idea of the force of this enormous volume of water may be given by mentioning the exploits of the steamer *Pioneer*, which on three consecutive occasions attacked the Yeh T'an when at its worst, and, though steaming a good fourteen knots, failed to ascend. She was obliged to lay out a long steel-wire hawser, and heave herself over by means of her windlass, the engines working at full speed at the same time. Hard and heavy was the heave, gaining foot by foot, with a tension on the hawser almost to breaking strain in a veritable battle against the dragon of the river. Yet so complete are the changes which are wrought by the great variation in the level of the river, that this formidable mid-level rapid completely disappears at high level.

After we had left this rapid—and right glad were we to get away—we came, after a couple of hours' run, to the Niu K'eo, or Buffalo Mouth Reach, quiet enough during the low-water season, but a wild stretch during high river, where many a junk is caught by the violently gyrating swirls, rendered unmanageable, and dashed to atoms on some rocky promontory or boulder pile in as short a space of time as it takes to write it. It was here that the *Woodlark*, one of the magnificent gunboats which patrol the river to safeguard the interests of the Union Jack in this region, came to grief on her maiden trip to Chung-king. One of these strong swirls caught the ship's stern, rendering her rudders useless for the moment, and causing her to sheer broadside into the foaming rapid. The engines were immediately reversed to full speed astern; but the swift current, combined with the momentum of the ship, carried her willy-nilly to the rock-bound shore, on which she crumpled her bows as if they were made of tin. Fortunately she was built in water-tight sections; her engineers removed the forward section, straightened out the crumpled plates, riveted them together, and bolted the section back into its place again so well, that on arrival at Chung-king not a trace of the accident was visible.

※

Upon arrival at Kweifu one bids farewell to the Gorges. This town, formerly a considerable coaling center, overlooks most beautiful hillocks, with cottage gardens cultivated in every accessible corner, and a wide sweep of the river.

We landed with difficulty. "Chor, chor!" yelled the trackers, who marked time to their cry, swinging their arms to and fro at each short step; but they almost gave up the ghost. However, we did land, and so did our boy, who bought excellent provisions and meat, which, alas! too soon disappeared. The mutton and beef gradually grew less and daily blackened, wrapped up in opposite corners of the cabin, under the protection from the wet of a couple of sheets of the "Pink 'Un."

From Kweifu to Wan Hsien there was the same kind of scenery—the clear river winding among sand-flats and gravel-banks, with occasional stiff rapids. But after having been in a *wu-pan* for several days, suffering that which has been detailed, and much besides, the journey got a bit dreary. These, however, are ordinary circumstances; but when one has been laid up on a bench of a bed for three days with a high temperature, a legacy of several years in the humid tropics, the physical discomfort baffles description. Malaria, as all sufferers know, has a tendency to cause trouble as soon as one gets into cold weather, and in my case, as will be seen in subsequent parts of this book, it held faithfully to its best traditions. Fever on the Yangtze in a *wu-pan* would require a chapter to itself, not to mention the kindly eccentricities of a companion whose knowledge of malaria was most elementary and whose knowledge of nursing absolutely *nil*. But I refrain. As also do I of further talk about the Yangtze gorges and the rapids.

From Kweifu to Wan Hsien is a tedious journey. The country opens out, and is more or less monotonously flat. The majority of the dangers and difficulties, however, are over, and one is able to settle down in comparative peace. Fortunately for the author, nothing untoward happened, but travelers are warned not to be too sanguine. Wrecks have happened within a few miles of the destination, generally to be accounted for by the unhappy knack the Chinese boatman has of taking all precautions where the dangerous rapids exist, and leaving all to chance elsewhere. Some two years later, as I was coming down the river from Chung-king in December, I counted no less than nine wrecks, one boat having on board a cargo for the China Inland Mission authorities of no less than 480 boxes. The contents were spread out on the banks to dry, while the boat was turned upside down and repaired on the spot.

❦

A hopeless cry is continually ascending in Hong-Kong and Shanghai that trade is bad, that the palmy days are gone, and that one might as well leave business to take care of itself.

And it is not to be denied that increased trade in the Far East does not of necessity mean increased profits. Competition has rendered buying and selling, if they are to show increased dividends, a much harder task than some of the older merchants had when they built up their businesses twenty or thirty years ago. There is no comparison. But Hong-Kong, by virtue of her remarkably favorable position geographically, should always be able to hold her own; and now that the railway has pierced the great province of Yuen-nan, and brought the provinces beyond the navigable Yangtze nearer to the outside world, she should be able to reap a big harvest in Western China, if merchants will move at the right time. More often than not the Britisher loses his trade, not on account of the alleged reason that business is not to be done, but because, content with his club life, and with playing games when he should be doing business, he allows the German to rush past him, and this man, an alien in the colony, by persistent plodding and other more or less commendable traits of business which I should like to detail, but for which I have no space, takes away the trade while the Britisher looks on.

The whole of the trade of the three western provinces—Yuen-nan, Kweichow and Szech'wan—has for all time been handled by Shanghai, going into the interior by the extremely hazardous route of these Yangtze rapids, and then over the mountains by coolie or pack-horse. This has gone on for centuries. But now the time has come for the Hong-Kong trader to step in and carry away the lion share of the greatly increasing foreign trade for those three provinces by means of the advantage the new Tonkin-Yuen-nan Railway has given him.

The railway runs from Haiphong in Indo-China to Yuen-nan-fu, the capital of Yuen-nan province. And it appears certain to the writer that, with such an important town three or four days from the coast, shippers will not be content to continue to ship via the Yangtze, with all its risk. British and American merchants, who carry the greater part of the imports to Western China, will send their goods direct to Hong-Kong, where transhipment will be made to Haiphong, and thence shipped by rail to Yuen-nan-fu, the distributing center for inland trade. To my mind, Hong-Kong merchants might control the whole of the British trade of Western China if they will

46

only push, for although the tariff of Tonkin may be heavy, it would be compensated by the fact that transit would be so much quicker and safer. But it needs push.

The history of our intercourse with China, from the days of the East India Company till now, is nothing but a record of a continuous struggle to open up and develop trade. Opening up trade, too, with a people who have something pathetic in the honest persistency with which their officials have vainly struggled to keep themselves uncontaminated from the outside world. Trade in China cannot be left to take care of itself, as is done in Western countries. However invidious it may seem, we must admit the fact that past progress has been due to pressure. Therefore, if the opportunities were placed near at hand to the Hong-Kong shipper, he would be an unenterprising person indeed were he not to avail himself of the opportunity. Shanghai has held the trump card formerly. This cannot be denied. But I think the railway is destined to turn the trade route to the other side of the empire. It is merely a question as to who is to get the trade—the French or the British. The French are on the alert. They cannot get territory; now they are after the trade.

It is my opinion that it would be to the advantage of the colony of Hong-Kong were the Chamber of Commerce there to investigate the matter thoroughly. Now is the time.

# Third Journey: Chung-King to Sui-Fu (Via Luchow)

## CHAPTER V

*Beginning of the overland journey. The official halo around the caravan. The people's goodbyes. Stages to Sui-fu. A persistent coolie. My boy's indignation, and the sequel. Kindness of the people of Chung-king. The Chung-king Consulate. Need of keeping fit in travelling in China. Walking tabooed. The question of "face" and what it means. Author runs the gauntlet. Carrying coolie's rate of pay. The so-called great paved highways of China, and a few remarks thereon. The garden of China. Magnificence of the scenery of Western China. The tea-shops. The Chinese coolie's thirst and how the author drank. Population of Szech-wan. Minerals found. Salt and other things. The Chinese inn: how it holds the palm for unmitigated filth. Description of the rooms. Szech-wan and Yuen-nan caravanserais. Need of a camp bed. Toileting in unsecluded publicity. How the author was met at market towns. How the days do not get dull.*

In a manner admirably befitting my rank as an English traveler, apart from the fact that I was the man who was endeavoring to cross China on foot, I was led out of Chung-king *en route* for Bhamo alone, my companion having had to leave me here.

It was Easter Sunday, a crisp spring morning.

First came a public sedan-chair, bravely borne by three of the finest fellows in all China, at the head of which on either side were two uniformed persons called soldiers—incomprehensible to one who has no knowledge of the interior, for they bore no marks whatever of the military—whilst uniformed men also solemnly guarded the back. Then came the grinning coolies, carrying that meager portion of my worldly goods which I had anticipated would have been engulfed in the Yangtze. And at the head of all, leading them on as captains do the Salvation Army, was I myself, walking along triumphantly, undoubtedly looking a person of weight, but somehow peculiarly unable to get out of my head that little adage apropos the fact that when the blind shall lead the blind both shall fall into a ditch! But Chinese decorum forbade my falling behind. I had determined to walk across China, every inch of the way or not at all; and the chair coolies, unaware of my intentions presumably, thought it a great joke when at the western gate, through which I departed, I gave instructions that one hundred cash be doled out to each man for his graciousness in escorting me through the town.

All the people were in the middle of the streets—those slippery streets of interminable steps—to give me at parting their blessings or their curses, and only with difficulty and considerable shouting and pushing could I sufficiently take their attention from the array of official and civil servants who made up my caravan as to effect an exit.

The following were to be stages:—

| | | |
|---|---|---|
| 1st day—Ts'eo-ma-k'ang | 80 li. | |
| 2nd day—Uein-ch'uan hsien | 120 " | |
| 3rd day—Li-shih-ch'ang | 105 " | |
| 4th day—Luchow | 75 " | |
| 5th day—Lan-ching-ch'ang | 80 " | |
| 6th day—Lan-chi-hsien | 75 " | |
| 7th day—Sui-fu | 120 " | |

In my plainest English and with many cruel gestures, four miles from the town, I told a man that he narrowly escaped being knocked down, owing to his extremely rude persistence in accosting me and obstructing my way. He acquiesced, opened his large mouth to the widest proportions, seemed thoroughly to understand, but continued more noisily to prevent me from going onwards, yelling something at the top of his husky voice—a voice more like a fog-horn than a human voice—which made me fear that I had done something very wrong, but which later I interpreted ignorantly as impudent humor.

I owed nothing; so far as I knew, I had done nothing wrong.

"Hi, fellow! come out of the way! Reverse your carcass a bit, old chap! Get—! What the— who the—?"

"Oh, master, he wantchee makee much bobbery. He no b'long my pidgin, d— rogue! He wantchee catch one more hundred cash! He b'long one piecee chairman!"

This to me from my boy in apologetic explanation.

Then, turning wildly upon the man, after the manner of his kind raising his little fat body to the tips of his toes and effectively assuming the attitude of the stage actor, he cursed loudly to the uttermost of eternity the impudent fellow's ten thousand relatives and ancestry; which, although it called forth more mutual confidences of a like nature, and made T'ong (my boy) foam at the mouth with rage at such an inopportune proceeding happening so early in his career, rendering it necessary for him to push the man in the right jaw, incidentally allowed him to show his master just a little that he could do. The man had been dumped against the wall, but he was still undaunted. With thin mud dropping from one leg of his flimsy pantaloons, he came forward again, did this chair coolie, whom I had just paid off—for it was assuredly one of the trio—leading out again one of those little wiry, shaggy ponies, and wished to do another deal. He had, however, struck a snag. We did not come to terms. I merely lifted the quadruped bodily from my path and walked on.

Chung-king people treated us well, and had it not been for their kindness the terrible three days spent still in our *wu-pan* on the crowded beach would have been more terrible still.

At the Consulate we found Mr. Phillips, the Acting-Consul, ready packed up to go down to Shanghai, and Mr. H.E. Sly, whom we had met in Shanghai, was due to relieve him. Mr. J.L. Smith, of the Consular Service, was here also, just reaching a state of convalescence after an attack of measles, and was to go to Chen-tu to take up duty as soon as he was fit. But despite the topsy-turvydom, we were made welcome, and both Phillips and Smith did their best to entertain. Chung-king Consulate is probably the finest—certainly one of the finest—in China, built on a commanding site overlooking the river and the city, with the bungalow part over in the hills. It possesses remarkably fine grounds, has every modern convenience, not the least attractive features being the cement tennis-court and a small polo ground adjoining. I had hoped to see polo on those little rats of ponies, but it could not be arranged. I should have liked to take a stick as a farewell.

People were shocked indeed that I was going to walk across China.

Let me say here that travel in the Middle Kingdom is quite possible anywhere provided that you are fit. You have merely to learn and to maintain untold patience, and you are able to get where you like, if you have got the money to pay your way;[6] but walking is a very different thing. It is probable that never previously has a traveler actually walked across China, if we except the Rev. J. McCarthy, of the China Inland Mission, who some thirty

---

6    This refers to the main roads There are many places in isolated and unsurveyed districts where it is extremely difficult and often impossible to get along at all—E.J.D.

years or so ago did walk across to Burma, although he went through Kwei-chow province over a considerably easier country. Not because it is by any means physically impossible, but because the custom of the country—and a cursed custom too—is that one has to keep what is called his "face." And to walk tends to make a man lose "face."

A quiet jaunt through China on foot was, I was told, quite out of the question; the uneclipsed audacity of a man mentioning it, and especially a man such as I was, was marvelled at. Did I not know that the foreigner *must* have a chair? (This was corroborated by my boy, on his oath, because he would have to pay the men.) Did I not know that no traveler in Western China, who at any rate had any sense of self-respect, would travel without a chair, not necessarily as a conveyance, but for the honor and glory of the thing? And did I not know that, unfurnished with this undeniable token of respect, I should be liable to be thrust aside on the highway, to be kept waiting at ferries, to be relegated to the worst inn's worst room, and to be generally treated with indignity? This idea of mine of crossing China on foot was preposterous!

Even Mr. Hudson Broomhall, of the China Inland Mission, who with Mrs. Broomhall was extremely kind, and did all he could to fit me up for the journey (it is such remembrances that make the trip one which I would not mind doing again), was surprised to know that I was walking, and tried to persuade me to take a chair. But I flew in the face of it all. These good people certainly impressed me, but I decided to run the gauntlet and take the risk.

The question of "face" is always merely one of theory, never of fact, and the principles that govern "face" and its attainment were wholly beyond my apprehension. "I shall probably be more concerned in saving my life than in saving my face," I thought.

Therefore it was that when I reached a place called Fu-to-gwan I discarded all superfluities of dress, and strode forward, just at that time in the early morning when the sun was gilding the dewdrops on the hedgerows with a grandeur which breathed encouragement to the traveler, in a flannel shirt and flannel pants—a terrible breach of foreign etiquette, no doubt, but very comfortable to one who was facing the first eighty li he had ever walked on China's soil. My three coolies—the typical Chinese coolie of Szech'wan, but very good fellows with all their faults—were to land me at Sui-fu, 230 miles distant (some 650 li), in seven days' time. They were to receive four hundred cash per man per day, were to find themselves, and if I reached Sui-fu within the specified time I agreed to *kumshaw* them to the extent of an extra thousand.[7] They carried, according to the arrangement, ninety catties apiece, and their rate of pay I did not consider excessive until I found that each man sublet his contract for a fourth of his pay, and trotted along light-heartedly and merry at my side; then I regretted that I had not thought twice before closing with them.

It is probable that the solidity of the great paved highways of China have been exaggerated. I have not been on the North China highways, but have had considerable experience of them in Western China, Szech'wan and Yuen-nan particularly, and have very little praise to lavish upon them. Certain it is that the road to Sui-fu does not deserve the nice things said about it by various travelers. The whole route from Chung-king to Sui-fu, paved with flagstones varying in width from three to six or seven feet—the only main road, of course—is creditably regular in some places, whilst other portions, especially over the mountains, are extremely bad and uneven. In some places, I could hardly get along at all, and my boy would call out as he came along in his chair behind me—

"Master, I thinkee you makee catch two piecee men makee carry. This b'long no proper road. P'raps you makee bad feet come."

And truly my feet were shamefully blistered.

One had to step from stone to stone with considerable agility. In places bridges had fallen in, nobody had attempted to put them into a decent state of repair—though this is never done in China—and one of the features of every day was the wonderful fashion in which the mountain ponies picked their way over the broken route; they are as sure-footed as goats.

As I gazed admiringly along the miles and miles of ripening wheat and golden rape, pink-flowering beans, interspersed everywhere with the inevitable poppy, swaying gently as in a sea of all the dainty colors of the rainbow, I did not wonder that Szech'wan had been called the Garden of China. Greater or denser cultivation I had never seen. The amphitheater-like hills smiled joyously in the first gentle touches of spring and enriching green, each terrace being irrigated from the one below by a small stream of water regulated in the most primitive manner (the windlass driven by man power), and not a square inch lost. Even the mud banks dividing these fertile areas are made to yield on the sides cabbages and lettuces and on the tops wheat

---

7    This rate of four hundred cash per day per man was maintained right up to Tong-ch'uan-fu, although after Chao-t'ong the usual rate paid is a little higher, and the bad cash in that district made it difficult for my men to arrange four hundred "big" cash current in Szech'wan in the Yuen-nan equivalent. After Tong-ch'uan-fu, right on to Burma, the rate of coolie pay varies considerably. Three tsien two fen (thirty-two tael cents) was the highest I paid until I got to Tengyueh, where rupee money came into circulation, and where expense of living was considerably higher.—E.J.D.

and poppy. There are no fences. You see before you a forest of mountains, made a dark leaden color by thick mists, from out of which gradually come the never-ending pictures of green and purple and brown and yellow and gold, which roll hither and thither under a cloudy sky in indescribable confusion. The chain may commence in the south or the north in two or three soft, slow-rising undulations, which trend away from you and form a vapory background to the landscape. From these (I see such a picture even as I write, seated on the stone steps in the middle of a mountain path), at once united and peculiarly distinct, rise five masses with rugged crests, rough, and cut into shady hollows on the sides, a faint pale aureola from the sun on the mists rising over the summits and sharp outlines. Looking to the north, an immense curved line shows itself, growing ever greater, opening like the arch of a gigantic bridge, and binding this first group to a second, more complicated, each peak of which has a form of its own, and does in some sort as it pleases without troubling itself about its neighbor. The most remarkable point about these mountains is the life they seem to possess. It is an incredible confusion. Angles are thrown fantastically by some mad geometer, it would seem. Splendid banyan trees shelter one after toiling up the unending steps, and dotted over the landscape, indiscriminately in magnificent picturesqueness, are pretty farmhouses nestling almost out of sight in groves of sacred trees. Oftentimes perpendicular mountains stand sheer up for three thousand feet or more, their sides to the very summits ablaze with color coming from the smiling face of sunny Nature, in spots at times where only a twelve-inch cultivation is possible.

A dome raises its head curiously over the leaning shoulder of a round hill, and a pyramid reverses itself, as if to the music of some wild orchestra, whose symphonies are heard in the mountain winds. Seen nearer and in detail, these mountains are all in delicious keeping with all of what the imagination in love with the fantastic, attracted by their more distant forms, could dream. Valleys, gorges, somber gaps, walls cut perpendicularly, rough or polished by water, cavities festooned with hanging stalactites and notched like Gothic sculptures—all make up a strange sight which cannot but excite admiration.

Every mile or so there are tea-houses, and for a couple of cash a coolie can get a cup of tea, with leaves sufficient to make a dozen cups, and as much boiling water as he wants. Szech'wan, the country, its people, their ways and methods, and much information thereto appertaining, is already in print. It were useless to give more of it here—and, reader, you will thank me! But the thirst of Szech'wan—that thirst which is unique in the whole of the Empire, and eclipsed nowhere on the face of the earth, except perhaps on the Sahara—one does not hear about.

Many an Englishman would give much for the Chinese coolie's thirst—so very, very much.

I wonder whether you, reader, were ever thirsty? Probably not. You get a thirst which is not insatiable. Yours is born of nothing extraordinary; yours can be satisfied by a gulp or two of water, or perhaps by a drink—or perhaps two, or perhaps three—of something stronger. The Chinese coolie's thirst arises from the grilling sun, from a dancing glare, from hard hauling, struggling with 120 pounds slung over his shoulders, dangling at the end of a bamboo pole. I have had this thirst of the Chinese coolie—I know it well. It is born of sheer heat and sheer perspiration. Every drop of liquid has been wrung out of my body; I have seemed to have swum in my clothes, and inside my muscles have seemed to shrink to dry sponge and my bones to dry pith. My substance, my strength, my self has drained out of me. I have been conscious of perpetual evaporation and liquefaction. And I have felt that I must stop and wet myself again. I really *must* wet myself and swell to life again. And here we sit at the tea-shop. People come and stare at me, and wonder what it is. They, too, are thirsty, for they are all coolies and have the coolie thirst.

I wet myself. I pour in cup after cup, and my body, my self sucks it in, draws it in as if it were the water of life. Instantly it gushes out again at every pore. I swill in more, and out it rushes again, madly rushes out as quickly as it can. I swill in more and more, and out it comes defiantly. I can keep none inside me. Useless—I *cannot* quench my thirst. At last the thirst thinks its conquest assured, taking the hot tea for a signal of surrender; but I pour in more, and gradually feel the tea settling within me. I am a degree less torrid, a shade more substantial.

And then here comes my boy.

"Master, you wantchee makee one drink brandy-and-soda. No can catchee soda this side—have got water. Can do?"

Ah! shall I? Shall I? No! I throw it away from me, fling a bottle of cheap brandy which he had bought for me at Chung-king away from me, and the boy looks forlorn.

Tea is the best of all drinks in China; for the traveler unquestionably the best. Good in the morning, good at midday, good in the evening, good at night, even after the day's toil has been forgotten. To-morrow I shall have more walking, more thirsting, more tea. China tea, thou art a godsend to the wayfarer in that great land!

I endeavored to get the details of the population of the province of Szech'wan, the variability of the reports providing an excellent illustration of the uncertainty impending over everything statistical in China—estimates ranged from thirty-five to eighty millions.

The surface of this province is made up of masses of rugged mountains, through which the Yangtze has cut its deep and narrow channel. The area is everywhere intersected by steep-sided valleys and ravines. The world-famed plain of Chen-tu, the capital, is the only plain of any size in the province, the system of irrigation employed on it being one of the wonders of the world. Every food crop flourishes in Szech'wan, an inexhaustible supply of products of the Chinese pharmacopoeia enrich the stores and destroy the stomachs of the well-to-do; and with the exception of cotton, all that grows in Eastern China grows better in this great Garden of the Empire. Its area is about that of France, its climate is even superior—a land delightfully *accidentee*. Among the minerals found are gold, silver, cinnabar, copper, iron, coal and petroleum; the chief products being opium, white wax, hemp, yellow silk. Szech'wan is a province rich in salt, obtained from artesian borings, some of which extend 2,500 feet below the surface, and from which for centuries the brine has been laboriously raised by antiquated windlass and water buffalo.

The best conditions of Chinese inns are far and away worse than anything the traveler would be called upon to encounter anywhere in the British Isles, even in the most isolated places in rural Ireland. There can be no comparison. And my reader will understand that there is much which the European misses in the way of general physical comfort and cleanliness. Sanitation is absent *in toto*. Ordinary decency forbids one putting into print what the uninitiated traveler most desires to know—if he would be saved a severe shock at the outset; but everyone has to go through it, because one cannot write what one sees. All travelers who have had to put up at the caravanseries in Central and Western China will bear me out in my assertion that all of them reek with filth and are overrun by vermin of every description. The traveler whom misfortune has led to travel off the main roads of Russia may probably hesitate in expressing an opinion as to which country carries off the palm for unmitigated filth; but, with this exception, travelers in the Eastern Archipelago, in Central Asia, in Africa among the wildest tribes, are pretty well unanimous that compared with all these for dirt, disease, discomfort, an utter lack of decency and annoyance, the Chinese inn holds its own. And in no part of China more than in Szech'wan and Yuen-nan is greater discomfort experienced.

The usual wooden bedstead stands in the corner of the room with the straw bedding (this, by the way, should on no account be removed if one wishes to sleep in peace), sometimes there is a table, sometimes a couple of chairs. If these are steady it is lucky, if unbroken it is the exception; there are never more. Over the bedstead (more often than not, by the way, it is composed of four planks of varying lengths and thickness, placed across two trestles) I used first to place my oilskin, then my *p'u-k'ai*, and that little creeper which rhymes with hug did not disturb me much. Rats ran round and over me in profusion, and, of course, the best room being invariably nearest to the pigsties, there were the usual stenches. The floor was Mother Earth, which in wet weather became mud, and quite a common thing it was for my joys to be enhanced during a heavy shower of rain by my having to sleep, almost suffocated, mackintosh over my head, owing to a slight break in the continuity of the roof—my umbrella being unavailable, as one of my men dropped it over a precipice two days out. For many reasons a camp-bed is to Europeans an indispensable part of even the most modest traveling equipment. I was many times sorry that I had none with me.

The inns of Szech'wan, however, are by many degrees better than those of Yuen-nan, which are sometimes indescribable. Earthen floors are saturated with damp filth and smelling decay; there are rarely the paper windows, but merely a sort of opening of woodwork, through which the offensive smells of decaying garbage and human filth waft in almost to choke one; tables collapse under the weight of one's dinner; walls are always in decay and hang inwards threateningly; wicked insects, which crawl and jump and bite, creep over the side of one's rice bowl—and much else. Who can describe it? It makes one ill to think of it.

Throughout my journeyings it was necessary for my toileting, in fact, everything, to be performed in absolute unalloyed publicity. Three days out my boy fixed up a cold bath for me, and barricaded a room which had a certain amount of privacy about it, owing to its secluded position; but even grown men and women, anxious to see what *it* was like when it had no clothes on, came forward, poked their fingers through the paper in the windows (of course, glass is hardly known in the interior), and greedily peeped in. This and the profound curiosity the people evince in one's every action and movement I found most trying.

It was my misfortune each day at this stage to come into a town or village where market was in progress. Catching a sight of the foreign visage, people opened their eyes widely, turned from me, faced me again with a little less of fear, and then came to me, not in dozens, but in hundreds, with open arms. They shouted and made signs, and walking excitedly by my side, they examined at will the texture of my clothes, and touched my boots with sticks to see whether the feet were encased or not. For the time I was their hero. When I walked into an inn business brightened immediately. Tea was at a premium, and only the richer class could afford nine cash instead of three to drink tea with the bewildered foreigner. The most inquisitive came behind me, rubbing their unshaven pates against the side of my head in enterprising endeavor to see through the sides of my spectacles. They would speak to me, yelling in their coarsest tones thinking my hearing was defective. I would motion then to go away, always politely, cleverly suppressing my sense of indignation at their conduct; and they would do so, only to make room for a worse crowd. The town's business stopped; people left their stalls and shops to glare aimlessly at or to ask inane and unintelligible questions about the barbarian who seemed to have dropped suddenly from the heavens. When I addressed a few words to them in strongest Anglo-Saxon, telling them in the name of all they held sacred to go away and leave me in peace, something like a cheer would go up, and my boy would swear them all down in his choicest. When I slowly rose to move the crowd looked disappointed, but allowed me to go forward on my journey in peace.

Thus the days passed, and things were never dull.

# CHAPTER VI

*Szech-wan people a mercenary lot. Adaptability to trading. None but na-*
*ture lovers should come to Western China. The life of the Nomad. The open-*
*ing of China, and some impressions. China's position in the eyes of her own*
*people. Industrialism, railways, and the attitude of the populace. Introduc-*
*tion of foreign machinery. Different opinions formed in different provinces.*
*Climate, and what it is responsible for. Recent Governor of Szech-wan's*
*tribute to Christianity. New China and the new student. Revolution-*
*ary element in Yuen-nan. Need of a new life, and how China is to get it.*
*Luchow, and a little about it. Fusong from the military. Necessity of the*
*sedan-chair. Cost of lodging. An impudent woman. Choice pidgin-English.*
*Some of the annoyances of travel. Canadian and China Inland missionaries.*
*Exchange of yarns. Exasperating Chinese life, and its effects on Europeans.*
*Men refuse to walk to Sui-fu. Experiences in arranging up-river trip. Un-*
*meaning etiquette of Chinese officials toward foreigners. Rude awakening*
*in the morning. A trying early-morning ordeal. Reckonings do not tally. An*
*eventful day. At the China Inland Mission. Impressions of Sui-fu. Ficti-*
*tious partnerships.*

*T*he people of Szech'wan, compared with other Yangtze provinces, must
be called a mercenary, if a go-ahead, one.

Balancing myself on a three-inch form in a tea-shop at a small
town midway between Li-shih-ch'ang and Luchow, I am endeavoring to
take in the scene around me. The people are so numerous in this province
that they must struggle in order to live. Vain is it for the most energetic
among them to escape from the shadow of necessity and hunger; all are
similarly begirt, so they settle down to devote all their energies to trade.
And trade they do, in very earnest.

59

Everything is labeled, from the earth to the inhabitants; these primitives, these blissfully "heathen" people, have become the most consummate of sharpers. I walk up to buy something of the value of only a few cash, and on all sides are nets and traps, like spider-webs, and the fly that these gentry would catch, as they see me stalk around inspecting their wares, is myself. They seem to lie in wait for one, and for an article for which a coolie would pay a few cash as many dollars are demanded of the foreigner. My boy stands by, however, magnificently proud of his lucrative and important post, yelling precautions to the curious populace to stand away. He hints, he does not declare outright, but by ungentle innuendo allows them to understand that, whatever their private characters may be, to him they are all liars and rogues and thieves. It is all so funny, that one's fatigue is minimized to the last degree by the humor one gets and the novel changes one meets everywhere.

Onward again, my men singing, perhaps quarreling, always swearing. Their language is low and coarse and vulgar, but happily ignorant am I.

The country, too, is fascinating in the extreme. A man must not come to China for pleasure unless he love his mistress Nature when she is most rudely clad. Some of her lovers are fascinated most in by-places, in the cool of forests, on the summit of lofty mountains, high up from the mundane, in the cleft of canons, everywhere that the careless lover is not admitted to her contemplation. It is for such that China holds out an inviting hand, but she offers little else to the Westerner—the student of Nature and of man can alone be happy in the interior. Forgetting time and the life of my own world, I sometimes come to inviolate stillnesses, where Nature opens her arms and bewitchingly promises embraces in soft, unending, undulating vastnesses, where even the watching of a bird building its nest or brooding over its young, or some little groundling at its gracious play, seems to hold one charmed beyond description. It is, some may say, a nomadic life. Yes, it is a nomadic life. But how beautiful to those of us, and there are many, who love less the man-made comforts of our own small life than the entrancing wonders of the God-made world in spots where nothing has changed. Gladly did I quit the dust and din of Western life, the artificialities of dress, and the unnumbered futile affectations of our own maybe not misnamed civilization, to go and breathe freely and peacefully in those far-off nooks of the silent mountain-tops where solitude was broken only by the lulling or the roaring of the winds of heaven. Thank God there are these uninvaded corners. The realm of silence is, after all, vaster than the realm of noise, and the fact brought a consolation, as one watched Nature effecting a sort of coquetry in masking her operations.

And as I look upon it all I wonder—wonder whether with the "Opening of China" this must all change?

The Chinese—I refer to the Chinese of interior provinces such as Szech-wan—are realizing that they hold an obscure position. I have heard educated Chinese remark that they look upon themselves as lost, like shipwrecked sailors, whom a night of tempest has cast on some lonely rock; and now they are having recourse to cries, volleys, all the signals imaginable, to let it be known that they are still there. They have been on this lonely isolated rock as far as history can trace. Now they are launching out towards progress, towards the making of things, towards the buying and selling of things—launching out in trade and in commerce, in politics, in literature, in science, in all that has spelt advance in the West. The modern spirit is spreading speedily into the domains of life everywhere—in places swiftly, in places slowly, but spreading inevitably, *si sit prudentia.*

Nothing will tend, in this particular part of the country, to turn it upside down and inside out more than the cult of industrialism. In a number of centers in Eastern China, such as Han-yang and Shanghai, foreign mills, iron works, and so on, furnish new employments, but in the interior the machine of the West to the uneducated Celestial seems to be the foe of his own tools; and when railways and steam craft appear—steam has appeared, of course, on the Upper Yangtze, although it has not yet taken much of the junk trade, and Szech'wan has her railways now under construction (the sod was cut at Ichang in 1909)[8]—and a single train and steamer does the work of hundreds of thousands of carters, coolies, and boatmen, it is wholly natural that their imperfect and short-sighted views should lead them to rise against a seeming new peril.

Whilst in the end the Empire will profit greatly by the inventions of the Occident, the period of transition in Szech'wan, especially if machines are introduced too rapidly and unwisely, is one that will disturb the peace. It will be interesting to watch the attitude of the people towards the railway, for Szech'wan is essentially the province of the farmer. Szech'wan was one of the provinces where concessions were demanded, and railways had been

---

8    I inspected the railway at Ichang in December, 1910, and found that a remarkable scheme was making very creditable progress. Around the main station centre there was an air of bustle and excitement, some 20,000 coolies were in employment there, all the buildings and equipment bore evidences of thoroughness, and the scheme seemed to be going on well. But in January of this year (1911) a meeting was held at Chen-tu, the proposed destination of the line, and the gentry then decided that as nothing was being done at that end the company should be requested to stop work at Ichang, and start laying the line from Chen-tu, at the other end. "All the money will be spent," they cried, "and we shall get nothing up this end!" If the money ran out and left the central portion of the line incomplete, it did not matter so long as each city had something for its money!—E.J.D.

planned by European syndicates, and where the gentry and students held mass meetings, feverishly declaring that none shall build Chinese lines but the people themselves. I have no space in a work of this nature to go fully into the question of industrialism, railways, and other matters immediately vital to the interests of China, but if the peace of China is to be maintained, it is incumbent upon every foreigner to "go slowly." Machines of foreign make have before now been scrapped, railways have been pulled up and thrown into the sea, telegraph lines have been torn down and sold, and on every hand among this wonderful people there has always been apparent a distinct hatred to things and ideas foreign. But industrially particularly the benefits of the West are being recognized in Eastern China, and gradually, if foreigners who have to do the pioneering are tactful, trust in the foreign-manufactured machine will spread to Western China, and enlarged industrialism will bring all-round advantages to Western trade.

Thus far there has been little shifting of the population from hamlets and villages to centers of new industries—even in the more forward areas quoted—but when this process begins new elements will enter into the Chinese industrial problem.

As we hear of the New China, so is there a "new people," a people emboldened by the examples of officials in certain areas to show a friendliness towards progress and innovation. They were not friendly a decade ago. It may, perhaps, be said that this "new people" were born after the Boxer troubles, and in Szech'wan they have a large influence.

Cotton mills, silk filatures, flour and rice mills employing western machinery, modern mining plants and other evidences of how China is coming out of her shell, cause one to rejoice in improved conditions. The animosity occasioned by these inventions that are being so gradually and so surely introduced into every nook and cranny of East and North China is very marked; but on close inspection, and after one has made a study of the subject, one is inclined to feel that it is more or less theoretical. So it is to be hoped it will be in Szech'wan and Far Western China.

Readers may wonder at the differences of opinions expressed in the course of these pages—a hundred pages on one may get a totally different impression. But the absolute differences of conditions existing are quite as remarkable. From Chung-king to Sui-fu one breathed an air of progress—after one had made allowance for the antagonistic circumstances under which China lives—a manifest desire on every hand for things foreign, and a most lively and intelligent interest in what the foreigner could bring. In many parts of Yuen-nan, again, conditions were completely reversed; and one finding himself in Yuen-nan, after having lived for some time at a port in the east of the Empire, would assuredly find himself surrounded by everything antagonistic to that to which he has become accustomed, and the people would seem of a different race. This may be due to the differences of climate—climate, indeed, is ultimately the first and the last word in the East; it is the arbiter, the builder, the disintegrator of everything. A leading writer on Eastern affairs says that the "climate is the explanation of all this history of Asia, and the peoples of the East can only be understood and accounted for by the measuring of the heat of the sun's rays. In China, with climate and weather charts in your hands, you may travel from the Red River on the Yuen-nan frontier to the great Sungari in lusty Manchuria, and be able to understand and account for everything."

However that may be, traveling in China, through a wonderful province like Szech'wan, whose chief entrepot is fifteen hundred miles from the coast, convinces one that she has come to the parting of the ways. You can, in any city or village in Szech'wan—or in Yuen-nan, for that matter, in a lesser degree—always find the new nationalism in the form of the "New China" student. Despite the opposition he gets from the old school, and although the old order of things, by being so strong as almost to overwhelm him, allows him to make less progress than he would, this new student, the hope of the Empire, is there. I do not wish to enter into a controversy on this subject, but I should like to quote the following from a speech delivered by Tseh Ch'un Hsuean, when he was leaving his post as Governor of Szech'wan:—

"The officials of China are gradually acquiring a knowledge of the great principles of the religions of Europe and America. And the churches are also laboring night and day to readjust their methods, and to make known their aims in their propagation of religion. Consequently, Chinese and foreigners are coming more and more into cordial relations. This fills me with joy and hopefulness.... My hope is that the teachers of both countries [Great Britain and America] will spread the Gospel more wisely than ever, that hatred may be banished, and disputes dispelled, and that the influence of the Gospel may create boundless happiness for my people of China. And I shall not be the only one to thank you for coming to the front in this good work.... May the Gospel prosper!"

There are various grades of people in China, among which the scholar has always come first, because mind is superior to wealth, and it is the intellect that distinguishes man above the lower order of beings, and enables him to provide food and raiment and shelter for himself and for others. At the time when Europe was thrilled and cut to the quick with news of the massacres of her compatriots in the Boxer revolts, the scholar was a dull, stupid fellow—day in day out, week in week out, month in month out, and year after year he ground at his classics. His classics were the *Alpha* and *Omega*; he worshipped them. This era has now passed away.

At the present moment there are upwards of twenty thousand Chinese students in Tokyo[9]—whither they went because Japan is the most convenient country wherein to acquire Western knowledge. The new learning, the new learning—they *must* have the new learning! No high office is ever again likely to be given but to him who has more of Western knowledge than Chinese knowledge. And mere striplings, nursed in the lap of the mission schools, and there given a good grounding in Western education, these are the men far more likely to pass the new examinations. In Yuen-nan, where little chance exists for the scholars to advance, the new learning has brought with it a revolutionary element, which would soon become dangerous were it by any means common. I have seen an English-speaking fellow, anxious to get on and under the impression that the laws of his country were responsible for keeping him back, write in the back of his exercise book a phrase against the imperial ruler that would have cost him his head had it come to the notice of the high authorities.

One will learn much if he travels across the Empire—facts and figures quite irreconcilable will arise, but even the man of dullest perception will be convinced that much of the reforming spirit in the people is only skin-deep, going no farther than the externals of life. It is at present, perhaps, merely a mad fermentation in the western provinces, wherefrom the fiercer it is the clearer the product will one day evolve itself. Such transitions are full of bewilderment to the European—bewildering to any writer who endeavors to tackle the Empire as a whole. Each province or couple of provinces should be dealt with separately, so diverse are the conditions.

But if China, from the highest to the lowest, will only embrace truth and love her for her own sake, so that she will not abate one jot of allegiance to her; if China will let truth run down through the arteries of everyday commercial, social, and political life as do the waterways through her marvelous country; if China will kill her retardative conservatism, and in its place erect honesty and conscience; if China will let her moral life be quickened—then her transition period, from end to end of the Empire, will soon end. Mineral, agricultural, industrial wealth are hers to a degree which is not true of any other land. Her people have an enduring and expansive power that has stood the test of more than four thousand years of honorable

---

9    This is not true to-day. There has been a great falling off in numbers.—E.J.D., February, 1911.]

history, and their activity and efficiency outside China make them more to be dreaded, as competitors, than any race or any dozen races of to-day.

But New China must have this new life.

Commerce, science, diplomacy, culture, civilization she will have in ever-increasing measure just in so much as she draws nearer to western peoples. But the new life can come from whence? From within or from without?

Luchow, into which I was led just before noon on the fourth day out of Chung-king, is the most populous and richest city on the Upper Yangtze.

Exceedingly clean for a Chinese city, possessing well-kept streets lined with well-stocked emporiums, bearing every evidence of commercial prosperity, it however lacks one thing. It has no hotel runners! I arrived at midday, crossing the river in a leaky ferry boat, under a blazing sun, my intention being to stop in the town at a tea-house to take a refresher, and then complete a long day's march, farther than the ordinary stage. But owing to some misunderstanding between the *fu-song*, sent to shadow the foreigner on part of his journey, and my boy, I was led through the busy city out into the open country before I had had a drink. And when I remonstrated they led me back again to the best inn, where I was told I should have to spend the night—there being nothing else, then, to be said.

May I give a word of advice here to any reader contemplating a visit to China under similar conditions? It is the custom of the mandarins to send what is called a *fu-song* (escort) for you; the escort comes from the military, although their peculiar appearance may lead you to doubt it. I have two of these soldier people with me to-day, and two bigger ragamuffins it has not been my lot to cast eyes on. They are the only two men in the crowd I am afraid of. They are of absolutely no use, more than to eat and to drink, and always come up smiling at the end of their stage for their *kumshaw*. During the whole of this day I have not seen one of them—they have been behind the caravan all the time; it would be hard to believe that they had sense enough to find the way, and as for escorting me, they have not accompanied me a single li of the way.[10]

Another nuisance, of which I have already spoken, is the necessity of taking a chair to maintain respectability. These things make travel in China not so cheap as one would be led to imagine. Traveling of itself is cheap enough, as cheap as in any country in the world. For accommodation for myself, for a room, rice and as much hot water as I want, the charge is a couple of hundred cash—certainly not expensive. In addition, there is gen-

---

10     This should not be taken to apply to the fu-song everywhere. I have found them to be the most useful on other occasions, but the above was written at Luchow as my experience of that particular day.—E.J.D.

erally a little "cha tsien" (tea money) for the cook. But it is the "face" which makes away with money, much more than it takes to keep you in the luxury that the country can offer—which is not much!

After I had had a bit of a discussion with my boy as to the room they wanted to house me in, a woman, brandishing a huge cabbage stump above her head, and looking menacingly at me, yelled that the room was good enough.

"What does she say, T'ong?"

"Oh, she b'long all same fool. She wantchee makee talkee talk. She have got velly long tongue, makee bad woman. She say one piecee Japan man makee stay here t'ree night. See? She say what makee good one piecee Japan man makee good one piecee English man. See? No have got topside, all same bottomside have got. Master, this no b'long my pidgin—this b'long woman pidgin, and woman b'long all same fool." T'ong ended up with an amusing allusion to the lady's mother, and looked cross because I rebuked him.

Gathering, then, that the lady thought her room good enough for me, I saw no other course open, and as the crowd was gathering, I got inside. Before setting out to call upon the Canadian missionaries stationed at the place, I held a long conversation with a hump-backed old man, an unsightly mass of disease, who seemed to be a traditional link of Luchow. I might say that this scholastic old wag spoke nothing but Chinese, and I, as the reader knows, spoke no Chinese, so that the amount of general knowledge derived one from the other was therefore limited. But he would not go, despite the frequent deprecations of T'ong and my coolies, and my vehement rhetoric in explanation that his presence was distasteful to me, and at the end of the episode I found it imperative for my own safety, and perhaps his, to clear out.

The Canadians I found in their Chinese-built premises, comfortable albeit. Five of them were resident at the time, and they were quite pleased with the work they had done during the last year or so—most of them were new to China. At the China Inland Mission later I found two young Scotsmen getting some exercise by throwing a cricket ball at a stone wall, in a compound about twenty feet square. They were glad to see me, one of them kindly gave me a hair-cut, and at their invitation I stayed the night with them.

What is it in the nature of the Chinese which makes them appear to be so totally oblivious to the best they see in their own country?

It is surely not because they are not as sensitive as other races to the magic of beauty in either nature or art. But I found traveling and living with such apparently unsympathetic creatures exasperating to a degree, and I did not wonder that the European whose lot had been cast in the interior, sometimes, on emerging into Western civilization, appears eccentric to his own countrymen. But this in passing.

I duly arrived at Lan-chi-hsien, and was told that Sui-fu, 120 li away, would be reached the next day, although I had my doubts. A deputation from the local "gwan" waited upon me to learn my wishes and to receive my commands. I was assured that no European ever walked to Sui-fu from Lan-chi-hsien, and that if I attempted to do such a thing I should have to go alone, and that I should never reach there. I remonstrated, but my boy was firm. He took me to him and fathered me. He almost cried over me, to think that I, that I, his master, of all people in the world, should doubt his allegiance to me. "I no 'fraid," he declared. "P'laps master no savee. Sui-fu b'long velly big place, have got plenty European. You wantchee makee go fast, catchee plenty good 'chow.' I think you catchee one piecee boat, makee go up the river. P'laps I think you have got velly tired—no wantchee makee more walkee—that no b'long ploper. That b'long all same fool pidgin."

And at last I melted. There was nothing else to do.

That no one ever walked to Sui-fu from this place the district potentate assured me in a private chit, which I could not read, when he laid his gunboat at my disposal.

This, he said, would take me up very quickly. In his second note, wherein he apologized that indisposition kept him from calling personally upon me—this, of course, was a lie—he said he would feel it an honor if I would be pleased to accept the use of his contemptible boat. But T'ong whispered that the law uses these terms in China, and that nobody would be more disappointed than the Chinese magistrate if I *did* take advantage of his unmeaning offer. So I took a *wu-pan*, and the following night, when pulling into the shadows of the Sui-fu pagoda, cold and hungry, I cursed my luck that I had not broken down the useless etiquette which these Chinese officials extend towards foreigners, and taken the fellow's gunboat.

The *wu-pan*, they swore to me, would be ready to leave at 3:30 a.m. the day following. My boy did not venture to sleep at all. He stayed up outside my bedroom door—I say bedroom, but actually it was an apartment which in Europe I would not put a horse into, and the door was merely a wide, worm-eaten board placed on end. In the middle of the night I heard a noise—yea, a rattle. The said board fell down, inwards, almost upon me. A light was flashed swiftly into my eyes, and desultory remarks which suddenly escaped me were rudely interrupted by shrill screams. My boy was singing.

"Master," he cried, pulling hard-heartedly at my left big toe to wake me, "come on, come on; you wantchee makee get up. Have got two o'clock. Get up; p'laps me no wakee you, no makee sleep—no b'long ploper. One man makee go bottomside—have catchee boat. This morning no have got tea—no can catch hot water makee boil."

And soon we were ready to start. Punctually to the appointed hour we were at the bottom of the steep, dark incline leading down to the river bank.

But my reckonings were bad.

The *laoban* and the other two youthful members of the half-witted crew had not yet taken their "chow," and this, added to many little discrepancies in their reckoning and in mine, kept me in a boiling rage until half-past six, when at last they pushed off, and nearly capsized the boat at the outset. The details of that early morning, and the happenings throughout the long, sad day, I think I can never forget—from the breaking of tow-lines to frequent stranding on the rocks and sticking on sandbanks, the orders wrongly given, the narrow escape of fire on board, the bland thick-headedness of the ass of a captain, the collisions, and all the most profound examples of savage ignorance displayed when one has foolish Chinese to deal with. We reached half-way at 4:30 p.m., with sixty li to do against a wind. Hour after hour they toiled, making little headway with their misdirected labor, wasting their energies in doing the right things at the wrong time, and wrong things always, and long after sundown Sui-fu's pagoda loomed in the distance. At 11:00 p.m., stiff and hungry, and mad with rage, I was groping my way on all fours up the slippery steps through unspeakable slime and filth at the quayhead, only to be led to a disgusting inn as dirty as anything I had yet encountered. It was hard lines, for I could get no food.

An invitation, however, was given me by the Rev. R. McIntyre, who with his charming wife conducts the China Inland Mission in this city, to come and stay with them. The next morning, after a sleepless night of twisting and turning on a bug-infested bed, I was glad to take advantage of the missionary's kindness. I could not have been given a kindlier welcome.

Sui-fu has a population of roughly 150,000, and the overcrowding question is not the least important. It is situated to advantage on the right bank of the Yangtze, and does an immense trade in medicines, opium, silk, furs, silverwork, and white wax, which are the chief exports. Gunboats regularly come to Sui-fu during the heavy rains.

Just outside the city, a large area is taken up with grave mounds—common with nearly every Chinese city. Mr. McIntyre and Mr. Herbert, who was passing through Sui-fu *en route* for Ta-chien-lu, where he is now working, showed me around the city one afternoon, and one could see everything typical of the social life of two thousand years ago. The same narrow lanes succeed each other, and the conviction is gradually impressed upon the mind that such is the general trend of the character of the city and its people. There were the same busy mechanics, barbers, traders, wayside cooks, traveling fortune-tellers, and lusty coolies; the wag doctor, the bane of the gullible, was there to drive his iniquitous living; now and then the scene's monotony was disturbed by the presence of the chair and the retinue of a city mandarin. Yet with all the hurry and din, the hurrying and the scurrying in doing and driving for making money, seldom was there an accident or interruption of good nature. There was the same romance in the streets that one reads of at school—so much alike and yet so different from what one meets in the Chinese places at the coast or in Hong-Kong or Singapore. In Sui-fu, more than in any other town in Western China which I visited, had the native artist seemed to have lavished his ingenuity on the street signboards. Their caligraphy gave the most humorous intimation of the superiority of the wares on sale; many of them contained some fictitious emblem, adopted as the name of the shop, similar to the practice adopted in London two centuries ago, and so common now in the Straits Settlements, where bankrupts are allowed considerable more freedom than would be possible if fictitious registration were not allowed. I refer to the Registration of Partnerships.

# Fourth Journey: Sui-Fu to Chao-T'ong-Fu (Via Lao-Wa-T'an)

## CHAPTER VII

*Chinese and simplicity of speech. Author and his caravan stopped. Advice to travelers. Farewell to Sui-fu. The postal service and tribute to I.P.O. Rushing the stages. Details of journey. Description of road to Chao-t'ong-fu. Coolie's pay. My boy steals vegetables. Remarks on roads and railways. The real Opening of China. How the foreigner will win the confidence of the Chinese. Distances and their variability. Calculations uprooted. Author in a dilemma. The scenery. Hard going. A wayside toilet, and some embarrassment. Filth inseparable from Chinese humanity. About Chinese inns. Typewriter causes some fun. Soldiers guard my doorway. Man's own "inner room." One hundred and forty li in a day. Grandeur and solitude. Wisdom of traveling alone. Coolie nearly cuts his toe off. Street scene at Puerh-tu. The "dying" coolie. A manacled prisoner. Entertained by mandarins. How plans do not work out.*

He who would make most abundant excuses for the Chinese could not say that he is simple in his speech.

That speech is the chief revelation of the mind, the first visible form that it takes, is undoubtedly true: as the thought, so the speech. All social relations with us have their roots in mutual trust, and this trust is maintained by each man's sincerity of thought and speech. Apparently not so in China. There is so much craft, so much diplomacy, so much subtle legerdemain that, if he chooses, the Chinese may give you no end of trouble to inform yourself on the simplest subject. The Chinese, like so many cavillers and calumniators, all glib of tongue, who know better than any nation on earth how to turn voice and pen to account, have taken the utmost advantage of extended means of circulating thought, with the result that an Englishman such as myself, even were I a deep scholar of their language,

71

would have the greatest difficulty in getting at the truth about their own affairs.

As I was going out of Sui-fu my caravan and myself were delayed by some fellow, who held the attention of my men for a full quarter of an hour. I listened, understanding nothing. After another five minutes, by which time the conversation had assumed what I considered dangerous proportions, having the safety of my boy at heart, I asked—

"T'ong, what is it?"

"Half a sec.," he replied (having learnt this phrase from the gunboat men down the river). He did not, however, take his eyes from the man with whom he was holding the conversation. He then dived into my food-basket, wrenched off the top of a tin, and pulled therefrom two beautifully-marked live pigeons, which flapped their wings helplessly to get away, and resumed the conversation. Talk waxed furious, the birds were placed by the side of the road, and T'ong, now white with seeming rage, threatened to hit the man. It turned out that the plaintiff was the seller of the birds, and that T'ong had got them too cheap.

"That man no savee. He thinkee you, master, have got plenty money. He b'long all same rogue. I no b'long fool. I know, I know."

As the cover of the food-basket was closed down I noticed a cooked fowl, two live pheasants with their legs tied together, a pair of my own muddy boots, a pair of dancing pumps, and a dirty collar, all in addition to my little luxuries and the two pigeons aforesaid. Reader, if thou would'st travel in China, peep not into thy *hoh shih lan tsi* if thou would'st feed well.

T'ong, laughing derisively, waved fond and fantastic salutations to the disappointed vendor of pigeons, and moved backwards on tiptoe till he could see him no more; then we went noiselessly down a steep incline out into an open space of distracted and dishevelled beauty on our way to Chao-t'ong-fu.

From Chung-king I had stuck to the regular stages. I had done no hustling, but I decided to rush it to Chao-t'ong if I could, as the reports I heard about being overtaken by the rains in Yuen-nan were rather disquieting. I had taken to Sui-fu three times as long as the regular mail time, the service of which is excellent. Chung-king has no less than six local deliveries daily, thus eliminating delays after the delivery of the mails, and a daily service to the coast has also been established. A fast overland service to Wan Hsien now exists, by which the coast mails are transmitted between that port and Chung-king in the hitherto unheard-of time of two days—a traveler considers himself fortunate if he covers the same distance in eight days. There are fast daily services to Luchow (380 li distant) in one day, Sui-fu (655 li) in two days, Hochow (180 li) in one night, and Chen-tu (1,020 li) in three days. It is creditable to the Chinese Imperial Post Office that a letter posted at Sui-fu will be delivered in Great Britain in a month's time.

It was a dull, chilly morning that I left Sui-fu, leading my little procession through the city on my way to Anpien, which was to be reached before sundown. My coolies—probably owing to having derived more pecuniary advantage than they expected during the journey from Chung-king—decided to re-engage, and promised to complete the fourteen-day tramp to Chao-t'ong-fu, two hundred and ninety miles distant, if weather permitted, in eleven days. We were to travel by the following stages:—

| | LENGTH OF STAGE | HEIGHT ABOVE SEA |
|---|---|---|
| 1st day—Anpien | 90 li | — |
| 2nd day—Huan-chiang | 55 li | — |
| 3rd day—Fan-ih-ts'uen | 70 li | — |
| 4th day—T'an-t'eo | 70 li | — |
| 5th day—Lao-wa-t'an | 140 li | 1,140 ft. |
| 6th day—Teo-sha-kwan | 60 li | 4,000 ft. |
| 7th day—Ch'i-li-p'u | 60 li | 1,900 ft. |
| 8th day—Ta-wan-tsi | 70 li | — |
| 9th day—Ta-kwan-ting | 70 li | 3,700 ft. |
| 10th day—Wuchai | 60 li | 7,000 ft. |
| 11th day—Chao-t'ong-fu | 100 li | 6,400 ft. |

I knew that I was in for a very hard journey. The nature of the country as far as T'an-t'eo, ten li this side of which the Szech'wan border is reached, is not exhausting, although the traveler is offered some rough and wild climbing. The next day's stage, to Lao-wa-t'an, is miserably bad. At certain places it is cut out of the rock, at others it runs in the bed of the river, which is dotted everywhere with roaring rapids (as we are ascending very quickly), and when the water is high these roads are submerged and often impassable. In some places it was a six-inch path along the mountain slope, with a gradient of from sixty to seventy degrees, and landslips and rains are ever changing the path.

Lao-wa-t'an is the most important point on the route. One of the largest Customs stations in the province of Yuen-nan is here situated at the east end of a one-span suspension bridge, about one hundred and fifty feet in length. No ponies carrying loads are allowed to cross the bridge, the roads east of this being unfit for beasts of burden. There is then a fearful climb to a place called Teo-sha-kwan, a stage of only sixty li. The reader should not mentally reduce this to English miles, for the march was more like fifty miles than thirty, if we consider the physical exertion required to scale the treacherous roads. Over a broad, zigzagging, roughly-paved road, said to have no less than ninety-eight curves from bottom to top, we ascend for thirty li, and then descend for the remainder of the journey through a narrow defile along the northern bank of the river, the opposite side being a vertical sheet of rock rising to at least a thousand feet sheer up, very similar to the gorges of the Mekong at the western end of the province, which I crossed in due course.

To Ch'i-li-p'u, high up on the mountain banks, the first twenty-five li is by the river. At the half-way place a fearful ascent is experienced, the most notable precipice on the route between Sui-fu and Yuen-nan-fu, up a broad zigzag path, and as I sat at dinner I could see neither top nor bottom owing to the overhanging masses of rock: this is after having negotiated an ascent quite as steep, but smaller. To Ta-kwan-hsien a few natural obstacles occur, although the road is always high up on the hill-sides. I crossed a miserable suspension bridge of two spans. The southern span is about thirty feet, the northern span eighty feet; the center is supported by a buttress of splendid blocks of squared stone, resting on the rock in the bed of the river, one side being considerably worn away by the action of the water. The longer span was hung very slack, the woodwork forming the pathway was not too safe, and the general shaky appearance was particularly uninviting.

From Ta-kwan-hsien to Wuchai is steady pulling. Once in an opening in the hill we passed along and then ascended an exceedingly steep spur on one side of a narrow and very deep natural amphitheatre, formed by surrounding mountains. We then came to a lagoon, and eventually the brow of the hill was reached. Thus the Wuchai Valley is arrived at, where, owing to a collection of water, the road is often impassable to man and beast. Often during the rainy season there is a lagoon of mud or water formed by the drainage from the mountains, which finds no escape but by percolating through the earth and rock to a valley on the east of, and below, the mountains forming the eastern boundary of the Wuchai Valley. To Chao-t'ong is fairly level going.

Considering the road, it was not unnatural that my men gibbed a little at the eleven-day accomplishment. I had a long parley with them, however, and agreed to reward them to the extent of one thousand cash among the three if they did it. Their pay for the journey, over admittedly some of the worst roads in the Empire, was to be four hundred cash per man as before, with three hundred and thirty-three cash extra if the rain did not prevent them from getting in in eleven days. They were in good spirits, and so was I, as we walked along the river-bank, where the poppy was to be seen in full flower, and the unending beds of rape alternated with peas and beans and tobacco. T'ong would persist in stealing the peas and beans to feed me on, and for the life of me I could not get him to see that he should not do this sort of thing. But how continually one was impressed with the great need of roads in Western China! It is natural that, walking the whole distance, I should notice this more than other travelers have done, and, to my mind, roads in this part of the country rank in importance before the railways.

To the foreign mind it is more to the interests of China that railways should be well and serviceably built than that the money should be squandered to no purpose. If the railway has rails, then in China it can be called a railway, and China is satisfied. So with the roads. If there is any passage at all, then the Chinese call it a road, and China is satisfied.

As one meanders through the country, watching a people who are equalled nowhere in the world for their industry, plodding away over the worst roads any civilized country possesses, he cannot but think, even looking at the question from the Chinese standpoint so far as he is able, that, were free scope once given for the infusion of Western energy and methods into an active, trade-loving people like the Chinese, China would rival the United States in wealth and natural resources. The Chinese knows that his country, the natural resources of the country and the people, will allow him to do things on a scale which will by and by completely overbalance the doings of countries less favored by Nature than his own. He knows that when properly developed his country will be one of the richest in the world, yet even when he is filled with such ideas he is just as cunctative as he has ever been. He has the idea that he should not commence to exhaust the wealth of his country before it is absolutely necessary.

Above all, he has now made up his mind that he himself, unaided by the foreigner, is going to develop it just as he likes and just when he likes.

The day of the foreign concession is gone. The Chinese now is paddling his own canoe, and it is only by cultivating his friendship, by proving to him by acts, and not by words, that the intrusion of privileged enterprises—such as great mining concessions and railway concessions, in which the foreigner demands that he be the only principal—is no longer contemplated, that the day will be won. But it is equally true that only by combining European and Chinese interests on the modern company system, the real Opening of China can be effected.

※

Distances are as variable as the wind in the Middle Kingdom.

The first forty li on this journey were much shorter than the last thirty, which took about twice as long to cover. I dragged along over the narrow path through the wheat fields, and, making for an old man, who looked as if he should know, I asked him the distance to my destination. His reply of twenty li I accepted as accurate, and I reckoned that I could cover this easily in a couple of hours. But at the end of this time we had, according to a casual wayfarer, five more li, and when we had covered at least four another rustic said it was "two and a bit." This answer we got from four different people on the way, and I was glad when I had completed the journey. One does not mind the two li so much—it is the "bit" which upsets one's calculations.

The following day, on the road to Huan-chiang, I lost myself—that is, I lost my men, and did not know the road. I got away into some quaint, secluded garden and sat down, tired and hot, under a tree in the shade, where a faint wind swung the heavy foliage with a solemn sound, and the subdued and soothing music of a brook running between two banks of moss and turf must have sent me to sleep. It was with a dreary sense of ominous foreboding that I woke, as if in expectation of some disaster. Not a living creature was visible, and I doubted the possibility of finding anyone in such a spot. Never, surely, was there a silence anywhere as here! Seized with a solemn fear, my presence there seemed to me a strange intrusion. I looked around, moved forward a little, hastened my steps to get away, but whence or how I knew not. I knew this was a country of erratic distances—it was now getting on for sunset—and the continuous toiling up and down the sides of the difficult mountains had tired me. All of a sudden I heard a noise, heard someone fall, looked round and beheld T'ong, perspiration pouring down his back and front.

"Oh, master, this b'long velly much bobbery. I makee velly frightened. I think p'laps master wantchee makee run away." And then, after a time: "You no wantchee catch 'chow'?"

"Chow?"

No, I could easily have gone without food for that night. I was lost, and now was found. I had no money, could not speak the language, was fatigued beyond words. What would have become of me?

Miniature turret-like hills hemmed us in as in a huge park, with a narrow winding pathway, steep as the side of a house, leading to the top of the mountain beyond, and then descending quite as rapidly to Fan-ih-ts'uen. The coolies told me the next day the road would be worse, and so it turned out to be.

At 5:00 a.m. a thick drizzly rain was falling, just sufficient to make the flagstones slippery as ice, and the European contrivances which covered my feet stood no chance at all compared with the straw sandals of the native. I could not get any big enough around here to put over my boots. My carriers had gone ahead, and as I was passing a paddy field one leg went from under me, and I was up to my middle in thin wet mud. In this I had to trudge seven miles before I could get other garments from the coolie, changing my trousers behind a piece of matting held up in front of me by my boy! All enjoyed the fun—except myself. Little boys tried to peer around the side of the matting, and, as T'ong tried to kick them away, the matting would drop and expose me to public view. But I had to change, and that was most important to me.

Later on, my ugly coolie—the ugliest man in or out of China, I should think, ugly beyond description—dropped my bedding as he was crossing the river, and I had the pleasure of sleeping on a wet bed at T'an-teo.

I must ask the reader's pardon for again referring to Chinese inns. I should not have made any remark upon this awful hovel had not the man laid a scheme to charge me three times as much as he should—a scheme, be it said, in which my boy took no part. It was truly a fearful den, where man and beast lived in promiscuous and insupportable filth. The dung-heap charms the sight of this agricultural people, without in the slightest wounding their olfactory nerves, and these utilitarians think there is no use seeking privacy to do what they regard as beneficial and productive work. The bed here was the worst I had had offered me. The mattress, upon which every previous traveler for many years had left his tribute of vermin, was not fit for use, there were myriads of filthy insects, and I found myself obliged to stop and have some clothes boiled, and for comfort's sake rubbed my body with Chinese wine. Filth there was everywhere. It seemed inseparable from the people, and a total apathy as regards matter in the wrong place pervaded all classes, from the highest to the lowest. The spring is opening, and my hard-worked coolies doff their heavy padded winter clothing, parade their naked skin, and are quite unconscious of any disgrace attending the exhibition of the itch sores which disfigure them.

I remember, however, that I am in China, and must not be disgusted.

And should any reader be disgusted at the disjointed character of this particular portion of my common chronicle, I would only say in apology that I am writing under the gaze of a mystified crowd, each of whom has a word to say about my typewriter—the first, undoubtedly, that he has ever seen. This machine has caused the greatest surprise all along the route, and it is on occasions when the Chinese sees for the first time things of this intimate mechanical nature that he gives one the impression that he is a little boy. The people crowd into my room; they cannot be kept out, although at the present moment I have stationed my two soldiers in the doorway where

I am writing, so as to get a little light, to keep them from crowding actually upon me.

It has been said that all of us have an innermost room, wherein we conceal our own secret affairs. In China everything is so open, and so much must be done in public, that it would surprise one to know that the Chinese have an inner room. The European traveler in this region must have no inner room, either, for the people seem to see down deep into one's very soul. But it is when one wanders on alone, as I have done to-day, doing two days in one, no less than one hundred and forty li of terrible road through the most isolated country, that one can enjoy the comfort of one's own loneliness and own inner room. The scenery was picturesque, much like Scotland, but the solitude was the best of all. I had left office and books and manuscripts, and was on a lonely walk, enjoying a solitude from which I could not escape, a reverie which was passed not nearly so much in thinking as in feeling, a feeling to nature-lovers which can never be completely expressed in words. It was indeed a refuge from the storms of life, and a veritable chamber of peace. And this, to my mind, is the way to spend a holiday. Robert Louis Stevenson tells us in one of his early books what a complete world two congenial friends make for themselves in the midst of a foreign population; all the hum and the stir goes on, and these two strangers exchange glances, and are filled with an infinite content Some of us would rather be alone, perhaps; for on a trip such as I am making now, in order to be happy with a companion you must have one who is thoroughly congenial and sympathetic, one who understands your unspoken thought, who is willing to let you have your way on the concession of the same privilege. Selfishness in the slightest degree should not enter in. But such a man is difficult to find, so I wander on alone, happy in my own solitude. Here I have liberty, perfect liberty.

I was stopped on my way to Lao-wa-t'an at a small town called Puerh-tu, the first place of importance after having come into Yuen-nan. A few li before reaching this town, one of my men cut the large toe of his left foot on a sharp rock, lacerating the flesh to the bone. I attended to him as best I could on the road, paid him four days' extra pay, and then had a bit of a row with him because he would not go back. He avowed that carrying for the foreigner was such a good thing that he feared leaving it! Upon entering Puerh-tu, however, he fell in the roadway. A crowd gathered, a loud cry went up from the multitude, and in the consternation and confusion which ensued the people divided themselves into various sections.

Some rushed to proffer assistance to the fallen man (this was done because I was about; he would have been left had a foreigner not been there), others gathered around me with outrageous adulation and seeming words of welcome. Meanwhile, I thought the coolie was dying, and, fearful and unnatural as it seems, it is nevertheless true that at all ages the Chinese find a peculiar and awful satisfaction in watching the agonies of the dying. By far the larger part of the mob was watching him dying, as they thought. But no, he was still worth many dead men! He slowly opened his eyes, smiled, rose up, and immediately recognized a poor manacled wretch, then passing under escort of several soldiers, who stopped a little farther down, followed by a mandarin in a chair.

On this particular day, more than a customary morbid diversion was thus apparent among the motley-garbed mass of men and women, and the ignominious way in which that prisoner was treated was horrible to look upon. The perpetual hum of voices sounded like the noise made by a thousand swarming bees. The band of soldiers guarding the prisoner suddenly halted, whilst the mandarin conferred with the chief, after which he advanced slowly towards me.

I was on the point of telling him in English that I had done nothing against the law, so far as I knew.

He bowed solemnly, during which time I, attempting the same, had much trouble from bursting out laughing in his face. He beckoned to me, and then rushed me bodily into a house, where, in the best room, I found another official and his two sons. T'ong followed as interpreter. The mandarin explained that I was wanted to stay the night, that a theatrical entertainment had been arranged particularly for my benefit, that he wished I would take their photographs,[11] that one of them would like a cigarette tin with some cigarettes in it, and that one of them would like to sell me a thoroughbred, hard-working, magnificently-shaped, without-a-single-vice black pony, which they would part with for my benefit for the consideration of one hundred taels down (four times its value), which awaited my inspection without. I stood up and fronted them, and replied, through T'ong, that I could not stay the night, that I would be pleased to tolerate the howling of the theatre for one half of an hour, that it would have given me the greatest pleasure to take their photographs, but, alas! my films were not many. I handed them a cigarette tin, but quite forgot that they asked for cigarettes as well (I had none), and I explained that horse-riding was not one of my accomplishments, so that their quadruped would be of no use to me.

They looked glum, I smiled serenely. This is Chinesey.

---

11    The photographs were included in the original hardcover edition of the book but are not included in this edition —publisher

# Chapter VIII

*Szech-wan and Yuen-nan. Coolies and their loads. Exports and imports. Hints to English exporters. Food at famine rates. A wretched inn at Wu-chai. Author prevents murder. Sleeping in the rain. The foreign cigarette trade. Poverty of Chao-t'ong. Simplicity of life. Possible advantages of Chinese in struggle of yellow and white races. Foreign goods in Yuen-nan and Szech'wan. Thousands of beggars die. Supposed lime poisoning. Content of the people. Opium not grown. Prices of prepared drug in Tong-ch'uan-fu compared. Smuggling from Kwei-chow. Opium and tin of Yuen-nan. Remarkable bonfire at Yuen-nan-fu. Infanticide at Chao-t'ong. Selling of female children into slavery. Author's horse steps on human skull.*

*W*ere one uninformed, small observance would be necessary to detect the borderline of Szech'wan and Yuen-nan. The latter is supposed to be one of the most ill-nurtured and desolate provinces of the Empire, mountainous, void of cultivation when compared with Szech'wan, one mass of high hills conditioned now as Nature made them; and the people, too, ashamed of their own wretchedness, are ill-fed and ill-clad.

The greater part of the roads to be traversed now were constructed on projecting slopes above rivers and torrents, affluents of the Yangtze, and cross a region upon which the troubled appearance of the mountains that bristle over it stamps the impress of a severe kind of beauty. Such roads would not be tolerated in any country but China—I doubt if any but the ancient Chinese could have had the patience to build them. One could not walk with comfort; it was an impossible task. Far away over the earth, winding into all the natural trends of the mountain base, ran the highway, merrily tripping over huge boulders, into hollows and out of them, almost underground, but always, with its long white extended finger, beckoning me on by the narrow ribbon in the distance. True, although I was absolutely destitute of company, I had always the road with me, yet ever far from me. I could not catch it up, and sometimes, dreaming triumphantly that I had now come even with it where it seemed to end in some disordered stony mass, it would trip mischievously out again into view, bounding away into some tricky bend far down to the edge of the river, and rounding out of sight once more until the point of vantage was attained. Its twisting and turning, up and down, inwards, outwards, made humor for the full long day. With it I could not quarrel, for it did its best to help me with my weary men onwards over the now darkened landscape, and ever took the lead to urge us forward. If it came to a great upstanding mountain, with marked politeness it ran round by a circuitous route, more easily if of greater length; at other times it scaled clear up, nimbly and straight, turning not once to us in its self-appointed task, and at the top, standing like some fairy on a steeple-point, beckoned us on encouragingly. At times it became exhausted and stretched itself wearisomely out, measuring in width to only a few small inches, and overlooked the river at great height, telling us to ponder well our footsteps ere we go forward. To part company with the road would mean to die, for elsewhere was no foothold possible. So in this narrow faithful ledge, torn up by the heavy tread of countless horses' feet beyond Lao-wa-t'an (where horse traffic starts), we carefully ordered every step. Looking down, sheer down as from some lofty palace window, I saw the green snake waiting, waiting for me. Slipping, there would be no hope—death and the river alone lay down that treacherous mountain-side. And then, at times, pursuing that white-faced wriggling demon which stretched out far over the mist-swept landscape in incessant writhing and annoying contortions, we quite gave up the chase. It seemed leading me on to some unknown destiny. I knew not whither; only this I knew—that I must follow.

And so each hour and every hour was fraught with peril which seemed imminent. But He who guards the fatherless and helpless, feeds the poor and friendless, guarded the traveler in those days. Mishaps I had none, and when at night I reached those tiny mountain seats, perched majestically high for the most part and swept by all the winds of heaven, I seemed to be the lonely spectator and companionless watcher over mighty mountain-tops, which appeared every moment to be hesitating to take a gigantic dive into the roaring river several hundred feet below our lofty resting-place.

Some of the larger villages had the arrogant look of old feudal fortresses, and up the paths leading to them, cut out in a defile in the vertical cliffs, we passed with difficulty coolies carrying on their backs the enormous loads, which are the wonder of all who have seen them, their backs straining under the boomerang-shaped frames to which the merchandise was lashed. Hundreds passed us on their toilsome journey with tea, lamp-oil, skins, hides, copper, lead, coal and white wax from Yuen-nan, and with salt, English cotton, Chinese porcelain, fans and so on from Szech'wan. One false step, one slight slip, and they would have been hurled down the ravine, where far below, in the roaring cataract, dwarfed to the size of a toy boat, was a junk being cleverly taken down-stream. And down there also, one false move and the huge junk would have been dashed against the rocks, and banks strewn with the corpses of the crew. As it was, they were mere specks of blue in a background of white foam, their vociferating and yelling being drowned by the roar of the waters. On the road, passing and re-passing, I saw coolies on the way to Yuen-nan-fu with German cartridges and Japanese guns, the packing, so different generally to British goods which come into China, being particularly good. This is one of the cries of the importer in China against the British manufacturer; and if the latter knew more of Chinese transport and the manner in which the goods are handled in changing from place to place, one would meet fewer broken packages on the road in this land of long distances.

A friend of mine, needing a typewriter, wrote home explicit instructions as to the packing. "Pack it ready to ship," he wrote, "then take it to the top of your office stairs, throw it down the stairs, take machine out and inspect, and if it is undamaged re-pack and send to me. If damaged, pack another machine, subject to the same treatment until you are convinced that it can stand being thus handled and escape injury." This is how goods coming to Western China should be sent away.

Gradually the days brought harder toil. The mountains grew higher, some covered with forests of pine trees, which natural ornament completely changed the aspect of the country. Torrents foamed noisily down the gorges, veiled by the curtain of great trees; sometimes, on a ridge, a field of buckwheat, shining in the sun, looked like the beginning of the eternal snows.

Food was at famine rates. Eggs there were in abundance, pork also; but it was not to be wondered at that the traveler, having seen the conditions under which the pigs are reared, refrained from the luxury of Yuen-nan roast pig. My men fed on maize. The faces of the people were pinched and wan, unpleasant to look upon, bearing unmistakable signs of poverty and misery, and they seemed too concerned in keeping the wolf from the door to attend to me. At Ta-kwan they treated themselves to a *sheng* of rice apiece—here the *sheng* is 1.8 catties, as against 11 catties in the capital of the province.

At Wuchai, the last stage before reaching Chao-t'ong-fu, the room of the inn had three walls only, and two of these were composed of kerosene tins, laced together with bamboo stripping. (Probably the oil tins had been stolen from the mission premises at Chao-t'ong.) Through the whole night it rained as it had never rained before, but, instead of feeling miserable, I tried to see the humor of the situation. One can get humor from the most embarrassing circumstances, and my chief amusement arose from a small business deal between one of my coolies, who had sublet his contract to a poor fellow returning in the rain, who had arranged to carry the ninety cat-ties ninety li for a fourth of the original price arranged between my coolie and myself. For one full hour they argued at a terrible speed as to the rate of exchange in the Szech'wan large and the Yuen-nan small cash, and this was only interrupted when a poor man, deaf and dumb, and of hideous appearance, seeing the foreigner in his contemptible town, rushed in with a carrying pole and felled his grumbling townsman at my feet.

My intervention probably averted murder—at any rate, it seemed as though murder would have taken place very soon but for my interference. The whole populace gathered, of course, and the fight waged fiercely until well on into the night. But wrapping myself in my mackintosh, and putting my paper umbrella at the right angle, I went to sleep with the rain dripping on me as they were indulging in final pleasantries regarding each other's ancestry.

The first thing I saw at Chao-t'ong the next day was the foreign ciga-rette, sold at a wayside stall by a vendor of monkey nuts and marrow seeds. No trade has prospered in Yuen-nan during the past two years more than the foreign cigarette trade, and the growing evil among the children of the common people, both male and female, is viewed with alarm. From Tachien-lu to Mengtsz, from Chung-king to Bhamo, one is rarely out of sight of the well-known flaring posters in the Chinese characters advertis-ing the British cigarette. Some months ago a couple of Europeans were sent out to advertise, and they stuck their poster decorations on the walls of temples, on private houses and official residences, with the result that the people were piqued so much as to tear down the bills immediately. In Yuen-nan, especially since the exit of opium, this common cigarette is smoked by high and low, rich and poor. I have been offered them at small feasts, and when calling upon high officials at the capital have been offered a packet of cigarettes instead of a whiff of opium, as would have been done formerly. One is not, of course, prepared to say whether such a trade is desirable or not, but it merely needs to be made known that towards the middle of the present year (1910) a proclamation was issued from the Viceroy's *yamen* at Yuen-nan-fu speaking in strongest terms against the increasing habit of smoking foreign cigarettes, to show the trend of official opinion on the subject. After having referred to the enormous advances made in the imports of cigarettes, the proclamation deplored the general tendency of the people to support such an undesirable trade, and exhorted the citizens to turn from their evil ways. We cannot stop the importation of cigarettes, it read, but there is no need for our people to buy.

At Chao-t'ong I stayed with the Rev. Dr. Savin, and spent a very pleasant two days' rest here in his hospitable hands. It was in this district I first came across goitre, the first time I had seen it in my life. It is a terrible disfigurement.

Poor indeed is the whole of this neighborhood. Poverty, thin and wanting food to eat, stalks abroad dressed in a rag or two, armed with a staff to keep away the snarling dogs, and a broken bowl to gather garbage.

Even the better class, who manage to afford their maize and bean curds, are to be praised for the extreme simplicity which everywhere vividly marks their monotonous lives. Indeed, this is true of the whole area through which I have traveled. No furniture brings confusion to their rooms, no machinery distresses the ear with its groaning or the eye with its unsightliness, no factories belch out smoke and blacken the beauty of the sky, no trains screech to disturb sleepers and frighten babies. The simplest of simple beds—in most cases merely a few boards with a straw mattress placed thereon—the straw sandal on the foot, wooden chopsticks in place of knives and forks, the small variety of foods and of cooking utensils, the simple homespun cotton clothing—much of this finds favor in the eye of the English traveler. The Chinese, of all Orientals, teach us how to live without furniture, without impedimenta, with the least possible amount of clothing in the case of the poorer classes, and I could not fail to be impressed by the advantage thus held by this great nation in the struggle of life. It may serve them in good stead in the struggle of the Yellow Man against the White Man, to which I refer at a later period in this book; also does it incidentally show up the real character of some of the weaknesses of our own civilization, and when one is in China, living near the people, one is forced to reflect upon the useless multiplicity of our daily wants. We must have our daily stock of bread and butter and meats, glass windows and fires, hats, white shirts and woolen underwear, boots and shoes, trunks, bags and boxes, bedsteads, mattresses, sheets and blankets—most of which a Chinese can do without, and indeed is actually better off without.[12]

This is not true in every class, however; for whilst there is no denying the charm of the simpler civilization, many of the Chinese of Szech'wan and Yuen-nan glory in goods of foreign manufacture, no matter if to them is not disclosed the proper purpose of any particular article adopted.

Rice will not grow here in great quantities, owing to the scarcity of water; therefore the people feed on maize, and are thankful to get it.

Chao-t'ong is the centre of a large district devastated by recurring seasons of plague, rebellion and famine, when thousands die annually from starvation in the town and on the level uplands surrounding it. The beggars on one occasion, becoming so numerous, were driven from the streets, confined within the walls of the temple and grounds beyond the South Gate, and there fed by common charity. Huddled together in disease and rags and unspeakable misery, they died in thousands, and the Chinese say that of five thousand who crossed the temple threshold two thousand never came out alive.

This happened some twenty years ago. The unfortunate victims had for their food a rice porridge, mixed with which was a subtance alleged to have been lime, the common belief being that the majority of those who perished died from the effect of poisoning. Outside the city boundary hundreds of the dead were flung into huge pits, and even now the inhabitants refer to the time when children were exchanged *ad libitum* for a handful of rice or even less.

During my stay in this city, I heard on all hands some of the most blood-curdling stories of the dire distress which, like a dark cloud, still menaces the people, some of which are too dreadful for public print.

But I suppose these poor people are content. If they are, they possess a virtue which produces, in some measure at all events, all those effects which the alchemist usually ascribes to what he calls the philosopher's stone; and if their content does not bring riches, it banishes the desire for them. Years ago the people could entertain some small hope of prosperity now and again. If the opium crop were good, money was plentiful. But now no opium is grown, and the misery-stricken people have lost all hope of better times,

---

12    Anyone who contemplates a tramp across China must not get the idea that he can still continue the uses of civilization. For the most part he will have to live pretty well as a Chinese the whole time, and he will find, as I found, that it is easy to give up a thing when you know the impossibility of getting it.—E.J.D.

and seem to have sunk in many instances to the lowest pangs of distressful poverty.[13]

Reader, alarm not yourself! I am not here to lead you into a long harangue on opium—it presents too thorny a subject for me to handle. I am not a partisan in the opium traffic; my mission is not essentially to denounce it; I am not impelled by an irresistible desire to investigate facts and put them before you. There is practically no opium in Yuen-nan to talk about.

This is absolute fact—not a Chinese fact, but good old British truth (although British truth when it touches upon opium has been very, very perverted since we first commenced to transact opium trade with this great country). With the exception of one small patch, some ten miles away from the main road between Yuen-nan-fu and Tali-fu, I saw no poppy whatever in the province. This does not mean, however, that no opium is to be had.

During the past three weeks[14] no less than five cases of attempted suicide by opium poisoning have come under my personal notice in the town in which I am residing, and there have doubtless been fifty more which have not. If there is no opium, where do the people so easily secure it in endeavors to take their lives upon the slightest provocation? Last year the price of opium here on the streets, although its sale was "illegal," was over three tsien (about nine-pence) the Chinese ounce of prepared opium. At the present time, in the same city, many men would be willing to do a deal for any quantity you like for less than two tsien. Cases of smuggling are frequent. One gets accustomed to hear of large quantities being smuggled through in most cunning ways, and it all goes to show that the *people* of Yuen-nan are not, as some of China's enlightened statesmen and some of the ranting faddists of England and America would have us believe, falling over one another in their zeal to free the province from the drug.

The other day some men passed through several towns, on the way to the capital, carrying three coffins. In the first was a corpse, the other two were

---

13    This was written later. I have altered my views since I have traveled from end to end of Yuen-nan. The disappearance of opium, on the contrary, apart from the moral advantage to the people, has done much to place them in a better position financially. In Tali-fu I found not a single shop on the main street "to let," and the trade of the place had gone ahead considerably, and this was a city which people generally supposed would suffer most on account of the non-growth of opium.—E.J.D.

14    May, 1910. As a matter of fact the date makes no difference, because unfortunately the number of suicides from opium does not seem to have decreased materially in Western China since the opium crusade was started. Upon the slightest provocation a Chinese woman in Yuen-nan will take her life, and it is probable that for the five cases which came to my notice through the mission house there were treble that number which did not—E.J.D.

packed with opium. Being suspected at Yuen-nan-fu, the first coffin was opened, and the carriers, making as much row as they could because their coffin had been burst open, secured a fair "squeeze" to hold their tongues, and the second and third coffins were passed unexamined. Quite common is it for men to travel in armed bands from the province of Kwei-chow, traveling by night over the mountains by lantern-light, and hiding by day from any possible official searchers.

Opium, which is and always has been so heavily taxed, does not in general follow the ordinary trade routes on which *likin* stations are numerous, but is carried by these armed bands over roads where the native Customs stations are few, and so poorly equipped as to yield readily to superior force, where the men are compelled to accept a composition much below the official rate.

Opium smoking is still common in Western China among people who can afford it. At the time of the crusade against it, wealthy people laid in stocks enough to last them for years; and, so long as there is smuggling from other provinces, which do grow it, into those which do not, there will be no danger of the absolute extermination being carried successfully into effect. Kwei-chow, in common with the western provinces, has undeservedly secured the credit for having practically abolished the poppy; but at the present moment (December, 1909) she is at a loss to know what to do with her supply, and that is the reason why people of Yuen-nan are making bargains in opium smuggled over the border. Much has yet to be done. To prevent the growth of a plant which has been in China for at least twelve centuries, which has had medicinal uses for nine, and whose medicinal properties have been put in the capsule for six, is not an easy matter, far more difficult, in fact, than the average Englishman and even those who rant so much about the whole business upon little knowledge can imagine. Opium has been made in China for four centuries, and although used then with tobacco, has been smoked since the middle of the seventeenth century.[15]

A few years ago Yuen-nan had only two articles of importance with which to pay for extra provincial products consumed, namely, opium and tin. The latter came from a spot twenty miles from Mengtsz, and the value of the output now runs to approximately three million taels. Opium came from all parts of the province and went in all directions, that portion sent to the Opium Regie at Tonkin sometimes being close to three thousand

---

15    This was written at the end of 1909 Now, in July, 1910, things are changed wonderfully. The rapidity with which China is driving out the poppy from province after province is truly remarkable. In Szech'wan, in April, 1909, I passed through miles and miles of poppy along the main road—to-day there is none to be seen It is to be hoped that Great Britain will do her part as faithfully as China is doing hers.

piculs, and the quantity going by land into China being very much greater. Yuen-nan opium was known at Canton and Chin-kiang in 1863. In 1879, the production was variously estimated at from twelve thousand to twenty-two thousand piculs; in 1887 it had risen to approximately twenty-seven thousand piculs, and since then to the time of the reform no less certainly than thirty thousand piculs.

One afternoon, in November of 1909, the execution ground of Yuen-nan-fu was the scene of a remarkably daring proceeding by the officials in the campaign for the total suppression of opium in the province. No less than 20,040 ounces of prepared opium were publicly destroyed by fire in the presence of an enormous crowd of people. The officials of the city were present in person, and everywhere the event was looked upon as the greatest public demonstration that the people had ever seen.

The missionary of whom I inquired denied that the infanticide at Chao-t'ong was very great—things must be improving!

Previous to my arrival at the city I had instructed my English-speaking boy to make inquiries in the city, and to let me know afterwards, whether girls were still sold publicly.

"Have got plenty," he exclaimed, in describing this wholesale selling of female children into slavery. "I know, I know; you wantchee makee buy. Can do! You wantchee catch one piecee small baby, can catchee two, three tael. Wantchee one piecee very much tall, big piecee, can catch fifty dollar."

Continuing, he told me that prices were fairly high, a girl who could boast good looks and who had reached an age when her charms were naturally the strongest fetching the alarming amount of three hundred taels. This was the highest figure reached, whilst small children could be had for anything up to twenty. This wholesale disposal of young girls, although the traffic was in some quarters emphatically denied to exist—a denial, however, which was all moonshine—is one of the chief sorrows of the district. And well it might be; for thousands of children are disposed of in the course of a year for a few taels by heartless parents, who watch them being carried away, like so much merchandise, to be converted into silver, in many cases in this poverty-stricken district merely to satisfy the craving for opium of some sodden wretch of a man who calls himself a father. Time and time again, long after I myself passed through Chao-t'ong, did I see little girls from three to ten years of age being conveyed by pack-horse to the capital, balanced in baskets on either side of the animal. This and the terrible infanticide which exists in all poor districts of China menaces the lives of all well-wishers of the entire province of Yuen-nan.

In the particular district of which I speak it is not an uncommon sight to see little children being torn to pieces by dogs, the scavengers of the Empire, perhaps by the very dogs that had been their playmates from birth. I have been riding many times and found that my horse had stepped on a human skull, and near by were the bones the dogs had left as the remains of the corpse.

※

Note.—I should mention that, since the above was written, I have lived and travelled a good deal around Chao-t'ong-fu, being the only European traveller who has ever penetrated the country to the east of the main road, by which I had now come down.

# CHAPTER IX

## The Chao-T'ong Rebellion of 1910

*Digression from travel. How rebellions start in China. Famous Boxer motto. Way of escape shut off. Riots expected before West can be won into the confidence of China. Boxerism and students of the Government Reform Movement. Author's impressions formed within the danger zone. More Boxerism in China than we know of. Causes of the Chao-t'ong Rebellion. Halley's Comet brings things to a climax. Start of the rioting. Arrival of the military. Number of the rebels. They hold three impregnable positions, and block the main roads. European ladies travel to the city in the dead of night. A new ch'en-tai takes the matter in hand. Rumors and suspense. Stations of the rebels. A night attack. Sixteen rebels decapitated. Officials alter their tactics. Fighting on main road. Superstition regarding soldiers. One of the leaders captured by a headman. Chapel burnt down and caretaker rescued by military. Li the Invincible under arms. Huang taken prisoner. Two leaders killed. Rising among the Miao. Mission work at a standstill. Child-stealing, and the Yuen-nan Railway rumor. Barbaric punishment. Tribute to Chinese officials. British Consul-General. Resume of the position. An unfortunate incident.*

*D*espite the fact that this chapter was the last written, it has been thought wise to place it here. It deals with the Chao-t'ong Rebellion, of which the outside world, even when it was at its height, knew little, but which, so recently as a couple of months prior to the date of writing, threatened to spell extermination to the foreigners in North-East Yuen-nan. And the reader, too, may welcome a digression from travel.

In spite of all that has been written in previous and subsequent chapters, and in face of the universal cry of the progress China is speedily realizing, of the stoutest optimism characteristic of the statesman and of the student of Chinese affairs, a feeling of deep gloom at intervals overcomes one in the interior—a fear of some impending trouble. There is a rumor, but one smiles at it—there are always rumors! Then there are more rumors, and a feeling of uneasiness pervades the atmosphere; a local bubble is formed, it bursts, the whole of one's trust in the sincerity of the reform of China and her people is brushed away to absolute unbelief in a few days, and it means either a sudden onrush and brutal massacre of the foreigners, or the thing blows over after a short or long time of great strain, and ultimately things assume a normality in which the detection of the slightest ruffle in the surface of social life is hardly traceable.

Such was the Chao-t'ong Rebellion, luckily unattended by loss of life among the foreigners. It is not yet over,[16] but it is believed that the worst is past.

At the end of 1909 probably no part of the Empire seemed more peaceful. Two months afterwards the heads of the Europeans were demanded; missionaries were guarded by armed soldiers in their homes inside the city walls, and forbidden to go outside; native Christians were brutally maltreated and threatened with death if they refused to turn traitor to their beliefs; thousands of generally law-abiding men, formed into armed bands, were defiantly setting at naught the law of the land, and the whole of the main road over which I had passed from Sui-fu to Tong-ch'uan-fu (a distance of over four hundred miles) was blocked by infuriated mobs, who were out to kill,—their motto the famous ill-omened Boxer motto of 1900: "Exalt the dynasty; destroy the foreigner."

"Kill, kill, kill!" ran the cry for miles around the countryside, and a fearful repetition of the bloody history of ten years ago was daily feared. Providential, however, was it that no foreigner was traveling at the time in these districts, and that those who, ignorant of the troubles, desired to do so were stopped at Yuen-nan-fu by the Consuls and at Sui-fu by the missionaries. It is a matter for gratitude also that throughout the riots, specially safeguarded by the great Providence of God, no lives of Europeans were lost; and owing to the praiseworthy and obvious attitude of the missionaries in this area in endeavoring to keep the thing as quiet as possible, and the notoriously conservative manner in which consular reports upon such matters are preserved in Governmental lockers, practically nothing has been heard of the uprising.

At times during the four slow-moving months, however, the situation became, as I shall endeavor to show, complicated in every way. The escape of the foreigners was made absolutely impossible by the fact that the whole

16    July, 1910.

of the roads, even those over the rough mountains leading south, were blocked successfully by the rebelling forces, and, when the deep gloom settled finally over the city, the fate of the Westerners seemed sealed and their future hopeless. All round the foreigners' houses the people, infected with that strange, unaccountable, national hysteria, so terrible in the Chinese temperament, rose up to burn and kill. Mayhap it means little to the man who reads. Massacres have always been common enough in China, he will say; and there are thousands of people in Europe to-day who know no more about China than what the telegrams of massacres of European missionaries have told them. Years ago one almost expected this sort of thing; but at the present day, when China is popularly supposed to be working honestly to gain for herself an honorable place among the nations, it is surely not to be expected in the ordinary run of things in days of peace.

But we know that such visions are common to every European in Inland China, and even at the coast men talk continually of and believe that riots are going to happen in the near future. Merchant, missionary, traveler and official all agree that there is yet more trouble ahead before the West will be won into the confidence of China and *vice versa*. The people who are studying the Reform Movement of the Young China, however, and who stolidly refuse to study with it the general attitude of the common people, laugh and dismiss with contempt the subject of the possibility of further outbreaks of Boxerism in the outlying parts of the Empire. But they should not laugh. The European cannot afford to laugh, and, if he be a sensible fellow, knows that he cannot afford to treat with contempt the opinions of the people who know. The more we understand the vast interior of China and the conservatism and peculiarities of character of the people of that interior, the less disposed shall we be to jest, the less disposed to ridicule, what I would characterize as the strongest and most deadly of the hidden menaces of the Celestial Empire.

One does not wish to be pessimistic, but it is foolish to close one's eyes to bare fact.

At the moment I am writing, in the middle of China, I know that I am safe enough here, but I do not disguise from myself that the wildest reports are still current within a quarter of a mile from me about me and my own kind in this peaceful city of Tong-ch'uan-fu. And it takes very little to light the fuse and to cause a terrible explosion here, in common with other places in this province. A man might be quite safe one day and lose his head the next if he did not, at times when the rebellious element is apparent, conform strictly to the general wishes and accepted customs of the people among whom he is living.

No, we cannot afford to laugh. We must seek the opinion of those people who were confined within the walls of Chao-t'ong city—the silence of their own homes broken up by the distant uproar of a frantic chorus of yells and angry disputations, sounding, as it were, their very death-knell, as if they were to form a manacled procession dragging their chains of martyrdom to their own slow doom—before we show contempt for the opinion of those who would tell the truth. There is more of Boxerism in the far-away interior parts of China than we know of.

Even as late as the middle of January of the year 1910 there was no rumor of any uprising. About this time, however, to supply a serious deficiency in the revenue caused by the dropping of the opium tax, since that drug had ceased to be grown, a general poll-tax was levied, which the people refused to pay, and at the same time they demanded that they be allowed again to grow the poppy. Among the population of Chao-t'ong-fu, or more particularly among the people around the city, especially the tribespeople, this additional tax was supposed to have been caused by the Europeans, and other wild rumors concerning the Tonkin-Yuen-nan Railway (to be opened in the following April), which gained currency with remarkable rapidity, added to the unrest. It required only that brilliant phenomenon of the heavens, with its wonderful tail—none other than Halley's Comet—to bring the whole to a climax. This was altogether too much for the superstitious Chinese, and he looked upon the comet as some evil omen organized and controlled by the foreigner especially for the working of his own selfish ends in the Celestial Empire; and a number believed it to be a heavenly sign for the Chinese to strike.

That the riot was being started was plain, but the first definite news the foreigners received was on February 5th, when an I-pien (one of the tribes), whose little girl attended the mission school, was captured and compelled to join the rebelling forces between T'o-ch-i (on the River of Golden Sand[17]) and Sa'i-ho, in a westerly direction from the town. A march would take place on the fifteenth of that month, the Europeans would be assassinated, their houses would be burned and looted—so ran the rumor. By this date, for two days' march in all directions from Chao-t'ong, the rebels had camped, and a motley crowd they were—Mohammendans, Chinese, I-pien, Hua Miao, and other hooligans. Mobilization was effected by spies taking round secret cases (the *ch'uandan*) containing two pieces of coal and a feather—a simile meaning that the rebels were to burn like fire and fly like birds. Meanwhile, military forces had been dispatched from Yuen-nan-

---

17    The local name for the Yangtze.

fu, the capital (twelve days away), and from Ch'u-tsing-fu (seven or eight days away), and these, to the strength of a thousand, now came to the city, and it was thought that the brigadier-general would be able to cope with the trouble now that he had so many armed troops. Soldiers patrolled the city walls (which, by the way, had to be built up so that the soldiers might be able to get decent patrol), more were stationed on the premises of the Europeans, and every defensive precaution was taken. The officials were in daily communication by telegraph with the Viceroy, and at first the riot was kept well in hand by Government authorities.

But the rebels had by this time got together no less than three thousand men, and were holding three impregnable positions on the adjacent hills, and had effectually cut off communication by the main road. Despite their numbers, they were afraid to strike, however, and lucky it was for the city that the leaders were not sufficiently trusted by their followers, many of them pressed men—men who had joined the rebelling ranks merely to save their own necks and their houses. At this time the *pen-fu* (a sort of mayor of the city) demanded that the missionaries working among the Hua Miao, and two lady workers paying a visit to that place, should return from Shih-men-K'an (70 li away), as he could not protect them in the country. A special messenger was dispatched, demanding instant departure, and in the dead of night—a bitter wintry night, icy, dark, slippery, and cold—these ladies came under cover to the city.

They reached the mission premises without molestation.

By this time a new *ch'en-tai* (brigadier-general) had arrived from the capital, having been sent as a man who could handle the situation successfully. He was a Liu Ta Ren, who had previously held office in the city, and whose cunning a Scotland Yard detective might envy.[18]

Rumors grew more and more serious; the mandarins went all round the countryside endeavoring to pacify the people, and the foreigners could do nothing but "sit tight" through these most trying days. The suspense of

18   This Liu was a remarkable man, quite unlike the average mandarin. He got the name of Liu Ma Pang, a disrespectful term, meaning that he was fond of using the stick. On a journey towards Chao-t'ong, some years ago, he went on ahead of his retinue of men and horses, and arriving at an inn at Tong-ch'uan-fu, asked the ta si fu—the general factotum—for the best room, and proceeded to walk into it. "No you don't," yelled the ta si fu, "that's reserved for Liu Ma Pang, and you're not to go in there." After some time Liu's men arrived, and calling one or two, he said, "Take this man" (pointing to the surprised ta si fu) "and give him a sound thrashing." He stood by and saw the whacking administered, after which he said, "That's for speaking disrespectfully of a mandarin." Then, "Give him a thousand cash," adding, "That's for knowing your business."

Some years ago Liu was the means of saving the life of the late Mr. Litton (mentioned later in this book), at the time he was British Consul at Tengyueh, when there was fighting down in the south of Yuen-nan with the Wa's.—E.J.D.

being shut up in one's house during a time of trouble of this nature, hearing every rumor which lying tongues create, and unable to get at the facts, is far worse than being in the thick of things, although this would have at once been fatal. But one needs to have lived in China during such a time to understand the awful tension which riots occasion.

The rioters were stationed as follows:—

    1. Weining, in Kwei-chow, to the southeast 1,000 men

    2. Kiang-ti Hill, in Yuen-nan, to the south 1,000 men

    3. Several places around the city, to the west as far as the River of Golden Sand 1,000 men

On March 13th a night attack was expected. Breathless, the foreigners waited in their suspense, but it passed off without serious damage being done. On the Sunday, the missionaries, almost at their wits' end with mingled fear and excitement, occasioned by the strain which weeks of anxiety must bring to the strongest, feared whether their services would be got through in peace.

Meetings were being held all around the city, and gradually the mandarins gained small successes. Prisoners—miserable specimens of men fighting for they hardly knew what—were captured and brought to the city, and, on March 16th, sixteen human heads, thrown in one gruesome mass into a common basket, with upturned eyes gaping into the great unknown, hideous-looking and bearing still the brutish stare of hysterical craving and morbid rage, were carried by an armed squad of military to the *yamen*.

They made a ghastly picture when hung over the gate of the city to put the fear of death into the hearts of their brutal compatriots. The officials, hard-worked and themselves feeling the strain of the whole business, and incidentally fearful for the safety of their own heads, were perturbed all this time by rumors coming from Weining, the mutineers of which were alleged to be the fiercest of the three bands. Up to now the officials had been playing a conciliating game. They had been trying vainly to pacify, but now they found that they had to prove their energies and their benevolence by acting the part of tyrants rather than of administrators of mercy, by warring rather than by peace-making, by fighting and forcing rather than by conciliating and persuading.

On Easter Tuesday, fighting took place on the main road to the north, when the *pen-fu* and his men achieved a creditable success. The rebels almost to a man were taken, and among the prisoners was a girl who had been distributing the beans, a lovely damsel of eighteen, said to have been the fiancee of the leader of that band. Both her legs were shot through and she was considerably mutilated; but although the *pen-fu* thought this sufficient punishment, instructions came from the capital that she must die. She was accordingly taken outside the city and beheaded. This caused some consternation among the rebels, as the death of the girl was looked upon as an omen of direct misfortune.

For a very long time she had been going around the country dropping beans into the ground outside any houses she came across, the superstition being that wherever a bean was dropped there in the very spot, perhaps at the very moment, for aught that we know, an invincible warrior would spring up. She had dropped some millions of beans, but the ranks were not swelled as a consequence.

The *ch'en-tai* had also been out all night, and as men were captured so they were beheaded on the spot without mercy and their heads subsequently hung outside the city gates. The headman of a small village—some forty li from the city—succeeded in capturing one of the leaders, and great credit was due to him; but soon the leader was rescued again by his followers, who then brutally killed and mutilated the body of the headman, causing him to undergo the ignominy of having his tongue and his heart cut out. Fighting was going on everywhere, and by the end of March things were at their height. The fact that rain was badly needed tended only to aggravate the situation, and that lustrous comet made things worse. Day by day miserable processions brought the wounded into the city, and the last day of the month, taken by sudden fright and almost getting out of hand, the panic-stricken people raised the cry that the rebels were marching direct for the city gates. Through the capital tactics adopted by the mandarins, however, this was prevented; but, on the following day, the chapel belonging to the United Methodist Mission at an out-station was burnt to the ground and the houses of the people razed and looted. The caretaker, a faithful Hua Miao convert, was taken, stripped of his clothing, and threatened with an awful death if he did not betray the foreigners. He refused manfully to divulge any information whatsoever, and was on the point of being sacrificed, when the *ch'en-tai* came unexpectedly upon the scene with his military. He released the Miao, captured thirty-six rebels, killed sixteen more where they stood, and carried away many of their horses and the dreaded Boxer flag around which the men rallied.

And now comes the smartest thing I heard of throughout the rebellion.

A man named Li was the most dreaded of the trio of rebel chiefs, a man of marvelous strength, and who seemed to be able to fascinate his men and get them to do anything he wished—and Liu, the *ch'en-tai*, set himself the task of capturing him. Disguising himself in the garb of a pedlar, Liu went out towards Li's camp, and met three spies on the look-out for a possible clue to the foreigners; they asked him where the *ch'en-tai* was and all about him, declaring that if he did not tell them all he knew they would take him to Li, and that he would then lose his head. Just behind were a few of Liu's best soldiers. Strolling up quite casually as if they knew least in the world of what was going on, they made their arrest, and clapped the handcuffs on them before their captives knew it. Liu ordered that two be beheaded immediately, which was done, and the other man was kept to show where Li's camp was and where Li himself was hiding.

And in this way Li the Invincible was captured also. This was the master-stroke of the situation. Li was brought back to the city with many other prisoners and a few heads, guarded by a strong body of the military.

Almost simultaneously, Huang, one of the other rebel chiefs, was captured; and at dusk one evening Li was put to death by the slow process. Afraid that if he were taken outside the city his followers might possibly re-capture him, he was murdered outside the chief *yamen*, about ten hacks being necessary by process adopted to sever the head from the body. Only two men have been put to death inside the walls since the city of Chao-t'ong was built, over two hundred years ago. After death had taken place, Li was served in the same way as he had served the village headman, and his heart and his tongue were taken from his body. Huang was killed in the usual way, and his head placed in a frame on the city gate.

And so there died two of the bravest men who have headed rebellions in this part of country of late years. Both were handsome fellows, of magnificent physique and undaunted courage, worthy of fighting for a better cause. It seemed so strange that two such men should have had to die in the very bloom of life, when every strong sinew and drop of blood must have rebelled at such premature dissolution, and by a death more hideous than imagination can depict or speech describe, just at a time in China's awakening when such fellows might have made for the uplifting of their country. And they died because they hated the foreigner.

After further desultory fighting, the remaining leader, losing heart, fled into Kwei-chow province, and for a time was allowed to wander away; but later, a sum of a thousand taels was offered for him, dead or alive, and I have no doubt of the reward proving too great a bait for his followers. He has probably been given up.[19] In the month of May the Miao people rose to prolong the rioting, but their efforts did not come to much, although guerilla warfare was prolonged for several weeks, and British subjects were not allowed to travel over the main road beyond Tong-ch'uan-fu for some

19 He was captured some months afterwards, I believe, at Mengtsz.—E.J.D.

time after; indeed, as I write (July 1st, 1910), permission for the missionaries to move about is still withheld.

Then, following the rebellion, rumors spread all over the province to the effect that the foreigners were on the look-out for children, and were buying up as many as they could get at enormous prices to *ch'i* the railway to Yuen-nan-fu, which by this time had been opened to the public. Daily were little children brought to the missionaries and offered for sale. Child-stealing became common; the greatest unrest prevailed again. Members of the Christian churches suffered persecution, and adherents kept at a safe distance. Scholars forsook the mission schools. Foreigners cautiously kept within their own premises as much as they could. Mission work was at a standstill, and all looked once more grave enough. Two women, caught in the act of stealing children at Chao-t'ong, were taken to the *yamen*, hung in cages for a time as a warning to others, and then made to walk through the streets shouting, "Don't steal children as I have; don't steal children as I have." If they stopped yelling, soldiers scourged them.

A man was lynched in the public streets in that city for stealing a child, and only by the adoption of the most stringent measures, which in England would be considered barbaric, were the mandarins able successfully to deal with the rumors and the trouble thereby caused. Even far away down on the Capital road, children ran from me, and mothers, catching sight of me, would cover up their little ones and run away from me behind barred doors, so that the foreigner should not get them.

This latter trouble was felt pretty well throughout the length and breadth of Yuen-nan, and it must have been very disappointing to Christian missionaries who had been working around the districts of Tong-ch'uan-fu and Chao-t'ong-fu for over twenty years, and had got into close contact with scores of men and women, to see these very people taking away their children so that they should not be bought up by the very missionaries whose ministrations they had listened to for years.

In course of time, things settled down again, but at the time my manuscript leaves me for the publisher the danger zone has not been greatly reduced.

In concluding my few remarks on this serious outbreak, the like of which it is to be hoped will not be seen again in this province, it is only fair to chronicle the excellent behavior of the Chinese officials and of the Viceroy of Yuen-nan in dealing with the situation. Although he is not, I believe, generally liked by the people as their ruler, Li Chin Hsi did all he could to quell the riots speedily, and saw to it that all the officials in whose districts the rebellion was raging, and who made blunders during its progress, were degraded in rank. It is difficult for Europeans thoroughly to grasp the situation. From Chao-t'ong to Yuen-nan-fu, the viceregal seat, is twelve days' hard going, and all communication was done by telegraph—seemingly easy enough; but one must not discount the slow Chinese methods of doing things. Most of the troops were twelve days away, and in China—in backward Yuen-nan especially—to mobilize a thousand men and march them over mountains a fortnight from your base is not a thing to be done at a moment's notice. By the time they would arrive, it might have been possible for all the foreigners to have been massacred and their premises demolished, especially as the exits were blocked on all sides. But no time was lost and no pains were saved; and although the Chao-t'ong foreign residents, who suffered in suspense more than most missionaries are called upon to suffer, may differ with me in this opinion, I believe that not one of the officials who took part in endeavors to keep the riots from assuming more actually dangerous proportions could have done more than was done. If a man neglected his duty he lost his button, and he deserved nothing else.

In Mr. P. O'Brien Butler, the able British Consul-General, the British subjects had the greatest confidence. He might have erred in having declined from harassing the Chinese Foreign Office to grant permission and protection to Britishers who wished to travel after the leaders of the rebellion had been captured, but he undoubtedly erred on the right side.

An unfortunate incident for the United Methodist missionaries was the fact that the Rev. Charles Stedeford, who was sent out by the Connexion to visit the whole of the mission fields, was able to come only so far as Tong-ch'uan-fu, and was forced to return to Europe without having seen any of the magnificent work among the Hua Miao.

After my manuscript went forward to my publishers, permission to travel and protection were granted to British subjects again on the main road leading up to the Yangtze Valley. The author was the first Britisher to go from Tong-ch'uan-fu to Chao-t'ong-fu, and as I write, as late as the middle of July, 1910, I am of the opinion that it is unwise to travel over this road for a long time to come, unless it is absolutely imperative to do so. At Kiang-ti I had considerable trouble in getting a place to sleep, and I was glad when I had passed Tao-ueen.

At the invitation of missionaries working among them, I then spent some months in residence and travel in Miaoland, and only regret that an extended account of my experiences is not possible.

# CHAPTER X

## The Tribes of North-East Yuen-Nan, and Mission Work Among Them

Men who came through Yuen-nan twenty years ago wrote of its doctors and its medicines, its poverty and its infanticide. There seemed little else to speak of.

Although the tribes were here then—and in a rawer state even then than they are at the present time—little was known about them, and men had not yet developed the cult of putting their opinions upon this most absorbing topic into print. To-day, however, scores of men in Europe are eagerly devouring every line of copy they can get hold of bearing upon this fascinating ethnological study. Missionaries are plagued by inquiries for information respecting the tribes of Western China, and it is a curious feature of the situation that, with each article or book coming before the public contradiction follows contradiction, and very few people—not even those resident in the areas and working among the tribes—can agree absolutely upon any given points in their data. The numerous non-Chinese tribes I met in China formed one of the most interesting, and at the same time most bewildering, features of my travel; and I can quite agree with Major H.R. Davies,[20] who tackles the tribe question with considerable ability in his book on Yuen-nan, when he says that it is safe to assert that in hardly any part of the world is there such a large variety of languages and dialects as are to be found in the country which lies between Assam and the eastern border of Yuen-nan, and in the Indo-Chinese countries to the north of that region. The reason for it is generally ascribed to the physical characteristics of the country, the high mountain ranges and deep, swift-flowing rivers, which have brought about the differences in customs and language and the innumerable tribal distinctions so perplexing to him who would put himself in the position of an inquirer into Indo-Chinese ethnology. I know more than one gentleman in Yuen-nan at the present moment having under preparation manuscript upon this subject intended for subsequent publication, and I feel sure that their efforts will add valuable information to the all too limited supply now obtainable. In the meantime, I print my own impressions.

I should like it to be known here, however, that I do not in any way whatsoever put myself forward as an authority on the question. I had not, at the time this was written, laid myself out to make any study of the subject. But the fact that I have lived in North-East Yuen-nan for a year and a half, and have traveled from one end of the province to the other, in addition to having come across tribes of people in Szech'wan, may justify me in the eyes of the reader for placing on record my own impressions as a general contribution to this most exciting discussion. I also lived at Shih-men-K'an (mentioned in the last chapter), among the Hua Miao for several months, traveled fairly considerably in the unsurveyed hill country where they live, and am the only man, apart from two missionaries, who has ever been over that wonderful country lying to the extreme north-east of Yuen-nan. One trip I made, extending over three weeks, will ever remain with me as a memorable time, but I regret that I have no space in this volume for even the merest reference to my journey.

Some of my friends in China might say sarcastically that mankind is destined to arrive at years of discretion, and that I should have known better than to include in my book anything, however well founded, of a nature tending to continue the wordy strife touching this vexed question of Mission Work, and that no matter how strikingly set forth, this is an old and obsolete story, fit only to be finally done with. It is for such to bear with me in what I shall say. There are thousands of men in the West who are

---

20    Yuen-nan, The Link between India, and the Yangtze, by Major H.R. Davies, Cambridge University Press.

entirely ignorant of men in China other than the ordinary *Han Ren*, and if I enlighten them ever so little, then this chapter will have served an admirable end.

In North-East Yuen-nan the tribes I came most in contact with were:—

(i) The Miao or Miao-tze, as the Chinese call them; or the Mhong or Hmao, as they call themselves.

(ii) The I-pien (or E-pien), as the Chinese call them; or the Nou Su (or Ngo Su), as they call themselves.

Probably the Nou Su tribes are what Major Davies calls the Lolo Group in his third division of the great Tibeto-Burman Family; but I merely suggest it, as it strikes me that the other branches of that group, including the Li-su, the La-hu, and the Wo-ni, seem to be descendants of a larger group, of which the Nou Su predominate in numbers, language, and customs. However, this by the way.

It may not be common knowledge that in most parts of the Chinese Empire, even to-day, there are tribes of people, essentially non-Chinese, who still rigidly maintain their independence, governed by their own native rulers as they were probably forty centuries ago, long before their kingdoms were annexed to China Proper. There are white bones and black bones, noses long and flattened, eyes straight and oblique, swarthy faces, faces yellow and white, coal-black and brown hair, and many other physical peculiarities differentiating one tribe from another.

In many instances, these tribes, conquered slowly by the encroaching Chinese during the long and tedious term of centuries marking the growth of the Chinese Empire to its present immensity, are allowed to maintain their social independence under their own chiefs, who are subject to the control of the Government of China—which means that excessive taxation is paid to the *yamen* functionary, who extorts money from anybody and everybody he can get into his clutches, and then gives a free hand. Others, in a further state of civilization, have been gradually absorbed by the Chinese and are now barely distinguishable from the *Han Ren* (the Chinese). And others, again, adopting Chinese dress, customs and language, would give the traveler a rough time of it were he to suggest that they are any but pure Chinese. To the ethnological student, it is obvious that so soon as the Chinese have tyrannized sufficiently and in their own inimitable way preyed upon these feudal landlords enough to warrant their lands being confiscated, reducing a tribe to a condition in which, far removed from districts where co-tribesmen live, they have no *status*, the aboriginals throw in their lot gradually with the Chinese, and to all intents and purposes become Chinese in language, customs, trade and life. This absorption by the

Chinese of many tribes, stretching from the Burmese border to the eastern parts of Szech'wan, whilst an interesting study, shows that the onward march of civilization in China will sweep all racial relics from the face of this great awakening Empire.

But at the same time there are many branches of a tribal family, some found as far west as British Burma and all more or less scattered and disorganized as the result of this silent oppression going on through the years, who still are ambitious of preserving their independent isolation, particularly in sparsely-populated spheres far removed from political activity. So remote are the districts in which these principalities are found, that the Chinese themselves are entirely ignorant of the characteristics of these tribes. They say of one tribe which is scattered all over China Far West that they all have tails; and of another tribe that the men and women have two faces! And into the official records published by the Imperial Government the grossest inaccuracies creep concerning the origin of these peoples.

Yuen-nan and Szech'wan—and a great part of Kwei-chow in the main still untouched by the increased taxation necessary to provide revenue to uphold the reforms brought about by the forward movement in various parts of the Empire—are where the aboriginal population is most evident. This part of the Empire might be called the ethnological garden of tribes and various races in various stages of uncivilization. These secluded mountain areas, their unaltered conditions still telling forth the story of the world's youth, have been the cradle and the death-bed of nations, of vigorous and ambitious tribes bent on conquest and a career of glory.

## THE MIAO

Of the Miao, with its various sections, we know a good deal. Their real home has been pretty finally decided to be in Kwei-chow province, and they probably in former times extended far into Hu-nan, the Chinese of these provinces at the present time having undoubtedly a good deal of Miao blood in their veins. They are comparatively recent arrivals in Yuen-nan, but are gradually extending farther and farther to the west, maintaining their language and their dress and customs. I personally found them as far west as thirty miles beyond Tali-fu, a little off the main road, but Major Davies found them far up on the Tibetan border. He says: "The most westerly point that I have come across them is the neighborhood of Tawnio (lat. 23 deg. 40', long. 98 deg. 45'). Through Central and Northern Yuen-nan they do not seem to exist, but they reappear again to the north of this in Western Szech'wan, where there are a few villages in the basin of the Yalung River (lat. 28 deg. 15', long. 101 deg. 40')."

The Major was evidently ignorant of this Miao district of Chao-t'ong, to the north-east of the province. Stretching three days from Tong-ch'uan-fu right away on to Chao-t'ong, in a north line, Miao villages are met with fairly well the whole way; then, three days from Tong-ch'uan-fu, in a north-westerly direction, we come to the Miao village of Loh-In-shan; and then, striking south-west, through country absolutely unsurveyed part of the way, Sa-pu-shan is met. This last place is the headquarters of the China Inland Mission, where, at the present rate of progress, one might modestly estimate that in twenty years there will be no less than a million people receiving Christian teaching. These are not all Miao, however; there are besides La-ka, Li-su, and many other tribes with which we have no concern at the present moment.

So that it may be seen that from Yuen-nan-fu, the capital, in areas on either side of the main road leading up to the bifurcation of the Yangtze below Sui-fu, in a long, narrow neck running between the River of Golden Sand and the Kwei-chow border, Miao are met with constantly. And then, of course, over the river, in Szech'wan, they are met with again, and in Kwei-chow, farther west, we have their real home.

It is a far cry from Miao-land to Malaysia, but as I get into closer contact with the Miao people, the more do I find them in many common ways of everyday customs and points of character akin to the Malays and the Sakai (the jungle hill people of the Malay Peninsula), among whom I have traveled. Their modes of living contain many points in common. Ethnologists probably may smile at this assertion, the same as I, who have lived among the Miao, have smiled at a good deal which has come from the pens of men who have not.

In this area there are two great branches of the Miao race:—

(i) The Hua Miao—The Flowery (or White) Miao.

(ii) The Heh Miao—The Black Miao.

(Many photographs[21] of the Hua Miao are reproduced in this volume.)

The latter are considered as the superior of the two sections, speak a different tongue, and differ more or less widely in their methods, dress and customs, a study of which would lead one into a lifetime of interminable disquisitions, at the end of which one would be little more enlightened. Those who wish to study the question of inter-racial differences of the Miao are referred to Mr. Clarke's *Kwei-chow and Yuen-nan Provinces*, Prince Henri d'Orleans' *Du Tonkin aux Indes*, and Mr. Baber's works. Major Davies also gives some new information concerning this hill people, and

---

21    The photographs were included in the original hardcover edition of the book but are not included in this edition —publisher

is generally correct in what he says; but in his, as in all the books which touch upon the subject, the language tests vary considerably. In Chao-t'ong and the surrounding districts, for instance, the traveler would be unable to make any progress with the vocabulary which the Major has compiled. I was unable to make it tally with the spoken language of the people, and append a table showing the differences in the phonetic—and I do it with all respect to Major Davies. I ought to add that this is the language of the north-east corner of Yuen-nan; that of Major Davies is taken from page 339 of his book. He says that the words given by him will not be found to correspond in every case with those in the Miao vocabulary in the pocket of the cover of his book, and some have been taken from other Miao dialects!. However, the comparison will be interesting:—

| ENGLISH WORD | MAJOR DAVIES'S MIAO | N-E. YUEN-NAN MIAO |
|---|---|---|
| Man (human being) | Tan-neng, Tam-ming | Teh-neh. |
| Son | To, T'am-t'ong | Tu. |
| Eye | K'a-mwa, Mai | A-ma. |
| Hand | Api | Tee. |
| Cow | Nyaw, Nga | Niu. |
| Pig | Teng | Npa. |
| Dog | Klie, Ko | Klee. |
| Chicken | Ka, Kei | Ki. |
| Silver | Nya | Nieh. |
| River | Tiang | Glee. |
| Paddy | Mblei | Nglee. |
| Cooked Rice | Mao | Va. |
| Tree | Ndong | Ntao. |
| Fire | To | Teh. |
| Wind | Chwa, Chiang | Chta. |
| Earth | Ta | Ti. |
| Sun | Hno, Nai | Hnu. |
| Moon | Hla | Hlee. |
| Big | Hlo | Hlo. |
| Come | Ta | Ta. |
| Go | Mong | Mao. |

| ENGLISH WORD | MAJOR DAVIES'S MIAO | N-E. YUEN-NAN MIAO |
|---|---|---|
| Drink | Ho | Hao. |
| One | A, Yi | Ih. |
| Two | Ao | Ah. |
| Three | Pie, Po | Tsz. |
| Four | Pei, Plou | Glao. |
| Five | Pa | Peh. |
| Six | Chou | Glao. |
| Seven | Shiang, I | Shiang. |
| Eight | Yi, Yik | Yih. |
| Nine | Chio | Chia. |
| Ten | Ch'it | Kao. |

The Miao language was until a year or two ago only spoken; it was never written, and no one ever dreamed that it could be written. At the time of the great Miao revival, when thousands of Miao made a raid on the mission premises at Chao-t'ong, and implored the missionaries to come and teach them, it was found absolutely necessary that the language should be reduced to writing, and the whole of this extremely creditable work fell to the Rev. Samuel Pollard, who may be characterized as the pioneer of this Christianizing movement in North-East Yuen-nan.

In reducing the language to writing, however, considerable difficulty was complicated by the presence of "tones," so well known to all students of Chinese, itself said to be an invention of the Devil. Tones introduce another element or dimension into speech. The number of sounds, not being sufficient for the reproduction of all the spoken ideas, has been multiplied by giving these various sounds in different tones. It is as if the element of music were introduced according to rule into speech, and as if one had not only to remember the words in everything he wished to say, but the tune also.

The Miao people being so low down in the intellectual scale, and having never been accustomed to study, it was felt by the promoters of the written language that they should be as simple as possible, and hence they looked about for some system which could be readily grasped by these ignorant people. It was necessary that the system be absolutely phonetic and understood easily. By adapting the system used in shorthand, of putting the vowel marks in different positions by the side of the consonant signs, Mr. Pollard and his assistant found that they could solve their problem. The signs for the consonants are larger than the vowel signs, and the position of the latter by the side of the former gives the tone or musical note required.

At the present time there are thousands of Miao now able to read and write, and the work of this enterprising missionary has conferred an inestimable boon upon this people. When I went among the Miao I was able, after ten minutes' instruction, to stand up and sing their hymns and read their gospels with them. Miao women, who heretofore had never hoped to read, are now put in possession of the Word of God, and the simplicity of the written language enables them almost at once to read the Story of the Cross. Surely this is one of the outstanding features of mission work in the whole of China. I hope at some future date to publish a work devoted exclusively to my travels among the Hua Miao, for I feel that their story, no matter how simply written, is one of the great untold romances of the world. As a people, they are extremely fascinating in life and customs, emotional, large-hearted, and absolutely distinct from, with hardly a manner of daily life in common with, the Chinese.

## MISSION WORK AMONG THE MIAO

Whilst referring to mission work, it is a great privilege for the writer to add a word of most deserved eulogy of the United Methodist Mission at Chao-t'ong and Tongi-ch'uan-fu, and to the kindness shown by the missionaries towards me when I came, an absolute stranger, among them in May, 1909. It is to two members of this Mission that I owe a life-long debt of gratitude, for it was Mr. and Mrs. Evans, of Tong-ch'uan-fu, who saved my life, a week or two after I left Chao-t'ong, as is recorded in a subsequent chapter.

It was in the old days of the Bible Christian Mission—than which the individual members of no mission in the whole of China worked with more zeal and lower stipends—that a most interesting development in the mission took place.

The mass of the Miao are the serfs of the descendants of their ancient kings, who are large landowners, and the Miao are tenants. In 1905 the Miao heard of the Gospel, and came to listen to the preaching, and thousands came in batches at one time and another to the mission house. Their movements thus aroused suspicion among the Chinese, there was a good deal of persecution and personal violence, and at one time it looked as if there might be serious trouble. But the danger quieted down. The chieftain gave land, the Miao contributed one hundred pounds sterling, and themselves put up a chapel large enough to accommodate six hundred people. A year later, a thousand at a time crowded their simple sanctuary, and in 1907 nearly six thousand were members or probationers, and the work has steadily progressed ever since.

I am indebted to the Rev. H. Parsons, who had charge of the work at the time I passed through this district, and whose guest I was for several months, for the following interesting details regarding the methods adopted in the running of this enormous mission field. Mr. Parsons is assisted in his work by his genial wife, who is a most ardent worker, and a capable Miao linguist. Mrs. Parsons regularly addresses congregations of several hundreds of Miao, and has traveled on journeys often with her husband; and such work as hers, with several others in this mission, is a testimony to the wisdom of a system advocating the increase of the number of lady workers on the mission field in China.

## THE NOU-SU (OR I-PIEN)

There is a class of people around Chao-t'ong who are called Nou-su, a people who, although occupying the Chao-t'ong Plain at the time the Chinese arrived, are believed not to be the aboriginals of the district. What I actually know about this people is not much. I have heard a good deal, but it must not be understood that I publish this as absolutely the final word. People who have lived in the district for many years do not agree, so that for a mere traveler the task of getting infallible data would be quite formidable.

No tribe is more widely known than the Nou-su, with their innumerable tribal distinctions and hereditary peculiarities so perplexing to the inquirer into Far Western China ethnology.

The Nou-su are a very fine, tall race, with comparatively fair complexions, suggesting a mixture of Mongolian with some other straight-featured people. Of their origin, however, little can be vouched for, and with it we will have nothing to do here. But at the present time the Nou-su provide a good deal of interest from the fact that their power as tyrannic landlords and feudal chiefs is fast dying, and it may be that in a couple of decades, or a still shorter time, a people who, by obstinate self-reliance and great dislike to the Chinese, have remained unaffected by the absorbing spirit of the arbitrary Chinese, will have passed beyond the vale of personality. Even now, however, they own and rule enormous tracts of country (notably that part lying on the right bank of the River of Golden Sand) in north-east Yuen-nan. Some are very wealthy. One man may own vast tracts bigger than Yorkshire. In this tract there may be one hundred villages, all paying tribute to him and subject to the vagaries of his vilest despotism. From his tyranny his struggling tenantry have no redress. So long as the I-pien (the local name of the Nou-su) greases the palm of the squeezing Chinese mandarin in whose nominal control the district extends, he may run riot as he pleases. Social law and order are unknown, justice is a complete contradiction in terms, and whilst one is in the midst of it, it is difficult to realize that in China to-day—the China which all the world believes to be awakening—there exists a condition of things which will allow a man to torture, to plunder, to murder, and to indulge to the utmost degree the whims of a Neronic and devilish temperament.

Slave trading is common. If a tenant cannot pay his tribute, he sells himself for a few taels and becomes the slave of his former landlord, and if he would save his head treads carefully.

In the early days, when different clans were driven farther into the hills, they each clinched as much land as they could. In course of time, by petty quarrels, civil wars, and common feuds, the Nou-su were gradually thinned out. The Miao-tsi—the men of the hills and the serfs of the landlords, who four thousand years ago were a powerful race in their own kingdom—became the tenants of the Nou-su, whose rule is still marked by the grossest infamy possible to be practiced on the human race. All the methods of torture which in the old days were associated with the Chinese are still in vogue, in many cases in an aggravated form. I have personally seen the tortures, and have listened to the stories of the victims, but it would not bear description in print.

It must not, however, be understood that to be a Nou-su is to be a landlord. By no means. For in the gradual process of the survival of the fittest, when the weaker landlords were murdered by their stronger compatriots and their lands seized, only a small percentage of the tribe in this area have been able to hold sway. However, wherever there are landlords in this part of the country, they are always Nou-su or Chinese. The Miao—or, at least, the Hua Miao, own no lands, and are body and soul in the tyrannic clutch of the tyrannic I-pien. Then, again, in the Nou-su tribe there are various hereditary distinctions enabling a man to claim caste advantage. There are the Black Bones, as they style themselves, the aristocrats of the race, and the White Bones, the lower breeds, who obey to the letter their wealthier brethren—or anybody who has authority over them.

The Nou-su, who are a totally different race and a much better class than the Miao, are believed to been driven from the Chao-t'ong Plain, preferring migration to fighting, and many trekked across the Yangtze (locally called the Kin-sha) river into country now marked on good maps as the Man-tze country. It appears that the following are the two important branches:—

(i) The Black (Na-su)—Farmers and landowners.
(ii) The White (Tu-su) Generally slaves.
Other minor classes are:—

(i) The Lakes (or Red Nou-su)—Mostly blacksmiths.

(ii) The A-u-tsi Mostly felt-makers, who rightly or wrongly claim relationship with the Chinese.

(iii) Another class, who are mostly basket-makers.

The two great divisions, however, are the White and the Black. The latter class, themselves the owners of land, claim that all the White were originally slaves, and that those who are now free have escaped at some previous period from servitude. Men, as usual among such tribes, are scarcely distinguishable from the ordinary *Han Ren*. It is the women, with their peculiar head-dress and picturesque skirts, who maintain the distinguishing features of the race. For the most part, the Nou-su are not idolaters; no idols are in their houses. That portion of the tribe which migrated across the Yangtze, secure among the mountains, has never ceased to harass the Chinese, who now dwell on land which the Nou-su themselves once tilled, or at least inhabited; but they have been driven into remoter districts, and are only found away from the highways of Chinese travel. The race, too, is dying out—in this area at all events—and the Nou-su themselves reckon that their numbers have decreased by one-half during the last thirty years. This is one of the saddest facts. The insanitation of their dwellings, their rough diet, and frequent riotings in wine, opium and other evils, are quickly playing havoc in their ranks, giving the strong the opportunity of enriching themselves at the expense of the weak, with frequent fighting about the division of land.

Europeans who can speak the language of the Nou-su are numbered on the fingers of one hand.

To one who has traveled in this neighborhood for any length of time, it must be apparent that the unique method generally adopted by the Nou-su, that is, the landlord class, to get rich quickly is to kill off their next-door neighbor. The lives these men live with nothing but scandal and licentiousness to pass their time, are grossly and horribly wicked when viewed by the broadest-minded Westerner. They all live in fear of their lives, and are each afraid of the others, all entertaining a secret hatred, and all ever on the alert to devise some safe scheme to murder the owner of some land they are anxious of annexing to their own—and in the doing of the deed to save their own necks. If they succeed, they are accounted clever men. As I write, I hear of a man, quite a youngster, himself an exceedingly wealthy man, who killed his brother and confiscated his property with no compunction whatever. When tackled on the subject, he said he could do nothing else, for if he had not killed his brother his brother would have killed him

Yet there is no sense of crime as we of the West understand it, and nothing is feared from the Chinese law. A man kills a slave, tortures him to death, and when the Chinese mandarin is appealed to, if he is at all, he looks wise and says, "I quite see your point, but I can do nothing. The murdered man was the landlord's slave," and, with a gentle wave of his three-inch fingernail, he explains how a man may kill his slave, his wife, or his son—and the law can do nothing. That is, if he compensates the mandarin.

A Nou-su looked upon a girl one day, when he was out collecting tribute. She was handsome, and he instructed his men to take her. She refused. A sum of one hundred ounces of silver was offered to anyone who would kidnap her and carry her off to his harem. Eventually he got the girl, and had her father tortured and then put to death because he would not deliver his daughter over to him. Yet there is no redress.

Nou-su women, their feet unbound, with high foreheads and well-cut features, with fiery eyes set in not unkindly faces, tall and healthy, would be considered handsome women in any country in Europe. They rarely intermarry with other tribes. A good deal of affection certainly exists sometimes between husband and wife and between parents and children, but the looseness of the marriage relation leads to unending strife.

Many Europeans, travelers and missionaries, have been murdered in the country inhabited by the independent Lolo people. Although I have not personally been through any of that country, I have been on the very outskirts and have lived for a long time among the people there. I found them a pleasant hospitable race, fairly easy to get on with. And it must not be averred that, because they consider their natural enemy, the Chinese, the man to be robbed and murdered, and because they kill off their fellow-landlords in order the more quickly to get rich, that they treat all strangers alike. Among the Europeans who have suffered death at their hands, it is probable that in some way the cause was traceable to their own bearing towards the people—either a total lack of knowledge of their language or an attitude which caused suspicion.

Among the Nou-su, strong as this feudal life still is, the Chinese are fast gaining permanent influence. Their dissolute and drunken and inhuman daily practices are tending to work out among this people their own destruction, and in years to come in this neighborhood the traveler will be perplexed at finding here and there a fine specimen of an upstanding Chinese, with clean-cut face, straight of feature and straight of limb, with a peculiar Mongol look about him. He will be one of the surviving specimens of a race of people, the Nou-su, whose forgotten historical records would do much to clear up the doubt attaching to Indo-China and Tibet-Burma ethnology.

The first Nou-su chieftain to come to Chao-t'ong, a man who was renowned as a tryannical brute, was one Ien Tsang-fu, who frequently gouged out the eyes of those who disobeyed his commands; and his descendants are said to have inherited a good many of this tyrant's vices. The landlords prey upon their weaker brethren, and at last, with infinite sagacity, the Chinese Government steps in to stop the quarrels, confiscates the whole of the property, and thus reduces the Nou-su land to immediate control of Chinese authorities.

"The Nou-su are, of course, entirely dependent upon the land for their living. They till the soil and rear cattle, and the greatest calamity that can come upon any family is that their land shall be taken from them. To be landless involves degradation as well as poverty, and very severe hardship is the lot of men who have been deprived of this means of subsistence. For those who own no land, but who are merely tenants of the Tu-muh,[22] there seems to be no security of tenure; but still, if the wishes and demands of the landlords are complied with, one family may till the same farm for many successive generations. The terms on which land is held are peculiar. The rental agreed upon is nominal. Large tracts of country are rented for a pig or a sheep or a fowl, with a little corn per year. Beside this nominal rent, the landlord has the right to make levies on his tenants on all special occasions, such as funerals, weddings, or for any other extraordinary expenses. He can also require his tenants with their cattle to render services. This system necessarily leads to much oppression and injustice. It is also said that if a family is hard pressed by a Tu-muh and reduced to extreme poverty, they will make themselves over to him on condition that a portion of his land be given them to cultivate. Such people are called caught slaves, as distinguished from hereditary, and the eldest children become the absolute property of the landlord and are generally given as attendants upon his wife and daughters.

"Every farmer owns a large number of slaves, who live in the same compound as himself. These people do all the work of the farm, while the master employs himself as his fancy leads him. Over these unfortunate people the owner has absolute control. All their affairs are managed by him. His girl slaves he marries off to other men's slave boys, and similarly obtains wives for his male slaves. The lot of these unfortunate people is hard beyond description. Being considered but little more valuable than the cattle they tend, the food given to them is often inferior to the corn upon which

---

22    Literally "Eyes of the Earth"—the landlords.

the master's horse is fed. The cruel beatings and torturings they have been subject to have completely broken their spirit, and now they seem unable to exist apart from their masters. Very seldom do any of them try to escape, for no one will give them shelter, and the punishment awarded a recaptured slave is so severe as to intimidate the most daring. These poor folk are born in slavery, married in slavery, and they die in slavery. It is not uncommon to meet with Chinese slaves, both boys and girls, in Nou-su families. These have either been kidnapped and sold, or their parents, unable to nourish them, have bartered them in exchange for food. Their purchasers marry them to Tu-su, and their lot is thrown in with the slave class. One's heart is wrung with anguish sometimes as he thinks of what cruelty and wretchedness exist among the hills of this benighted district. Even here, however, light is beginning to shine, for some adherents of the Christian religion have changed their slaves into tenants, thus showing the way to the ultimate solution of this difficult problem.

"The life in a Nou-su household is not very complex. The cattle are driven out early in the morning, as soon as the sun has risen. They remain out until the breakfast hour, and then return to the stables and rest during the heat of the day, going out again in the cool hours. The food of the household is prepared by the slaves, under the direction of the lady of the house. There is no refined cooking, for the Nou-su despises well-cooked food, and complains that it never satisfies him. He has a couplet which runs: 'If you eat raw food, you become a warrior; if you eat it cooked, you suffer hunger.' No chairs or tables are found in a genuine Nou-su house. The food is served up in a large bowl placed on the floor. The family sit around, and each one helps himself with a large wooden spoon. At the present time the refinements of Chinese civilization have been adopted by a large number of Nou-su, and the homes of the wealthier people are as well furnished as those of the middle-class Chinese of the district. The women of the households also spend much time making their own and their children's clothes. The men have adopted Chinese dress, but the women, in most cases, retain their tribal costume with its large turban-like head-dress, its plaited skirt and intricately embroidered coat. All this is made by hand, and the choicest years of maidenhood are occupied in preparing the clothes for the wedding-day.

"The Nou-su, it would seem, used not to beg a wife, but rather obtained her by main force. At the present day, while the milder method generally prevails, there are still survivals of the ancient custom. The betrothal truly takes place very early, even in infancy, and at the ceremony a fowl is killed, and each contracting party takes a rib; but as the young folk grow to marriageable age, the final negotiations have to be made. These are purposely prolonged until the bridegroom, growing angry, gathers his friends and makes an attack on the maiden's home. Arming themselves with cudgels, they approach secretly, and protecting their heads and shoulders with their felt cloaks, they rush towards the house. Strenuous efforts are made by the occupants to prevent their entering, and severe blows are exchanged. When the attacking party has succeeded in gaining an entrance, peace is proclaimed, and wine and huge chunks of flesh are provided for their entertainment.

"Occasionally during these fights the maiden's home is quite dismantled. The negotiations being ended, preparations are made to escort the bride to her future home. Heavily veiled, she is supported on horseback by her brothers, while her near relatives, all fully armed, attend her. On arriving at the house, a scuffle ensues. The veil is snatched from the bride's face by her relatives, who do their utmost to throw it on to the roof, thus signifying that she will rule over the occupants when she enters. The bridegroom's people on the contrary try to trample it upon the doorstep, as an indication of the rigor with which the newcomer will be subjected to the ruling of the head of the house. Much blood is shed, and people are often seriously injured in these skirmishes. The new bride remains for three days in a temporary shelter before she is admitted to the home. A girl having once left her parent's home to become a wife, waits many years before she pays a return visit. Anciently the minimum time was three years, but some allow ten or more years to elapse before the first visit home is paid. Two or three years are then often spent with the parents. Many friends and relatives attend any visitor, for with the Nou-su a large following is considered a sign of dignity and importance. When a child is born a tree is planted, with the hope that as the tree grows so also will the child develop.

"The fear of disease lies heavily upon the Nou-su people, and their disregard of the most elementary sanitary laws makes them very liable to attacks of sickness. They understand almost nothing about medicine, and consequently resort to superstitious practices in order to ward off the evil influences. When it is known that disease has visited a neighbor's house, a pole, seven feet long, is erected in a conspicuous place in a thicket some distance from the house to be guarded. On the pole an old ploughshare is fixed, and it is supposed that when the spirit who controls the disease sees the ploughshare he will retire to a distance of three homesteads.

"A fever called No-ma-dzi works great havoc among the Nou-su every year, and the people are very much afraid of it. No person will stay by the sick-bed to nurse the unfortunate victim. Instead, food and water are placed by his bedside and, covered with his quilt, he is left at the mercy of the disease. Since as the fever progresses the patient will perspire, heavy stones are placed on the quilt, that it may not be thrown off, and the sick person take cold. Many an unfortunate sufferer has through this strange practice died from suffocation. After a time the relatives will return to see what course the disease has taken. This fever seems to yield to quinine, for Mr. John Li has seen several persons recover to whom he had administered this drug. When a man dies, his relatives, as soon as they receive the news, hold in their several homes a feast of mourning called by them the Za. A pig or sheep is sacrificed at the doorway, and it is supposed that intercourse is thus maintained between the living persons and the late departed spirit. The near kindred, on hearing of the death of a relative, take a fowl and strangle it; the shedding of its blood is not permissible. This fowl is cleaned and skewered, and the mourner then proceeds to the house where the deceased person is lying, and sticks this fowl at the head of the corpse as an offering. The more distant relatives do not perform this rite, but each leads a sheep to the house of mourning, and the son of the deceased man strikes each animal three times with a white wand, while the Peh-mo (priest or magician) stands by, and announcing the sacrifice by calling 'so and so,' giving of course the name, presents the soft woolly offering.

"Formerly the Nou-su burned their dead. Said a Nou-su youth to me years ago, 'The thought of our friends' bodies either turning to corruption or being eaten by wild beasts is distasteful to us, and therefore we burn our dead.' The corpse is burnt with wood, and during the cremation the mourners arrange themselves around the fire and chant and dance. The ashes are buried, and the ground leveled. This custom is still adhered to among the Nou-su of the independent Lolo territory or more correctly Papu country of Western Szech'wan. The tribesmen who dwell in the neighborhood of Weining and Chao-t'ong have adopted burial as the means of disposing of their dead, adding some customs peculiar to themselves.

"On the day of the funeral the horse which the deceased man was in the habit of riding is brought to the door and saddled by the Pehmo. The command is then given to lead the horse to the grave. All the mourners follow, and marching or dancing in intertwining circles, cross and recross the path of the led horse until the poor creature, grown frantic with fear, rushes and kicks in wild endeavor to escape from the confusion. The whole company then raise a great shout and call, 'The soul has come to ride the horse, the soul has come to ride the horse.' A contest then follows among the women of the deceased man's household for the possession of this horse, which is henceforth regarded as of extreme value. It is difficult to discover much about the religion of the Nou-su, because so many of their ancient customs have fallen into disuse during the intercourse of the people with the Chinese. At the ingathering of the buckwheat, when the crop is stacked on the threshing floor, and the work of threshing is about to begin, the simple formula, 'Thank you, Ilsomo,' is used. Ilsomo seems to be a spirit who has control over the crops; whether good or evil, it is not easy to determine. Ilsomo is not God, for at present, when the Nou-su wish to speak of God, they use the word Soe, which means Master.

"In the independent territory of the Nou-su, to the west of Szech'wan, the term used for God is Eh-nia, and a Nou-su who has much intercourse with the independent people contends that there are three names indicative of God, each representing different functions if not persons of the Godhead. These names are: Eh-nia, Keh-neh, Um-p'a-ma. The Nou-su believe in ancestor worship, and perhaps the most interesting feature of their religion is the peculiar form this worship takes. Instead of an ancestral tablet such as the Chinese use, the Nou-su worship a small basket (lolo) about as large as a duck's egg and made of split bamboo. This 'lolo' contains small bamboo tubes an inch or two long, and as thick as an ordinary Chinese pen handle. In these tubes are fastened a piece of grass and a piece of sheep's wool. A man and his wife would be represented by two tubes, and if he had two wives, an extra tube would be placed in the 'lolo.' At the ceremony of consecration the Pehmo attends, and a slave is set apart for the purpose of attending to all the rites connected with the worship of the deceased person. The 'lolo' is sometimes placed in the house, but more often on a tree in the neighborhood or it may be hidden in a rock. For persons who are short-lived, the ancestral 'lolo' is placed in a crevice in the wall of some forsaken and ruined building. Every three years the 'lolo' is changed, and the old one burnt. The term 'lolo,' by which the Nou-su are generally known, is a contemptuous nickname given them by the Chinese in reference to this peculiar method of venerating their ancestors.

"Hill worship is another important feature of Nou-su religious life. Most important houses are built at the foot of a hill and sacrifice is regularly offered on the hill-side in the fourth month of each year. The Pehmo determines which is the most propitious day, and the Tumuh and his people proceed to the appointed spot. A limestone rock with an old tree trunk near is chosen as an altar, and a sheep and pig are brought forward by the Tumuh. The Pehmo, having adjusted his clothes, sits cross-legged before the altar, and begins intoning his incantations in a low muttering voice. The sacrifice is then slain, and the blood poured beneath the altar, and a handful of rice and a lump of salt are placed beneath the stone. Some person then gathers a bundle of green grass, and the Pehmo, having finished intoning, the altar is covered, and all return to the house. The Pehmo then twists the grass into a length of rope, which he hangs over the doorway of the house. Out of a piece of willow a small arrow is made, and a bow similar in size is cut out of a peach tree. These are placed on the doorposts. On a piece of soft white wood a figure of a man is roughly carved, and this, with two sticks of any soft wood placed cross-wise, is fastened to the rope hanging over the doorway, on each side of which two small sticks are placed. The Pehmo then proceeds with his incantation, muttering: 'From now, henceforth and for ever will the evil spirits keep away from this house.'

"Most Nou-su at the present time observe the New Year festival on the same date and with the same customs as the Chinese. Formerly this was not so, and even now in the remoter districts New Year's day is observed on the first day of the tenth month of the Chinese year. A pig and sheep are killed and cleaned, and hung in the house for three days. They are then taken down, cut up and cooked. The family sit on buckwheat straw in the middle of the chief room of the house. The head of the house invites the others to drink wine, and the feasting begins. Presently one will start singing, and all join in this song: 'How firm is this house of mine. Throughout the year its hearth fire has not ceased to burn, My food corn is abundant, I have silver and also cash, My cattle have increased to herds, My horses and mules have all white foreheads K'o K'o Ha Ha Ha Ha K'o K'o, My sons are filial, My wife is virtuous, In the midst of flesh and wine we sleep, Our happiness reaches unto heaven, Truly glorious is this glad New Year.' A scene of wild indulgence then frequently follows.

"The Nou-su possess a written language. Their books were originally made of sheepskin, but paper is now used. The art of printing was unknown, and many books are said to have been lost. The books are illustrated, but the drawings are extremely crude."[23]

---

23    A good deal of information in this chapter was obtained from an article by the Rev. C E Hicks, published in the Chinese Recorder for March, 1910. The portion quoted is taken bodily from this excellent article.

# Fifth Journey: Chao-T'ong-Fu to Tong-Ch'uan-Fu

## CHAPTER XI.

*Revolting sights compensated for by scenery. Most eventful day in the trip. Buying a pony, and the reason for its purchase. Author's pony kicks him and breaks his arm. Chastising the animal, and narrow escape from death. Rider and pony a sorry sight. An uneasy night. Reappearance of malaria. Author nearly forced to give in. Heavy rain on a difficult road. At Ta-shui-tsing. Chasing frightened pony in the dead of night. Bad accommodation. Lepers and leprosy. Mining. At Kiang-ti. Two mandarins, and an amusing episode. Laying foundation of a long illness. The Kiang-ti Suspension Bridge. Hard climbing. Tiffin in the mountains. Sudden ascents and descents. Description of the country. Tame birds and what they do. A non-enterprising community. Pleasant travelling without perils. Majesty of the mountains of Yuen-nan.*

Whilst in this district, as will have been seen, one has to steel himself to face some of the most revolting sights it is possible to imagine, he is rewarded by the grandeur of the scenic pictures which mark the downward journey to Tong-ch'uan-fu.

The stages to Tong-ch'uan-fu were as follows:—

|  | LENGTH OF STAGE | HEIGHT ABOVE SEA LEVEL |
|---|---|---|
| 1st day T'ao-ueen | 70 li. | — ft. |
| 2nd day Ta-shui-tsing | 30 " | 9,300 ft. |
| 3rd day Kiang-ti | 40 " | 4,400 " |
| 4th day Yi-che-shin | 70 " | 6,300 " |
| 5th day Hong-shih-ai | 90 " | 6,800 " |
| 6th day Tong-ch'uan-fu | 60 " | 7,250 " |

The Chao-t'ong plateau, magnificently level, runs out past the picturesque-ly-situated tower of Wang-hai-leo, from which one overlooks a stretch of water. A memorial arch, erected by the Li family of Chao-t'ong-fu, graces the main road farther on, and is probably one of the best of its kind in Yuen-nan, comparing favorably with the best to be found in Szech'wan, where monumental architecture abounds. Perhaps the only building of interest in Chao-t'ong is the ancestral hall of the wealthy family mentioned above, the carving of which is magnificent.

At the end of the first day we camped at the Mohammedan village of T'ao-ueen, literally "Peach Garden," but the peach trees might once have been, though now certainly they are not.

It was cold when we left, 38 deg. F., hard frost. All the world seemed buttoned up and great-coated; the trees seemed wiry and cheerless; the legs of the pack-horses seemed brittle, and I felt so. Breath issued visibly from the mouth as I trudged along. My boy and I nearly came to blows in the early morning. I wanted to lie on; he did not. If he could not entertain himself for half an hour with his own thoughts, I, who could, thought it no fault of mine. I was a reasoning being, a rational creature, and thought it a fine way of spending a sensible, impartial half-hour. But I had to get up, and then came the benumbed fingers, a quivering body, a frozen towel, and a floor upon which the mud was frozen stiff. Little did he know that he was pulling me out to the most eventful and unfortunate day of my trip.

At Chao-t'ong I had bought a pony in case of emergency—one of those sturdy little brutes that never grow tired, cost little to keep, and are unexcelled for the amount of work they can get through every day in the week. Its color was black, a smooth, glossy black—the proverbial dark horse—and when dressed in its English saddle and bridle looked even smart enough for the use of the distinguished traveler, who smiled the smile of pleasant ownership as it was led on in front all day long, seeming to return a satanic grin for my foolishness at not riding it.[24]

The first I saw of it was when it was standing full on its hind legs pinning a man between the railings and a wall in a corner of the mission premises. It looked well. Truly, it was a blood beast!

On the second day out, whilst walking merrily along in the early morning, the little brute lifted its heels, lodged them most precisely on to my right

---

24   The incredulous of my readers may question, and rightly so, "Then where did he get his saddle?" So I must explain that I met just out of Sui-fu a Danish gentleman (also a traveler) who wished to sell a pony and its trappings. As I had the arrangement with my boy that I would provide him with a conveyance, and did not like the idea of seeing him continually in a chair and his wealthy master trotting along on foot, I bought it for my boy's use. He used the saddle until we reached Chao-t'ong.

forearm with considerable force—more forceful than affectionate—sending the stick which I carried thirty feet from me up the cliffs. The limb ached, and I felt sick. My boy—he had been a doctor's boy on one of the gunboats at Chung-king—thought it was bruised. I acquiesced, and sank fainting to a stone. On the strength of my boy's diagnosis we rubbed it, and found that it hurt still more. Then diving into a cottage, I brought out a piece of wood, three inches wide and twenty inches long, placed my arm on it, bade my boy take off one of my puttees from one of my legs, used it as a bandage, and trudged on again.

Not realizing that my arm was broken, in the evening I determined to chastise the animal in a manner becoming to my disgust. Mounting at the foot of a long hill, I laid on the stick as hard as I could, and found that my pony had a remarkable turn of speed. At the brow of the hill was a twenty-yard dip, at the base of which was a pond.

Down, down, down we went, and, despite my full strength (with the left arm) at its mouth, the pony plunged in with a dull splash, only to find that his feet gave way under him in a clay bottom. He could not free himself to swim. Farther and farther we sank together, every second deeper into the mire, when just at the moment I felt the mud clinging about my waist, and I had visions of a horrible death away from all who knew me, I plunged madly to reach the side.

With one arm useless, it is still to me the one great wonder of my life how I escaped. Nothing short of miraculous; one of the times when one feels a special protection of Providence surrounding him.

Pulling the beast's head, after I had given myself a momentary shake, I succeeded in making him give a mighty lurch—then another—then another—and in a few seconds, after terrible struggling, he reached the bank. We made a sorry spectacle as we walked shamefacedly back to the inn, under the gaze of half a dozen grinning rustics, where my man was preparing the evening meal.

In the evening, on the advice of my general confidential companion, I submitted to a poultice being applied to my arm. It was bruised, so we put on the old-fashioned, hard-to-be-beaten poultice of bread. Whilst it was hot it was comfortable; when it was cold, I unrolled the bandage, threw the poultice to the floor, and in two minutes saw glistening in the moonlight the eyes of the rats which ate it.

Then I bade sweet Morpheus take me; but, although the pain prevented me from sleeping, I remember fainting. How long I lay I know not. Shuddering in every limb with pain and chilly fear, I at length awoke from a long swoon. Something had happened, but what? There was still the paper window, the same greasy saucer of thick oil and light being given by the same rush, the same rickety table, the same chair on which we had made the poultice—but what had happened? I rubbed my aching eyes and lifted myself in a half-sitting posture—a dream had dazzled me and scared my senses. And then I knew that it was malaria coming on again, and that I was once more her luckless victim.

Malignant malaria, mistress of men who court thee under tropic skies, and who, like me, are turned from thee bodily shattered and whimpering like a child, how much, how very much hast thou laid up for thyself in Hades!

Thank Heaven, I had superabundant energy and vitality, and despite contorted and distorted things dancing haphazard through my fevered brain, I determined not to go under, not to give in. My mind was a terrible tangle of combinations nevertheless—intricate, incongruous, inconsequent, monstrous; but still I plodded on. For the next four days, with my arm lying limp and lifeless at my side, and with recurring attacks of malaria, I walked on against the greatest odds, and it was not till I had reached Tong-ch'uan-fu that I learnt that the limb was fractured. Men may have seen more in four days and done more and risked more, but I think few travelers have been called upon to suffer more agony than befell the lot of the man who was crossing China on foot.

From T'ao-ueen there is a stiff ascent, followed by a climb up steep stone steps and muddy mountain banks through black and barren country. The morning had been cold and frosty, but rain came on later, a thick, heavy deluge, which swished and swashed everything from its path as one toiled painfully up those slippery paths, made almost unnegotiable. But my imagination and my hope helped me to make my own sunshine. There is something, I think, not disagreeable in issuing forth during a good honest summer rain at home with a Burberry well buttoned and an umbrella over one's head; here in Yuen-nan a coat made it too uncomfortable to walk, and the terrific wind would have blown an umbrella from one's grasp in a twinkling. If we are in the home humor, in the summer, we do not mind how drenching the rain is, and we may even take delight in getting our own legs splashed as we glance at the "very touching stockings" and the "very gentle and sensitive legs" of other weaker ones in the same plight. But here was I in a gale on the bleakest tableland one can find in this part of Yuen-nan, and a sorry sight truly did I make as I trudged "two steps forward, one step back" in my bare feet, covered only with rough straw sandals, with trousers upturned above the knee, with teeth chattering in malarial shivers, endeavoring between-times to think of the pouring deluge as a benignant enemy fertilizing fields, purifying the streets of the horrid little villages in which we spent our nights, refreshing the air!

Shall I ever forget the day?

Just before sundown, drenched to the skin and suffering horribly from the blues, we reached one single hut, which I could justly look upon as a sort of evening companion; for here was a fire—albeit, a green wood fire—which looked gladly in my face, talked to me, and put life and comfort and warmth into me for the ten li yet remaining of the day's hard journey.

And at night, about 8:30 p.m., we at last reached the top of the hill, actually the summit of a mountain pass, at the dirty little village of Ta-shui-tsing. Not for long, however, could I rest; for I heard yells and screams and laughs. That pony again! Every one of my men were afraid of it, for at the slightest invitation it pawed with its front feet and landed man after man into the gutter, and if that failed it stood upright and cuddled them around the neck. Now I found it had run—saddle, bridle and all—and none volunteered to chase. So at 9:30, weary and bearing the burden of a terrible day, which laid the foundation of a long illness to be recorded later, I found it my unpleasant duty to patrol the hill from top to bottom, lighting my slippery way with a Chinese lantern, chasing the pony silhouetted on the sky-line. Ta-shui-tsing is a dreary spot with no inn accommodation at all,[25] a place depopulated and laid waste, gloomy and melancholy. I managed, however, after promising a big fee, to get into a small mud-house, where the people were not unkindly disposed. I ate my food, slept as much as I could in the few hours before the appearing of the earliest dawn on the bench allotted to me, feeling thankful that to me had been allowed even this scanty lodging. But I could not conscientiously recommend the place to future travelers—a dirty little village with its dirty people and its dirty atmosphere. At the top of the pass the wind nearly removed my ears as I took a final glance at the mountain refuge. Mountains here run south-west and north-east, and are grand to look upon.

The poorest people were lepers, the beggars were all dead long ago. In Yuen-nan province leprosy afflicts thousands, a disease which the Chinese, not without reason, dread terribly, for no known remedy exists. Burning the patient alive, which used often to be resorted to, is even now looked upon as the only true remedy. Cases have been known where the patient, having been stupefied with opium, has been locked in a house, which has then been set on fire, and its inmate cremated on the spot.

Mining used to be carried on here, so they told me; but I was not long in concluding that, whatever was the product, it has not materially affected the

---

25    A new inn has been built since.—E.J.D.

world's output, nor had it greatly enriched the laborers in the field. When I got into civilization I found that coal of a sulphurous nature was the booty of ancient days. There may be coal yet, as is most probable, but the natives seemed far too apathetic and weary of life to care whether it is there or not.

Passing Ta-shui-tsing, the descent narrows to a splendid view of dark mountain and green and beautiful valley. We were now traveling away from several ranges of lofty mountains, whose peaks appeared vividly above the drooping rain-filled clouds, onwards to a range immediately opposite, up whose slopes we toiled all day, passing *en route* only one uninhabited hamlet, to which the people flee in time of trouble. After a weary tramp of another twenty-five li—the Yuen-nan li, mind you, the most unreliable quantity in all matters geographical in the country—I asked irritatedly, as all travelers must have asked before me, "Then, in the name of Heaven, where is Kiang-ti?"[26] It should come into view behind the terrible steep decline when one is within only about a hundred yards. It is roughly four thousand feet below Ta-shui-tsing.

Kiang-ti is an important stopping place, with but one forlorn street, with two or three forlorn inns, the best of which has its best room immediately over the filthiest stables, emitting a stench which was almost unbearable, that I have seen in China. It literally suffocates one as it comes up in wafts through the wide gaps in the wood floor of the room. There are no mosquitoes here, but of a certain winged insect of various species, whose distinguishing characteristics are that the wings are transparent and have no cases or covers, there was a formidable army. I refer to the common little fly. There was the house fly, the horse fly, the dangerous blue-bottle, the impecunious blow fly, the indefatigable buzzer, and others. One's delicate skin got beset with flies: they got in one's ears, in one's eyes, up one's nose, down one's throat, in one's coffee, in one's bed; they bade fair to devour one within an hour or two, and brought forth inward curses and many swishes of the 'kerchief.

The village seemed a death-trap.

Glancing comprehensively at one another as I entered the higher end of the town, a party of reveling tea-drinkers hastily pulled some cash from their satchels to settle accounts, and made a general rush into the street, where they awaited noisily the approach of a strangely wondrous and imposing spectacle, one that had not been seen in those parts for many days. The tramper, tired as he could be, at length approached, but the crowd had increased so enormously that the road was completely blocked. Tradesmen

---

26    Pronounced Djang-di. Famous throughout Western China for its terrible hill, one of the most difficult pieces of country in the whole of the west.

with their portable workshops, pedlars with their cumbersome gear and pack-horses could not pass, but had to wait for their turn; there were not even any tortuous by-streets in this place whereby they might reach their destination. Children lost themselves in the crush, and went about crying for their mothers. A party of travelers, newly arrived from the south by caravan route, got wedged with their worn-out horses and mules in the thick of the mob, and could not move an inch. As far as the eye could reach the blue-clad throng heaved restlessly to and fro under the blaze of the brilliant sun which harassed everyone in the valley, and, moving slowly and majestically in the midst of them all, came the foreigner. As they caught sight of me, my sandalled feet, and the retinue following on wearily in the wake, the populace set up an ecstatic yell of ferocious applause and turned their faces towards the inn, in the doorway of which one of my soldier-men was holding forth on points of more or less delicacy respecting my good or bad nature and my British connection. At that moment, the huge human mass began to move in one predetermined direction, and then a couple of mandarins in their chairs joined the swarming rabble. I had to sit down on the step for five minutes whilst my boy, with commendable energy, cleared these two mandarins, who had come from Chen-tu and were on their way to the capital, out of the best room, because his master wanted it.

As he finished speaking, there came a loud crashing noise and a shout— my pony had landed out just once again, and banged in one side of a chair belonging to these traveling officials. They met me with noisy and derisive greetings, which were returned with a straight and penetrating look.

No less than fifty degrees was the thermometrical difference in Ta-shui-tsing and Kiang-ti. Here it was stifling. Cattle stood in stagnant water, ducks were envied, my room with the sun on it became intolerable, and I sought refuge by the river; my butter was too liquid to spread; coolies were tired as they rested outside the tea-houses, having not a cash to spend; my pony stood wincing, giving sharp shivers to his skin, and moving his tail to clear off the flies and his hind legs to clear off men. As for myself, I could have done with an iced soda or a claret cup.

Very early in the morning, despite malaria shivers, I made my way over the beautiful suspension bridge which here graces the Niu Lan,[27] a tributary of the Yangtze, up to the high hills beyond.

This bridge at Kiang-ti is one hundred and fifty feet by twelve, protected at one end by a couple of monkeys carved in stone, whilst the opposite

---

27    This river, the Niu Lan, comes from near Yang-lin, one day's march from Yuen-nan-fu. It is being followed down by two American engineers as the probable route for a new railway, which it is proposed should come out to the Yangtze some days north of Kiang-ti.

end is guarded by what are supposed to be, I believe, a couple of lions—and not a bad representation of them either, seeing that the workmen had no original near at hand to go by.

From here the ascent over a second range of mountains is made by tortuous paths that wind along the sides of the hills high above the stream below, and at other times along the river-bed. The river is followed in a steep ascent, a sort of climbing terrace, from which the water leaps in delightful cascades and waterfalls. A four-hour climb brings one, after terrific labor, to the mouth of the picturesque pass of Ya-ko-t'ang at 7,500 feet. In the quiet of the mountains I took my midday meal; there was about the place an awe-inspiring stillness. It was grand but lonely, weird rather than peaceful, so that one was glad to descend again suddenly to the river, tracing it through long stretches of plain and barren valley, after which narrow paths lead up again to the small village of Yi-che-shin, considerably below Ya-ko-t'ang. It is the sudden descents and ascents which astonish one in traveling in this region, and whether climbing or dropping, one always reaches a plain or upland which would delude one into believing that he is almost at sea-level, were it not for the towering mountains that all around keep one hemmed in in a silent stillness, and the rarefied air. Yi-che-shin, for instance, standing at this altitude of considerably over 6,000 feet, is in the center of a tableland, on which are numerous villages, around which the fragrance of the broad bean in flower and the splendid fertility now and again met with makes it extremely pleasant to walk—it is almost a series of English cottage gardens. Here the weather was like July in England—or what one likes to imagine July should be in England—dumb, dreaming, hot, lazy, luxurious weather, in which one should do as he pleases, and be pleased with what he does. As I toiled along, my useless limb causing me each day more trouble, I felt I should like to lie down on the grass, with stones 'twixt head and shoulders for my pillow, and repose, as Nature was reposing, in sovereign strength. But I was getting weaker! I saw, as I passed, gardens of purple and gold and white splendor; the sky was at its bluest, the clouds were full, snowy, mountainous.

Then on again to varying scenes.

Inns were not frequent, and were poor and wretched. The country was all red sandstone, and devoid of all timber, till, descending into a lovely valley, the path crossed an obstructing ridge, and then led out into a beautiful park all green and sweet. The country was full of color. It put a good taste in one's mouth, it impressed one as a heaven-sent means of keeping one cheerful in sad dilemma. The gardens, the fields, the skies, the mountains, the sunset, the light itself—all were full of color, and earth and heaven seemed of one opinion in the harmony of the reds, the purples, the drabs, the blacks, the browns, the bright blues, and the yellows. Birds were as tame as they were in the Great Beginning; they came under the table as I ate, and picked up the crumbs without fear. Peasant people sat under great cedars, planted to give shade to the travelers, and bade one feel at home in his lonely pilgrimage. Then one felt a peculiar feeling—this feeling will arise in any traveler—when, surmounting some hill range in the desert road, one descries, lying far below, embosomed in its natural bulwarks, the fair village, the resting-place, the little dwelling-place of men, where one is to sleep. But when towards nightfall, as the good red sun went down, I was led, weary and done-up, into one of the worst inns it had been my misfortune to encounter, a thousand other thoughts and feelings united in common anathema to the unenterprising community.

Tea was bad, rice we could not get, and all night long the detestable smells from the wood fires choked our throats and blinded our eyes; glad, therefore, was I, despite the heavy rain, to take a hurried and early departure the next morning, descending a thousand feet to a river, rising quite as suddenly to a height of 8,500 feet.

Now the road went over a mountain broad and flat, where traveling in the sun was extremely pleasant—or, rather, would have been had I been fit. Pack-horses, laden clumsily with their heavy loads of Puerh tea, Manchester goods, oil and native exports from Yuen-nan province, passed us on the mountain-side, and sometimes numbers of these willing but ill-treated animals were seen grazing in the hollows, by the wayside, their backs in almost every instance cruelly lacerated by the continuous rubbing of the wooden frames on which their loads were strapped. For cruelty to animals China stands an easy first; love of animals does not enter into their sympathies at all. I found this not to be the case among the Miao and the I-pien, however; and the tribes across the Yangtze below Chao-t'ong, locally called the Pa-pu, are, as a matter of fact, fond of horses, and some of them capable horsemen.

The journey across these mountains has no perils. One may step aside a few feet with no fear of falling a few thousand, a danger so common in most of the country from Sui-fu downwards. The scenery is magnificent—range after range of mountains in whatever direction you look, nothing but mountains of varying altitudes. And the patches of wooded slopes, alternating with the red earth and more fertile green plots through which streams flow, with rolling waterfalls, picturesque nooks and winding pathways, make pictures to which only the gifted artist's brush could do justice. Often, gazing over the sunlit landscape, in this land "South of the Clouds," one is held spellbound by the intense beauty of this little-known province, and one wonders what all this grand scenery, untouched and unmarred by the hand of man, would become were it in the center of a continent covered by the ubiquitous globe-trotter.

No country in the world more than West China possesses mountains of combined majesty and grace. Rocks, everywhere arranged in masses of a rude and gigantic character, have a ruggedness tempered by a singular airiness of form and softness of environment, in a climate favorable in some parts to the densest vegetation, and in others wild and barren. One is always in sight of mountains rising to fourteen thousand feet or more, and constantly scaling difficult pathways seven or eight or nine thousand feet above the sea. And in the loneliness of a country where nothing has altered very much the handiwork of God, an awe-inspiring silence pervades everything. Bold, grey cliffs shoot up here through a mass of verdure and of foliage, and there white cottages, perched in seemingly inaccessible positions, glisten in the sun on the colored mountain-sides. You saunter through stony hollows, along straight passes, traversed by torrents, overhung by high walls of rocks, now winding through broken, shaggy chasms and huge, wandering fragments, now suddenly emerging into some emerald valley, where Peace, long established, seems to repose sweetly in the bosom of Strength. Everywhere beauty alternates wonderfully with grandeur. Valleys close in abruptly, intersected by huge mountain masses, the stony water-worn ascent of which is hardly passable.

Yes, Yuen-nan is imperatively a country first of mountains, then of lakes. The scenery, embodying truly Alpine magnificence with the minute sylvan beauty of Killarney or of Devonshire, is nowhere excelled in the length and breadth of the Empire.

# Chapter XII

Yuen-nan's chequered career. Switzerland of China. At Hong-shih-ai. China's Golden Age in the past. The conservative instinct of the Chinese. How to quiet coolies. Roads. Dangers of ordinary travel in wet season. K'ung-shan and its mines. Tong-ch'uan-fu, an important mining centre. English and German machinery. Methods of smelting. Protestants and Romanists in Yuen-nan. Arrival at Tong-ch'uan-fu. Missionaries set author's broken arm. Trio of Europeans. Author starts for the provincial capital. Abandoning purpose of crossing China on foot. Arm in splints. Curious incident. At Lai-t'eo-po. Malaria returns. Serious illness of author. Delirium. Devotion of the missionaries. Death expected. Innkeeper's curious attitude. Recovery. After-effects of malaria. Patient stays in Tong-ch'uan-fu for several months. Then completes his walking tour.

*Y*uen-nan has had a checkered career ever since it became a part of the empire. In the thirteenth century Kublai Khan, the invincible warrior, annexed this Switzerland to China; and how great his exploits must have been at the time of this addition to the land of the Manchus might be gathered from the fact that all the tribes of the Siberian ice-fields, the deserts of Asia, together with the country between China and the Caspian Sea, acknowledged his potent sway—or at least so tradition says. She is sometimes right.

My journey continuing across more undulating country brought me at length to Hong-shih-ai (Red Stone Cliff), a tiny hamlet hidden away completely in a deep recess in the mountain-side, settled in a narrow gorge, the first house of which cannot be seen until within a few yards of entry. Inn accommodation, as was usual, was by no means good. It is characteristic of these small places that the greater the traffic the worse, invariably, is the accommodation offered. Travelers are continually staying here, but not one Chinese in the population is enterprising enough to open a decent inn. They have no money to start it, I suppose.

But it is true of the Chinese, to a greater degree than of any other nation, that their Golden Age is in the past. Sages of antiquity spoke with deep reverence of the more ancient ancients of the ages, and revered all that they said and did. And the rural Chinese to-day says that what did for the sages of olden times must do for him to-day. The conservative instinct leads the Chinese to attach undue importance to precedent, and therefore the people at Hong-shih-ai, knowing that the village has been in the same pitiable condition for generations, live by conservatism, and make no effort whatever to improve matters.

Fire in the inn was kindled in the hollow of the ground. There was no ventilation; the wood they burned was, as usual, green; smoke was suffocating. My men talked well on into the night, and kept me from sleeping, even if pain would have allowed me to. I spoke strongly, and they, thinking I was swearing at them, desisted for fear that I should heap upon their ancestors a few of the reviling thoughts I entertained for them.

I should like to say a word here about the roads in this province, or perhaps the absence of roads. They had been execrable, the worst I had met, aggravated by heavy rains. With all the reforms to which the province of Yuen-nan is endeavoring to direct its energies, it has not yet learned that one of the first assets of any district or country is good roads. But this is true of the whole of the Middle Kingdom. The contracted quarters in which the Chinese live compel them to do most of their work in the street, and, even in a city provided with but the narrowest passages, these slender avenues are perpetually choked by the presence of peripatetic vendors of every kind of article of common sale in China, and by itinerant craftsmen who have no other shop than the street. In the capital city of the province, even, it is a matter of some difficulty to the European to walk down the rough-paved street after a shower of rain, so slippery do the slabs of stone become; and he has to be alive always to the lumbering carts, whose wheels are more solid than circular, pulled by bullocks as in the days long before the dawn of the Christian Era. The wider the Chinese street the more abuses can it be put to, so that travel in the broad streets of the towns is quite as difficult as in the narrow alleys; and as these streets are never repaired, or very rarely, they become worse than no roads at all—that is, in dry weather.

This refers to the paved road, which, no matter what its faults, is certainly passable, and in wet weather is a boon. There is, however, another kind of road—a mud road, and with a vengeance muddy.

An ordinary mud or earth road is usually only wide enough for a couple of coolies to pass, and in this province, as it is often necessary (especially in the Yuen-nan-fu district) for one cart to pass another, the farmer, to prevent trespass on his crops, digs around them deep ditches, resembling those which are dug for the reception of gas mains. In the rainy season the fields are drained into the roads, which at times are constantly under water, and beyond Yuen-nan-fu, on my way to Tali-fu, I often found it easier and more speedy to tramp bang across a rice field, taking no notice of where the road ought to be. By the time the road has sunk a few feet below the level of the adjacent land, it is liable to be absolutely useless as a thoroughfare; it is actually a canal, but can be neither navigated nor crossed. There are some roads removed a little from the main roads which are quite dangerous, and it is not by any means an uncommon thing to hear of men with their loads being washed away by rivers where in the dry season there had been the roads.

The great lines of Chinese travel, so often impassable, might be made permanently passable if the governor of a province chose to compel the several district magistrates along the line to see that these important arteries are kept free from standing water, with ditches in good order at all seasons. But for the village roads—during my travels over which I have come across very few that could from a Western standpoint be called roads—there is absolutely no hope until such time as the Chinese village may come dimly to the apprehension that what is for the advantage of the one is for the advantage of all, and that wise expenditure is the truest economy—an idea of which it has at the present moment as little conception as of the average thought of the Englishman.

A hundred li to the east of Hong-shiih-ai, over two impassable mountain ranges, are some considerable mines, with antiquated brass and copper smelting works, and this place, K'ung-shan by name, with Tong-ch'uan-fu, forms an important center. As is well known, all copper of Yuen-nan goes to Peking as the Government monopoly, excepting the enormous amount stolen and smuggled into every town in the province.[28]

The smelting is of the roughest, though they are at the present moment laying in English machinery, and the Chinese in charge is under the impression that he can speak English; he, however, makes a hopeless jargon of it. This mining locality is sunk in the deepest degradation. Men and women live more as wild beasts than as human beings, and should any be unfortunate enough to die, their corpses are allowed to lie in the

---

28    In the capital there is a street called "Copper Kettle Lane," where one is able to buy almost anything one wants in copper and brass. Hundreds of men are engaged in the trade, and yet it is "prohibited." These "Copper Kettle Lanes" are found in many large cities.—E.J.D.

mines. Who is there that could give his time and energy to the removal of a dead man? Tong-ch'uan-fu should become an important town if the rich mineral country of which it is the pivot were properly opened up. Several times I have visited the works in this city, which, under the charge of a small mandarin from Szech'wan, can boast only the most primitive and inadequate machinery, of German make. A huge engine was running as a kind of pump for the accumulation of air, which was passed through a long thin pipe to the three furnaces in the outer courtyard. The furnaces were mud-built, and were fed with charcoal (the most expensive fuel in the district), the maximum of pure metal being only 1,300 catties per day. The ore, which has been roughly smelted once, is brought from K'ung-shan, is finely smelted here, then conveyed most of the way to Peking by pack-mule, the expense in thus handling, from the time it leaves the mine to its destination at Peking, being several times its market value. Nothing but copper is sought from the ore, and a good deal of the gold and silver known to be contained is lost.

I passed an old French priest as I was going to Tong-ch'uan-fu the next day. He was very pleased to see me, and at a small place we had a few minutes' chat whilst we sipped our tea. In Yuen-nan, I found that the Protestants and the Romanists, although seeing very little of each other, went their own way, maintaining an attitude of more or less friendly indifference one towards the other.

The last day's march to Tong-ch'uan-fu is perhaps the most interesting of this stage of my journey. Climbing over boulders and stony steps, I reached an altitude of 8,500 feet, whence thirty li of pleasant going awaited us all the way to Lang-wang-miao (Temple of the Dragon King). Here I sat down and strained my eyes to catch the glimpse of the compact little walled city, where I hoped my broken arm would be set by the European missionaries. The traveler invariably hastens his pace here, expecting to run down the hill and across the plain in a very short space; but as the time passed, and I slowly wended my way along the difficult paths through the rice fields, I began to realize that I had been duped, and that it was farther than it seemed. Two blushing damsels, maids goodly to look upon, gave me the sweetest of smiles as I strode across the bodies of some fat pigs which roamed at large in the outskirts of the city, the only remembrance I have to mar the cleanliness of the place.

At Tong-ch'uan-fu the Rev. A. Evans and his extremely hospitable wife set my arm and did everything they could—as much as a brother and sister could have done—to help me, and to make my short stay with them a most happy remembrance. It was, however, destined that I should be their guest for many months, as shall hereinafter be explained.

A trio of Europeans might have been seen on the morning of Monday, May 10, 1909, leaving Tong-ch'uan-fu on the road to Yuen-nan-fu, whither the author was bound. Mr. and Mrs. Evans, who, as chance would have it, were going to Ch'u-tsing-fu, were to accompany me for two days before turning off in a southerly direction when leaving the prefecture.

It was a fine spring morning, balmy and bonny. It was decided that I should ride a pony, and this I did, abandoning my purpose of crossing China on foot with some regret. I was not yet fit, had my broken arm in splints, but rejoiced that at Yuen-nan-fu I should be able to consult a European medical man. Comparatively an unproductive task—and perhaps a false and impossible one—would it be for me to detail the happenings of the few days next ensuing. I should be able not to look at things themselves, but merely at the shadow of things—and it would serve no profitable end.

Suffice it to say that two days out, about midday, a special messenger from the capital stopped Mr. Evans and handed him a letter. It was to tell him that his going to Ch'u-tsing-fu would be of no use, as the gentleman he was on his way to meet would not arrive, owing to altered plans. After consulting his wife, he hesitated whether they should go back to Tong-ch'uan-fu, or come on to the capital with me. The latter course was decided upon, as I was so far from well—I learned this some time afterwards. And now the story need not be lengthened.

At Lai-t'eo-po (see first section of the second book of this volume), malaria came back, and an abnormal temperature made me delirious. The following day I could not move, and it was not until I had been there six days that I was again able to be moved. During this time, Mr. and Mrs. Evans nursed me day and night, relieving each other for rest, in a terrible Chinese inn—not a single moment did they leave me. The third day they feared I was dying, and a message to that effect was sent to the capital, informing the consul. Meanwhile malaria played fast and loose, and promised a pitiable early dissolution. My kind, devoted friends were fearful lest the innkeeper would have turned me out into the roadway to die—the foreigner's spirit would haunt the place for ever and a day were I allowed to die inside.

But I recovered.

It was a graver, older, less exuberant walker across China that presently arose from his flea-ridden bed of sickness, and began to make a languid personal introspection. I had developed a new sensitiveness, the sensitiveness of an alien in an alien land, in the hands of new-made, faithful friends.

Without them I should have been a waif of all the world, helpless in the midst of unconquerable surroundings, leading to an inevitable destiny of death. I seemed declimatized, denationalized, a luckless victim of fate and morbid fancy.

It was malaria and her workings, from which there was no escape.

Malaria is supposed by the natives of the tropic belt to be sent to Europeans by Providence as a chastening for the otherwise insupportable energy of the white man. Malignant malaria is one of Nature's watch-dogs, set to guard her shrine of peace and ease and to punish woeful intruders. And she had brought me to China to punish me. As is her wont, Nature milked the manhood out of me, racked me with aches and pains, shattered me with chills, scorched me with fever fires, pursued me with despairing visions, and hag-rode me without mercy. Accursed newspapers, with their accursed routine, came back to me; all the stories and legends that I had ever heard, all the facts that I had ever learnt, came to me in a fashion wonderfully contorted and distorted; sensations welded together in ghastly, brain-stretching conglomerates, instinct with individuality and personality, human but torturingly inhuman, crowded in upon me. The barriers dividing the world of ideas, sensations, and realities seemed to have been thrown down, and all rushed into my brain like a set of hungry foxhounds. The horror of effort and the futility of endeavor permeated my very soul. My weary, helpless brain was filled with hordes of unruly imaginings; I was masterless, panic-driven, maddened, and had to abide for weeks—yea, months—with a fever-haunted soul occupying a fever-rent and weakened body.

At Yuen-nan-fu, whither I arrived in due course after considerable struggling, dysentery laid me up again, and threatened to pull me nearer to the last great brink. For weeks, as the guest of my friend, Mr. C.A. Fleischmann, I stayed here recuperating, and subsequently, on the advice of my medical attendant, Dr. A. Feray, I went back to Tong-ch'uan-fu, among the mountains, and spent several happy months with Mr. and Mrs. Evans.

Had it not been for their brotherly and sisterly zeal in nursing me, which never flagged throughout my illness, future travelers might have been able to point to a little grave-mound on the hill-tops, and have given a chance thought to an adventurer whom the fates had handled roughly. But there was more in this than I could see; my destiny was then slowly shaping.

Throughout the rains, and well on into the winter, I stayed with Mr. and Mrs. Evans, and then continued my walking tour, as is hereafter recorded.

During this period of convalescence I studied the Chinese language and traveled considerably in the surrounding country. Tong-ch'uan-fu is a city of many scholars, and it was not at all difficult for me to find a satisfactory teacher. He was an old man, with a straggly beard, about 70 years of age, and from him I learned much about life in general, in addition to his tutoring in Chinese. I had the advantage also of close contact with the missionaries with whom I was living, and on many occasions was traveling companion of Samuel Pollard, one of the finest Chinese linguists in China at that time. So that with a greatly increased knowledge of Chinese, I was henceforth able to hold my own anywhere. During this period, too, many days were profitably passed at the Confucian Temple, a picture of which is given in this volume.

❦ End of Book I ❧

# BOOK II

*The second part of my trip was from almost the extreme east to the extreme west of Yuen-nan—from Tong-ch'uan-fu to Bhamo, in British Burma. The following was the route chosen, over the main road in some instances, and over untrodden roads in others, just as circumstances happened:*

*Tong-ch'uan-fu to Yuen-nan-fu (the capital city) 520 li. Yuen-nan-fu to Tali-fu 905 li. Tali-fu to Tengyueh (Momien) 855 li. Tengyueh to Bhamo (Singai) 280 English miles approx.*

*I also made a rather extended tour among the Miao tribes, in country un-trodden by Europeans, except by missionaries working among the people.*

# First Journey: Tong-Ch'uan-Fu to the Capital

## CHAPTER XIII

*Stages to the capital. Universality of reform in China. Political, moral, social and spiritual contrast of Yuen-nan with other parts of the Empire. Inconsistencies of celestial life. Author's start for Burma. The caravan. To Che-chi. Dogs fighting over human bones. Lai-t'eo-p'o: highest point traversed on overland journey. Snow and hail storms at ten thousand feet. Desolation and poverty. Brutal husband. Horse saves author from destruction. The one hundred li to Kongshan. Wild, rugged moorland and mournful mountains. Wretchedness of the people. Night travel in Western China. Author knocks a man down. Late arrival and its vexations. Horrible inn accommodation. End of the Yuen-nan Plateau. Appreciable rise in temperature. Entertaining a band of inelegant infidels. European contention for superiority, and the Chinese point of view. Insoluble conundrums of "John's" national character. The Yuen-nan railway. Current ideas in Yuen-nan regarding foreigners. Discourteous fu-song and his escapades. Fright of ill-clad urchin. Scene at Yang-lin. Arrival at the capital.*

No exaggeration is it to say that the eyes of the world are upon China. It is equally safe to say that, whilst all is open and may be seen, but little is understood.

In the Far Eastern and European press so much is heard of the awakening of China that one is apt really to believe that the whole Empire, from its Dan to Beersheba, is boiling for reform. But it may be that the husk is taken from the kernel. The husk comprises the treaty ports and some of the capital cities of the provinces; the kernel is that vast sleepy interior of China. Few people, even in Shanghai, know what it means; so that to the stay-at-home European pardon for ignorance of existing conditions so much out of his focus should readily be granted.

From Shanghai, up past Hankow, on to Ichang, through the Gorges to Chung-king, is a trip likely to strike optimism in the breast of the most skeptical foreigner. But after he has lived for a couple of years in an interior city as I have done, with its antiquated legislation, its superstition and idolatry, its infanticide, its girl suicides, its public corruption and moral degradation, rubbing shoulders continually at close quarters with the inhabitants, and himself living in the main a Chinese life, our optimist may alter his opinions, and stand in wonder at the extraordinary differences in the most ordinary details of life at the ports on the China coast and the Interior, and of the gross inconsistencies in the Chinese mind and character. If in addition he has stayed a few days away from a city in which the foreigners were shut up inside the city walls because the roaring mob of rebels outside were asking for their heads, and he has had to abandon part of his overland trip because of the fear that his own head might have been chopped off *en route*, he may increase his wonder to doubt. The aspect here in Yuen-nan—politically, morally, socially, spiritually—is that of another kingdom, another world. Conditions seem, for the most part, the same yesterday, to-day, and for ever. And in his new environment, which may be a replica of twenty centuries ago, the dream he dreamed is now dispelled. "China," he says, "is *not* awaking; she barely moves, she is still under the torpor of the ages." And yet again, in the capital and a few of the larger cities, under your very eyes there goes on a reform which seems to be the most sweeping reform Asia has yet known.

Such are the inconsistencies, seemingly unchangeable, irreconcilable in conception or in fact; a truthful portrayal of them tends to render the writer a most inconsistent being in the eyes of his reader.

No one was ever sped on his way through China with more goodwill than was the writer when he left Tong-ch'uan-fu; but the above thoughts were then in his mind.

Long before January 3rd, 1910, the whole town knew that I was going to Mien Dien (Burma). Confessedly with a sad heart—for I carried with me memories of kindnesses such as I had never known before—I led my nervous pony, Rusty, out through the Dung Men (the East Gate), with twenty enthusiastic scholars and a few grown-ups forming a turbulent rear. As I strode onwards the little group of excited younkers watched me disappear out of sight on my way to the capital by the following route—the second time of trying:—

| | LENGTH OF STAGE | HEIGHT ABOVE SEA LEVEL |
|---|---|---|
| 1st day—Che-chi | 90 li. | 7,800 ft. |
| 2nd day—Lai-t'eo-p'o | 90 li. | 8,500 ft. |
| 3rd day—Kongshan | 100 li. | 6,700 ft. |
| 4th day—Yang-kai | 85 li. | 7,200 ft. |
| 5th day—Ch'anff-p'o | 95 li | 6,000 ft. |
| 6th day—The Capital | 70 li | 6,400 ft. |

My caravan consisted of two coolies: one carried my bedding and a small basket of luxuries in case of emergency, the other a couple of boxes with absolute necessities (including the journal of the trip). In addition, there accompanied me a man who carried my camera, and whose primary business it was to guard my interests and my money—my general factotum and confidential agent—and by an inverse operation enrich himself as he could, and thereby maintain relations of warm mutual esteem. They received thirty-two tael cents per man per diem, and for the stopping days on the road one hundred cash. None of them, of course, could speak a word of English.

The ninety li to Che-chi was mostly along narrow paths by the sides of river-beds, the intermediate plains having upturned acres waiting for the spring. At Ta-chiao (7,500 feet), where I stayed for my first alfresco meal at midday, the man—a tall, gaunt, ugly fellow, pockmarked and vile of face—told us he was a traveler, and that he had been to Shanghai. This I knew to be a barefaced lie. He voluntarily explained to the visitors, gathered to see the barbarian feed, what condensed milk was for, but he went wide of the mark when he announced that my pony,[29] hog-maned and dock-tailed (but Chinese still), was an American, as he said I was. A young mother near by, suffering from acute eye inflammation, was lying in a smellful gutter on a felt mat, two pigs on one side and a naked boy of eight or so on the other, whilst she heaped upon the head of the innocent babe she was suckling curses most horribly blood-curdling. Dogs—the universal scavengers of the awakening interior, to which merest allusion is barred by one's Western sense of decency—just outside Che-chi, where I stayed the night, had recently devoured the corpse of a little child. Its clothing was strewn in my path, together with the piece of fibre matting in which it had been wrapped, and the dogs were then fighting over the bones.

To Lai-t'eo-p'o was a day that men might call a "killer."

---

29    I took a pony because I had made up my mind to return into China after I had reached Burma. In Tong-ch'uan-fu a good pony can be bought for, say, L3—in Burma, the same pony would sell for L10. —E.J.D.

It is a dirty little place with a dirty little street, lying at the foot of a mountain known throughout Western China as one of the wildest of Nature's corners, nearly ten thousand feet high, a terrific climb under best conditions. A clear half-moon, and stars of a silvery twinkle, looked pityingly upon me as I started at 3 a.m., ignorant of the dangerously narrow defile leading along cliffs high up from the Yili Ho. In the dark, cautiously I groped along. Not without a painful emotion of impending danger, as I watched the stellular reflections dancing in the rushing river, did I wander on in the wake of a group of pack-ponies, and took my turn in being assisted over the broken chasms by the muleteers. Two fellows got down below and practically lifted the tiny animals over the passes where they could not keep their footing. Gradually I saw the nightlike shadows flee away, and with the dawn came signs of heavy weather.

Snow came cold and sudden. As we slowly and toilsomely ascended, the velocity of the wind fiercely increased; down the mountain-side, at a hundred miles an hour, came clouds of blinding, flinty dust, making the blood run from one's lips and cheeks as he plodded on against great odds. With the biting wind, howling and hissing in the winding ravines and snow-swept hollows, headway was difficult. Often was I raised from my feet: helplessly I clung to the earth for safety, and pulled at withered grass to keep my footing. The ponies, patient little brutes, with one hundred and fifty pounds strapped to their backs, came near to giving up the ghost, being swayed hopelessly to and fro in the fury. For hours we thus toiled up pathways seemingly fitter for goats than men, where leafless trees were bending destitute of life and helpless towards the valley, as the keen wind went sighing, moaning, wailing through their bare boughs and budless twigs.

Such a gale, wilder than the devil's passion, I have not known even on the North Atlantic in February.

At times during the day progression in the deepening snow seemed quite impossible, and my two men, worn and weary, bearing the burden of an excessively fatiguing day, well-nigh threw up the sponge, vowing that they wished they had not taken on the job.

But the scenery later in the day, though monotonously so, was grand. The earth was literally the color of deep-red blood, the crimson paths intertwining the darker landscape bore to one's imagination a vision of some bloody battle—veritable rivers of human blood. To cheer the traveler in his desolation, the sun struggled vainly to pierce with its genial rays through the heavy, angry clouds rolling lazily upwards from the black valleys, and enveloping the earth in a deep infinity of severest gloom. The cold was damp. In the small hemmed-in hollows, whereto our pathway led, the icy dew clung to one's hair and beard. From little brown cottages, with poor thatched roofs letting in the light, and with walls and woodwork long since uniformly rotten, men and women emerged, rubbing their eyes and buttoning up their garments, looking wistfully for the hidden sun.

At Shao-p'ai (8,100 feet) a brute of a fellow was administering cruellest chastisement to his disobedient yoke-fellow, who took her scourging in good part. I passed along as fast as I could to the ascent over which a road led in and around the mountain with alarming steepness, a road which at home would never be negotiated on foot or on horseback, but which here forms part of the main trade route. From the extreme summit one dropped abruptly into a protecting gorge, where falling cascades, sparkling like crystal showers in the feeble sunlight occasionally breaking through, danced playfully over the smooth-worn, slippery rocks; a stream foamed noisily over the loose stones, and leapt in rushing rapids where the earth had given way; there was no grass, no scenery, no life, and in the sudden turnings the hurricane roared with heavenly anger through the long deep chasms, over the twelve-inch river-beds at the foot.

At Lai-t'eo-p'o accommodation at night was fairly good. Men laughed hilariously at me when I raved at some carpenters to desist their clumsy hammering three feet above my head. Hundreds of dogs yelped unceasingly at the moon, and with the usual rows of the men in mutual invitation to "Come and wash your feet," or "Ching fan, ching fan," the draughts, the creaks and cracks, the unintermitting din, and so much else, one was not sorry to rise again with the lark and push onwards in the cold.

Down below this horrid town there is a plain; in this plain there is a hole fifty feet deep, and had my pony, which I was leading, not pulled me away from falling thereinto, my story would not now be telling.

To Kongshan (6,700 feet), past Yei-chu-t'ang (8,100 feet) and Hsiao-lang-t'ang (7,275 feet), one hundred li away, was a journey through country considerably more interesting, especially towards the end of the day, a peculiar combination of wooded slope and rough, rock-worn pathways.

Hsiao-lang-t'ang, twenty-five li from the end of the stage, overlooks a wide expanse of barren, uninviting moorland. Deep, jagged gullies break the uneven rolling of the mountains; dark, weird caverns of terrible immensity yawn hungrily from the surface of weariest desolation, ever widening with each turn. Mist hid the ugliest spots high up among the peaks, whose white summits, peeping sullenly from out this blue sea of damp haze, told a wondrous story of winter's withering all life to death, a spot than which in summer few places on earth would be more entrancing. But these mountains are breathing out a solitude which is eternal. Man here has never been.

143

Far away beyond lies the country of the aborigines; but even the Lolo, wild and rugged as the country, fearless of man and beast, have never dared to ascend these heights. They are mournful, cheerless, devoid of a single smile from the common mother of us all, lacking every feature by which the earth draws man into a spirit of unity with his God. Horrid, frowning waste and aimless discontinuity of land, harbinger of loneliness and of evil! People, poor struggling beings of our kind, here seemed mocked of destiny, and a hot raging of misery waged within them, for all that the heart might desire and wish for had to them been denied. If, indeed, the earth be the home of hope, and man's greatest possession be hope, then would it seem that these poor creatures were entirely cut off, shut out from life, wandering wearisomely through the world in one long battle with Nature whereby to gain the wherewithal to live in that grim desert. There were no exceptions, it was the common lot. Each day and every day did these men and women, with a stolidity of long-continued destitution, and temporal and spiritual tribulation, gaze upon that bare, unyielding country, pregnant only with aggravation to their own dire wretchedness.

In such spots, unhappily in Yuen-nan not few, does the mystery of life grow ever more mysterious to one whom distress has never harassed. A great pity seized my heart, but these poor people would probably have laughed had they known my thoughts.

As I passed they came uninterestedly to look upon me. They watched in expressive silence; they were silent because of poverty. And I, too, kept a seal upon my lips as I ate the good things here provided under the eyes of those to whom hunger had given none but a jealous outlook. Pitiful enough were it, thought I, merely to watch without allowing speech to escape further to taunt them. So I ate, and they looked at me. I came and went, but never a word was uttered by these men and women, or even by the children, whose most painful feeling seemed that of their own feebleness. They were indeed feeble units standing in a threatening infinitude of life, and their thoughts probably dwelt upon my luxury and wealth as mine could not help dwelling upon their hungry town of hungry men and famished children. Words cannot paint their poverty—men void of hope, of life, of purpose, of idea. Happy for them that they had known no other.

We ascended over a road of unspeakable torture to one's feet. Gazing down, far away into a seemingly bottomless abyss, we could faintly hear in the lulling of the wind the rush of a torrent, fed by a hundred mountain streams, which washed our path and in horrible disfigurement tore open the surface of the hill-sides.

The long day was drawing wearily to a close. As the sun was sinking beyond the uneven hills over which I was to climb before the descent to the town begins, the effect of the green and gold and red and brown produced a striking picture of sweet poetic beauty. I stood in contemplative admiration meditating, as I waited for my coolies, who sat moodily under a dilapidated roadside awning, nonchalantly picking out mouldy monkey-nuts from some coarse sweetmeat sold by a frowsy female. Then upwards we toiled in the dark, the weird groans of my exhausted men and the falling of the gravel beneath their sandalled feet alone breaking the hollow's gloom. Uncanny is night travel in China.

"Who knows but that ghosts, those fierce-faced denizens of the hills, may run against thee and bewitch thee," murmured one man to the others. They stopped, and I stopped with them. And in the darkness, pegging on alone at the mercy of these coolies, my own thoughts were not unsynchronistic.

At last, with no slight misgiving, we came down into the city's smoke. Dogs barked at me, and ran away like the curs they are. Midway down the stone footway my yamen runner too cautiously crept up to me in the dark, muttering something, and I floored him with my fist. Afterwards I learnt that he came to relieve me of the pony I was leading.

Every room in every wretched inn was occupied; opium fumes already issued from the doorways, and it was now pitch dark, so that I could scarce see the sallow faces of the hungry, uncouth crowd, to whom with no little irritation I tried to speak as I peered carefully into the caravanserai. Evident it certainly was that the duty lying nearest to me at that particular moment, to myself and all concerned therein, was to accept what I was offered, and not wear out my temper in grumbling. My boy, Lao Chang (an I-pien), the brick, expressed to me his regrets, and something like real sympathy shone out from his eyes in the dimness.

"Puh p'a teh, puh p'a teh" ("Have no fear, have no fear"), said he; and as I stood the while piling up cruellest torture upon my uncourtly host, he made off to prepare a downstair room (to lapse into modern boarding-house phraseology).

First through an outer apartment, dark as darkest night; on past the cat-erwauling cook and a few disreputable culinary hangers-on; asked to look out for a pony, which I could not see, but which I was told might kick me; then onward to my boy, who stood on a stool and dropped the grease of a huge red Chinese candle among his plaited hair, as he wobbled it above his head to light the way. He gripped me tenderly, took me to his bosom as it were, gave me one push, and I was there. He tarried not. What right had he to listen to what I in secret would say of the horrid keeper and his twice horrid shakedown inn? He passed out swiftly into outer darkness, uttering a groan I rudely interpreted as, "That or nothing, that or nothing."

It *was* a room, that is in so far as four sides, a floor and a ceiling comprise one. Of that I had no doubt. A sort of uncomely offshoot from the main inn building, built on piles in the earth after the fashion of the seashore houses of the Malay—but much dirtier and incomparably more shaky. For many a long year, longer than mine horrid host would care to recollect, this now unoccupied space had served admirably as the common cooking-room—the ruined fireplace was still there; later, it had been the stable—the ruined horse trough was still there. At one extreme corner only could I stand upright; long sooty cobwebs graced the black wood beams overhead, hanging as thick as icicles in a mountain valley; each step I took in fear and trembling (the slightest move threatened to collapse the whole dilapidation). Four planks, four inches wide at the widest part and of varying lengths and thicknesses, placed on a pile of loose firewood at the head and foot, comprised the bedstead on which I tremulously sat down. Upon this improvised apology for a bed, under my mosquito curtains (no traveler should be without them in Western China), I washed my blistered feet on an ancient *Daily Telegraph*, whilst my cook saw to my evening meal. His bringing in the rice tallied with my laying the tablecloth in the same place where I had washed my feet—the one available spot.

As I ate, rats came brazenly and picked up the grains of rice I dropped in my inefficient handling of chopsticks, and in scaring off these hardened, hungry vermin I accidentally upset tea over my bed, whilst at the same moment a clod-hopping coolie came in with an elephant tread, with the result that my European reading-lamp lost its balance from the top of a tin of native sugar and started a conflagration, threatening to make short work of me and my belongings—not to mention that horrid fellow and his inn.

During the night the moments throbbed away as I lay on my flea-ridden couch—moments which seemed long as hours, and no gleaming rift broke the settled and deepening blackness of my hateful environs. Every thing and every place was full of the wearisome, depressing, beauty-blasting commonplace of Interior China. Stenches rose up on the damp, dank air, and throughout the night, through the opening of a window, I seemed to gaze out to a disconsolate eternity—gaping, empty, unsightly. Waking from my dozing at the hour when judgment sits upon the hearts of men, I sat in ponderous judgment upon all to whom the bungling of the previous day was due. There were the rats and mice, and cats and owls, and creaks and cracks—no quiet about the place from night to morning. Then came the barking of dogs, the noises of the cocks and kine, of horses and foals, of pigs and geese—the general wail of the zoological kingdom—cows bellowing, duck diplomacy, and much else. So that it were not surprising to learn that this distinguished traveler in these contemptible regions was sitting on a broken-down bridge, looking wearily on to the broken-down tower on the summit of a pretty little knoll outside Kungshan, thinking that it were well a score of such were added did their design embrace a warning to evade the place.

Having done some twenty li by moonlight, I managed with little difficulty to reach Yang-kai (6,350 feet) by 3.0 p.m. This road, which is not the main road to the capital, was purposely chosen; most travelers go through Yang-lin. The journey is comprised of pleasant ascents and descents over the latter portion of the great Yuen-nan Plateau, and a very appreciable difference in the temperature was here noticed. While the people at the northeast of the province, from which I had come, were shivering in their rags and complaining about the price of charcoal, the population here basked under Italian skies in a warm sun. From Lui-shu-ho (7,200 feet) the country was beautifully wooded with groves of firs and chestnuts.

At the inn to which I was led the phlegmatic proprietor, after wishing me peace, assumed unostentatiously the becoming attitude of a Customs official, and scrutinized with vigor the whole of my gear, from an empty Calvert's tooth-powder tin to my Kodak camera, showering particularly condescending felicitations upon my English Barnsby saddle and field-glasses thereto attached.

His excitement rose at once.

He called loudly for his confederates—a band of inelegant infidels—and bidding them stand one by one at given distances, he gaped at them through the glasses with the hilarity of a schoolboy and the stupidity of an owl. He jumped, he shouted, he waved his arms about me, and handing them back to me with both hands, shouted deafeningly in my ear that they were quite beyond his ken; and then he sucked his teeth disgustingly and spat at my feet. His associates were speechless, asses that they were, and could only stare, in horror or impudence I know not.

Meantime Lao Chang brought tea, and sallied forth immediately to fraternize among old friends. As I drank my tea, after having invited them one by one to join me, slowly and with a fitting dignity, the empty stare, destitute of sense or sincerity, of these six upstanding Chinese gentry, sucking at tobacco-pipes as long as their own overfed bodies, forced upon me a sense of my unfitness for the unknown conditions of the life of the place, a sense of loneliness and social unshelteredness in the sterile waste of their fashionable life. They spoke to me subsequently, and I bravely threw at them a Chinese phrase or two; but when the conversation got above my head, I told them, quietly but determinedly, that I could not understand, my English speech seemed vaguely to indicate a sudden collapse of the acquaintance, the opening of a gulf between us, destined to widen to the whole length and breadth of Yang-kai, swallowing up their erstwhile confidences. One of them facetiously remarked that the gentleman wished to eat his rice; and as they cleared out, falling over each other and the high step at the entrance to the room, I thought that no matter how old they are, Chinese are but little children. But had I treated them as little children I should have found that they were old men.

There was in me withal a sense of better rank in the eyes of this super-excellent few who worshipped, in "heathen" China, the Satan of Fashion. As a matter of fact, their rank had emerged from such long centuries ago that it seemed to me to be so identified with them that they were hardly capable of analysis of people such as myself. As I looked pityingly upon them and the involved simplicity of their immutable natures, I realized an unconquerable feeling of inborn rank and natural elevation in respect to nationality. This is, however, against my personal general conception of Eastern peoples, but I must admit I felt it this afternoon. And so perhaps it is with the majority of Europeans in the Far East, who, because they have no knowledge of the language or a familiarity with national customs and ideas, remain always aliens with the Easterner. They cannot sympathize with him in his joys and sorrows, his likes and dislikes, his prejudice and bias, or understand anything of his point of view. This is one of the hardest lessons for the European traveler in China who has little of the language. Because we do not understand him, we call the Chinese a heathen—it is easier.

Now, to the Chinese his country is the best in the world, his province better than any other of the eighteen, and the village in which he lives the most enviable spot in the province—the center of his universe. Speak disparagingly about that little circle, critically or sympathetically, and he is at once up against you. It may develop narrowness of mind and smallness of soul. We Westerners think we know that it does; and the fact that he allows his mental horizon to be bounded by such narrow confines appears to us to render him anything but a desirable citizen and a full-sized man. But no matter. The Chinese, on the other hand, regards as barbarians all those men who have never tasted the bliss of a true home in the Empire which is celestial—part of this feeling is patriotism and love of country, part is rank conceit. But Englishmen are saying that England is the most Christian country in the world for the very same reason!

Rationally speaking, John is the "old brother" of the world, oldest of any nation by very many centuries. In common with all other travelers and those who have lived with this man, and who have made his nature a serious study, apart from racial bias, I am perplexed with conundrums which cannot be solved. Some of the conundrums are perhaps superficial, and disappear with a deeper insight into his life; others are wrought into his being. Yet he has a fixedness of character, reaching in some directions to absolute crystallization; he possesses the virility of young manhood and many of the mutually inconsistent traits of late manhood and early youth. I wonder at his ignorance of merest rudimentary political economy—but why? This man explored centuries ago the cardinal theories of some of our present-day Western classics. However, I have to teach him the form of the earth and the natural causes of eclipses. He is frightened by ghosts, burns mock money to maintain his ancestors in the future state, worships a bit of rusty old iron as an infallible remedy for droughts; I have seen him shoot at clouds from the city walls to frighten away the rain—and I despise him for it all. As I revise this copy, a rumor is current in the town in which I am resting to the effect that foreigners are buying children and using their heads to oil the wheels of the new Yuen-nan railway, and I despise him for believing it. The Chinese will not fight, and I sneer at him; he abhors me because I do. I ridicule his manner of dress; he thinks mine grossly indecent. I consider his flat nose and the plaited hair and shaven skull as heathenish; but the Chinese, eating away with his to me ridiculous chopsticks, looks out from his quick, almond-shaped eyes and considers me still a foreign devil, although he is too cunning to tell me. His opinions of me are founded upon the narrow grounds of vanity and egotism; mine, although I do not admit it even to myself, from something very much akin thereto.[30]

I have been looked upon in far-away outposts of the Chinese Empire where foreigners are still unknown, as an example of those human monstrosities which come from the West, a creature of a very low order of the human species, with a form and face uncouth, with language a hopeless jargon, and with manners unbearably rude and obnoxious. Not that *I* personally answer accurately to this description, reader, any more than you would, but because I happen to be among a people who, as far back as Chinese opinion of foreigners can be traced, have considered themselves of a morality and intellectuality superior to yours and mine.

I write the foregoing because it sums up what may be termed the current ideas regarding Europeans, ideas the reverse of complimentary, which are

---

30    For further excellent descriptions of the Chinese nature I refer the reader to Chester Holcombe's China: Past and Present.—E.J.D.

the more unfortunate on account of the fact that they are held by the vast majority of a people forming a quarter of the whole human race. This is true, despite all the reform.

These ideas may be, and I trust they are, erroneous, but I know that I must keep in mind the extremely important desideratum in dealing with the Chinese that they look at me—my person, my manners, my customs, my theories, my things—through Chinese eyes, and although mistaken, misled, reach their own conclusions from their own point of view. This is what they have been doing for centuries, but we know that it all now is being subjected to slow change. The original stock, however, takes on no change whatever, and several generations must pass before this transfer of mental vision can be effected, when the Chinese will view all things and all peoples in their true light.

Next morning my three men were heavy. The lean fellow—I have christened him Shanks, a long, shambling human bag of bones—moved about painfully in a listless sort of way, betokening severe rheumatics; his joints needed oil. Four or five huge basins of steaming rice and the customary amount of reboiled cabbage, however, bucked him up a bit, and holding up a crooked, bony finger, he indicated intelligently that we had one hundred li to cover. Whilst engaged in conversation thus, sounds of early morning revelry reached me from below. My boy, his accustomed serenity now quite disturbed, held threateningly above the head of the yamen runner (who had given me a profound kotow the evening previous prior to taking on his duties) a length of three-inch sugar cane; he evidently meant to flatten him out. This I learned was because this shadower of the august presence wished to take Yang-lin (about 60 li away) instead of going to Ch'ang-p'o (100 li) as I intended. I got him in, looked him as squarely in the face as it is possible when a Chinese wants to evade your scrutiny, told him I wished to go to Ch'ang-p'o, and that I hoped I should have the pleasure of his company thus far. He replied with a grinning smile, which one could easily have taken for a smiling grin—

"Oh, yes, foreign mandarin, Ch'ang-p'o—100 li—foreign mandarin, foreign mandarin."

And I thought the incident closed. Such is the appalling gullibility of the Englishman in China.

We stopped for tea at a small hamlet ten li out. The place was deserted save for a small starving boy, whose chief attention was given to laborious endeavors to make his clothing meet in certain necessary areas. He evidently had never seen a foreigner. As he directed his optics towards me he winced visibly. He walked round me several times, fell over a grimy pail of soap-suds, stopped, gazed in enraptured enchantment with parted lips and outstretched arms as if he had begun to suspect what it was before him. To the eye of the beholder, however, he gazed as yet only on vacancy, but just as I was about to attempt self-explanation he was gone, tearing away down the hill as fast as his legs could carry him, the ragged remains of his father's trousers flapping gently in the breeze. As I rose to leave crackers frightened my pony, followed, in a few moments by a howling, hooting, unreasonable rabble from a temple near by. I found it was the result of a village squabble. I could scarce keep the order of my march as I left the tea-shop, so roughly was I handled by the irritated and impatient crowd, and had much ado to refrain from responding wrathfully to the repeated jeers of impudent, half-grown beggars of both sexes who helped to swell the riotous cortege. But through it all none of the insults were meant for me, so Lao Chang told me, and they did not mean to treat me with discourtesy.

Trees hollowed out and spanned from field to field served as gutters for irrigation; shepherds clad in white felt blankets sat huddled upon the ground behind huge boulders, oblivious of time and of the boisterous wind, while their sheep and goats grubbed away on the scanty grass the moorland provided; high up we saw forest fires, making the earth black and desolate; ruins almost everywhere recalled to one's mind the image of a past prosperity, which now were replaced by traces of misery, exterior influences which seemed to breed upon the traveler a deep discouragement. I came across some women mock-weeping for the dead: at their elbow two girls were washing clothes, and when little children, catching sight of me, ran to their mothers, the women stopped their hulla-baloo, had a good stare at me, exchanged a few words of mutual inquiry, and then resumed their bellowing.

Soon it became quite warm, and walking was pleasant. I was startled by the *fu-song*,[31] who invited me to go to a neighboring town for tea. My men were far behind. I was at his mercy, so I went. Soon I found myself passing through the city gates of Yang-lin, the very town I was trying to keep away from. The yamen fellow turned back at me and chuckled rudely to himself. I insisted that I did not wish to take tea; he insisted that I should—I must. He led me to an inn in the main street, arrangements were made to house me, old men and young lads gathered to welcome me as a lost brother, and the *fu-song* told me graciously that he was going to the magistrate. In cruel English, with many wildly threatening gestures, did I protest, and the people laughed acquiescingly.

"Puh tong, puh tong, you gaping idiots!" I repeated, and it caused more glee.

---

31    i.e. Yamen escort.

Swinging myself past them all, I dragged my stubborn pony through the mob to the gate by which I had entered. My men were not to be found. I did not know the road nor much of the language. I sat down on a granite pillar to undergo an embarrassing half-hour. Presently my men hailed me, and approaching, swore with imposing loftiness at the discomfited guide. My bull-dog coolie dropped his loads, the *fu-song* somehow lost his footing, I yelled "Ts'eo" ("Go"), and with a cheer the caravan proceeded.

The following day we were at the capital.

CHAPTER XIV

## Yuen-Nan-Fu, the Capital

*Access to Yuen-nan-fu. Concentrated reform. Tribute to Hsi Liang. Conservatism and progress. The Tonkin-Yuen-nan Railway. The Yuen-nan army. Author's views in 1909 and 1910 contrasted. Phenomenal forward march, and what it means. Danger of too much drill. International aspect on the frontier. The police. Street improvements. Visit to the gaol, and a description. The Young Pretender to the Chinese throne. How the prison is conducted. The schools. Visit to the university, and a description. Riot among the students. Visit to the Agricultural School, and a description. Silk industry of Yuen-nan.*

Yuen-nan-fu to-day is as accessible as Peking. After many weary years the Tonkin-Yuen-nan railway is now an accomplished fact, and links this capital city with Haiphong in three days.

Reform concentrates at the capital. The man who visited Yuen-nan-fu twenty, or even ten years ago, would be astounded, were he to go there now, at the improvements visible, on every hand. A building on foreign lines was then a thing unknown, and the conservative Viceroy, Tseng Kong Pao, the decapitator in his time of thousands upon thousands of human beings, would turn in his grave if he could behold the utter annihilation of his pet "feng shui," which has followed in the wake of the good works done by the late loved Viceroy, Hsi Liang.

The name of Hsi Liang is revered in the province of Yuen-nan as the most able man who has ever ruled the two provinces of Yuen-nan and Kweichow, a man of keen intellectuality and courtly manner, and notorious as being the only Mongolian in the service of China's Government. I lived

153

in Yuen-nan-fu for several weeks at a stretch, and since then have made frequent visits, and knowing the enormous strides being made towards acquiring Occidental methods, I now find it difficult to write with absolute accuracy upon things in general. But I have found this to be the case in all my travels. What is, or seems to be, accurate to-day of any given thing in a given place is wrong tomorrow under seemingly the same conditions; and although no theme could be more tempting, and no subject offer wider scope for ingenious hypothesis and profound generalization, one has to forego much temptation to "color" if he would be accurate of anything he writes of the Chinese. Eminent sinologues agree as to the impossibility of the conception of the Chinese mind and character as a whole, so glaring are the inconsistencies of the Chinese nature. And as one sees for himself in this great city, particularly in official life, the businesslike practicability on the one hand and the utter absurdity of administration on the other, in all modes and methods, one is almost inclined to drop his pen in disgust at being unable to come to any concrete conclusions.

Of no province in China more than of Yuen-nan is this true.

Reform and immovable conservatism go hand in hand. Men of the most dissimilar ambitions compose the *corps diplomatique*, and are willing to join hands to propagate their main beliefs; and when one writes of progress—in railways, in the army, in gaols, in schools, in public works, in no matter what—one is ever confronted by that dogged immutability which characterizes the older school.

So that in writing of things Yuen-nanese in this great city it is imperative for me to state bare facts as they stand now, and make little comment.

## The Railway

The Tonkin-Yuen-nan Railway, linking the interior with the coast, is one of the world's most interesting engineering romances. This artery of steel is probably the most expensive railway of its kind, from the constructional standpoint. In some districts seven thousand pounds per mile was the cost, and it is probable that six thousand pounds sterling per mile would not be a bad estimate of the total amount appropriated for the construction of the line from a loan of 200,000,000 francs asked for in 1898 by the Colonial Council in connection with the program for a network of railways in and about French Indo-China.

To Lao-kay there are no less than one hundred and seventy-five bridges.

The completion of this line realizes in part the ambition of a celebrated Frenchman, who—once a printer, 'tis said, in Paris—dropped into the political flower-bed, and blossomed forth in due course as Governor-General of Indo-China. When Paul Doumer, for it was he, went east in 1897, he felt it his mission to put France, politically and commercially, on as good a footing as any of her rivals, notably Great Britain. It did not take him long to see that the best missionaries in his cause would be the railways. At the time of writing (June, 1910) I cannot but think that profit on this railway will be a long time coming, and there are some in the capital who doubt whether the commercial possibilities of Yuen-nan justified this huge expenditure on railway construction. Whilst authorities differ, I personally believe that the ultimate financial success of the venture is assured. There are markets crying out to be quickly fed with foreign goods, and it is my opinion that the French will be the suppliers of those goods. British enterprise is so weak that we cannot capture the greater portion of the growing foreign trade, and must feel thankful if we can but retain what trade we have, and supply those exports with which the French have no possibility of competing.

## THE MILITARY

The foreigner in Yuen-nan-fu can never rest unless he is used to the sounds of the bugle and the hustling spirit of the men of war.

In standard works on Chinese armaments no mention is ever made of the Yuen-nan army, and statistics are hard to get. But it is evident that the cult of the military stands paramount, and it has to be conceded, even by the most pessimistic critics of this backward province, that the new troops are sufficiently numerous and sufficiently well-organized to crush any rebellion. This must be counted a very fair result, since it has been attained in about two years. A couple of years ago Yuen-nan had practically no army—none more than the military ragtags of the old school, whose chief weapon of war was the opium pipe. But now there are ten thousand troops—not units on paper, but men in uniform—well-drilled for the most part and of excellent physique, who could take the field at once. The question of the Yuen-nan army is one of international interest: the French are on the south, Great Britain on the west.

On June 2nd, 1909, I rode out to the magnificent training ground, then being completed, and on that date wrote the following in my diary:—

"I watched for an hour or two some thousand or so men undergoing their daily drill—typical tin soldiery and a military sham.

"Only with the merest notion of matters military were most of the men conversant, and alike in ordinary marching—when it was most difficult for them even to maintain regularity of step—or in more complicated drilling, there was a lack of the right spirit, no go, no gusto—scores and scores of them running round doing something, going through a routine, with the knowledge that when it was finished they would get their rice and be happy. Everyone who possesses but a rudimentary knowledge of the Chinese knows that he troubles most about the two meals every day should bring him, and this seems to be the pervading line of thought of seven-eighths of the men I saw on the padang at drill. Officers strutting about in peacock fashion, with a sword dangling at their side, showed no inclination to enforce order, and the rank and file knew their methods, so that the disorder and haphazardness of the whole thing was absolutely mutual.

"Whilst I was on the field gazing in anything but admiration on the scene, I was ordered out by one of the khaki-clad officers in a most unceremonious manner. Seeing me, he shouted at the top of his thick voice, 'Ch'u-k'ue, ch'u-k'ue' (an expression meaning 'Go out!'—commonly used to drive away dogs), and simultaneously waved his sword in the air as if to say, 'Another step, and I'll have your head.' And, of course, there being nothing else to do, I 'ch'u-k'ued,' but in a fashion befitting the dignity of an English traveler.

"The reorganization of the army, with the acceleration of warlike preparedness, has the advantage that it appeals to the embryonic feeling of national patriotism, and affords a tangible expression of the desire to be on terms of equality with the foreigner. That officer never had a prouder moment in his life than when he ordered a distinguished foreigner from the drilling ground, of which he was for the time the lordly comptroller. And it may be added that the foreigner can remember no occasion when he felt 'smaller,' or more completely shrivelled.

"Whilst it is safe to infer that the motives that underlie the significant access of activity in military matters in Yuen-nan differ in no way from those which have led to the feverish increase in armaments in other parts of the world, such ideas that have yet been formed on actual preparations for possible war are most crude. On paper the appointments in the army and the accuracy of the figures of the complement of rank and file admit of no question, but the practical utility of their labors is quite another matter, and a matter which does not appear to produce among the army officials any great mental disturbance in their delusion that they are progressing. Yuen-nan is in need of military reform, reform which will embrace a start from the very beginning, and one of the first steps that should be taken is that those who are to be in the position of administering training should find out something about western military affairs, and so be in a position of knowing what they are doing."

The above was my conscientious opinion in the middle of last year. Now—in June of 1910—I have to write of enormous improvements and revolutions in the drilling, in the armaments, in the equipment, in the general organization of the troops and the conduct of them. Yuen-nan is still peculiarly in her transition stage, which, while it has many elements of strength and many menacing possibilities, contains, more or less, many of the old weaknesses. All matters, such as her financial question, her tariff question, her railway question, her mining question, are still "in the air"—the unknown $x$ in the equation, as it were—but her army question is settled. There is a definite line to be followed here, and it is being followed most rigidly. Come what will, her army must be safe and sound. China is determined to work out the destiny of Yuen-nan herself, and she is working hard—the West has no conception how hard—so as to be able to be in a position of safeguarding—vigorously, if necessary—her own borders.

One question arises in my mind, however. Should there be a rebellion, would the soldiers remain true? This is vital to Yuen-nan. Skirmishings on the French border more or less recently have shown us that soldiers are wobblers in that area. The rank and file are chosen from the common people, and one would not be surprised to find, should trouble take place fairly soon, while they are still raw to their business, the soldiers turn to those who could give them most. It has been humorously remarked that in case of disturbances the first thing the Chinese Tommy would do would be to shoot the officers for treating him so badly and for drilling him so hard and long.

What is true of the capital in respect to military progress I found to be true also of Tali-fu.

A couple of years ago a company of drilled soldiers arrived there as a nucleus for recruiting units for the new army. Soon 1,500 men were enlisted. They were to serve a three years' term, were to receive four dollars per month, and were promised good treatment. The officers drilled them from dawn to dusk; deserters were therefore many, necessitating the detail of a few heads coming off to avert the trouble of losing all the men. It cost the men about a dollar or so for their rice, so that it will be readily seen that, with a clear profit of three dollars as a monthly allowance, they were better off than they would have been working on their land. Officers received from forty to sixty taels a month. Temples here were converted into barracks—a sign in itself of the altered conditions of the times—and I visited some extensive buildings which were being erected at a cost of eighty thousand gold dollars.

Military progress in this "backward province" is as great as it has been anywhere at any time in any part of the Chinese Empire.

## THE POLICE

Until a few years ago, as China was kept in law and order without the necessary evil of a standing army, so did Yuen-nan-fu slumber on in the Chinese equivalent for peace and plenty. As they now are, and taking into consideration that they were all picked from the rawest material, the police force of this capital is as able a body of men as are to be found in all Western China. Probably the Metropolitan police of dear old London could not be re-forced from their ranks, but disciplined and well-ordered they certainly are withal. Swords seem to take the place of the English bludgeon, and a peaked cap, beribboned with gold, is substituted for the old-fashioned helmet of blue; and if the time should ever come, with international rights, when Englishmen will be "run in" in the Empire, the sallow physiognomy and the dangling pigtail alone will be unmistakable proofs to the victim, even in heaviest intoxication, that he is not being handled by policemen of his awn kind—that is, if the Yuen-nan police shall ever have made strides towards the attainment of home police principles. However, in their place these men have done good work. Thieving in the city is now much less common, and gambling, although still rife under cover—when will the Chinese eradicate that inherent spirit?—is certainly being put down. One of the features of their work also has been the improvement they have effected in the appearance of the streets. Old customs are dying, and at the present time if a man in his untutored little ways throws his domestic refuse into the place where the gutter should have been, as in olden days, he is immediately pounced upon, reprimanded by the policeman on duty, and fined somewhat stiffly.

## THE GAOL

A great fuss was made about me when I went to visit the governor of the prison one wet morning. He met me with great ostentation at the entrance, escorting me through a clean courtyard, on either side of which were pretty flower-beds and plots of green turf, to a reception-room. There was nothing "quadlike" about the place. This reception-room, furnished on a semi-Occidental plan, overlooked the main prison buildings, contained foreign glass windows draped with white curtains, was scrupulously clean for China, and had magnificent hanging scrolls on the whitewashed walls. Tea was soon brewed, and the governor, wishing to be polite and sociable, told me that he had been in Yuen-nan-fu for a few months only, and that he considered himself an extremely fortunate fellow to be in charge of such an excellent prison—one of the finest in the kingdom, he assured me.

After we had drunk each other's health—I sincerely trust that the cute, courteous old chap will live a long and happy life, although to my way of thinking the knowledge of the evil deeds of all the criminals around me would considerably minimize the measure of bliss among such intensely mundane things—I was led away to the prison proper.

This gaol, which had been opened only a few months, is a remarkably fine building, and with the various workshops and outhouses and offices covers from seven to eight acres of ground inside the city. The outside, and indeed the whole place, bears every mark of Western architecture, with a trace here and there of the Chinese artistry, and for carved stone and grey-washed brick might easily be mistaken for a foreign building. It cost some ninety thousand taels to build, and has accommodation for more than the two hundred and fifty prisoners at present confined within its walls.

After an hour's inspection, I came to the conclusion that the lot of the prisoners was cast in pleasant places. The food was being prepared at the time—three kinds of vegetables, with a liberal quantity of rice, much better than nine-tenths of the poor brutes lived on before they came to gaol. Besworded warders guarded the entrances to the various outbuildings. From twenty to thirty poor human beings were manacled in their cells, condemned to die, knowing not how soon the pleasure of the emperor may permit of them shuffling off this mortal coil: one grey-haired old man was among the number, and to see him stolidly waiting for his doom brought sad thoughts.

The long-termed prisoners work, of course, as they do in all prisons. Weaving cloth, mostly for the use of the military, seemed to be the most important industry, there being over a score of Chinese-made weaving machines busily at work. The task set each man is twelve English yards per day; if he does not complete this quantity he is thrashed, if he does more he is remunerated in money. One was amused to see the English-made machine lying covered with dust in a corner, now discarded, but from its pattern all the others had been made in the prison. Tailors rose as one man when we entered their shop, where Singer machines were rattling away in the hands of competent men; and opposite were a body of pewter workers, some of their products—turned out with most primitive tools—being extremely clever. The authorities had bought a foreign chair, made of iron—a sort of miniature garden seat—and from this pattern a squad of blacksmiths were turning out facsimiles, which were selling at two dollars apiece. They were well made, but a skilled mechanic, not himself a prisoner, was teaching the men. Bamboo blinds were being made in the same room, whilst at the extreme end of another shed were paper dyers and finishers, carrying on a primitive work in the same primitive way that the Chinese did thousands of years ago. It was, however, exceedingly interesting to watch.

As we passed along I smelt a strong smell of opium. Yes, it was opium. I sniffed significantly, and looked suspiciously around. The governor saw and heard and smelt, but he said nothing. Opium, then, is not, as is claimed, abolished in Yuen-nan. Worse than this: whilst I was the other day calling upon the French doctor at the hospital, the vilest fumes exuded from the room of one of the dressers. It appeared that the doctor could not break his men of the habit. But we remember that the physician of older days was exhorted to heal himself.

Just as I was beginning to think I had seen all there was to be seen, I heard a scuffle, and saw a half-score of men surrounding a poor frightened little fellow, to whom I was introduced. He was the little bogus Emperor of China, the Young Pretender, to whom thousands of Yuen-nan people, at the time of the dual decease in recent Chinese history, did homage, and kotowed, recognizing him as the new emperor. The story, not generally known outside the province, makes good reading. At the time of the death of the emperor and empress-dowager, an aboriginal family at the village of Kuang-hsi-chou, in the southeast of Yuen-nan province, knowing that a successor to the throne must be found, and having a son of about eight years of age, put this boy up as a pretender to the Chinese throne, and not without considerable success. The news spread that the new emperor was at the above-named village, and the people for miles around flocked in great numbers to do him homage, congratulating themselves that the emperor should have risen from the immediate neighborhood in which they themselves had passed a monotonous existence. For weeks this pretense to the throne was maintained, until a miniature rebellion broke out, to quell which the Viceroy of Yuen-nan dispatched with all speed a strong body of soldiers.

Everybody thought that the loss of a few heads and other Chinese trivialities was to end this little flutter of the people. But not so. The whole of the family who had promoted this fictitious claim to the throne—father, mother, brothers, sisters—were all put to death, most of them in front of the eyes of the poor little fellow who was the victim of their idle pretext. The military returned, reporting that everything was now quiet, and a few days later, guarded by twenty soldiers, came this young pretender, encaged in one of the prison boxes, breaking his heart with grief. And it was he who was now conducted to meet the foreigner. He has been confined within the prison since he arrived at the capital, and the object seems to be to keep him there, training and teaching him until he shall have arrived at an age when he can be taught a trade. The tiny fellow is small for his eight years, and his little wizened face, sallow and delicate, has a plausible tale to tell. He is always fretting and grieving for those whose heads were shown to him after decapitation. However, he is being cared for, and it is doubtful whether the authorities—or even the emperor himself—will mete out punishment to him when he grows older. He did nothing; he knew nothing. At the present time he is going through a class-book which teaches him the language to be used in audience with the Son of Heaven—he will probably be taken before the emperor when he is old enough. But now he is not living the life of a boy—no playmates, no toys, no romps and frolics. He, like Topsy, merely grows—in surroundings which only a dark prison life can give him.

This was the first time I had even been in prison in China. This remark rather tickled the governor, and on taking my departure he assured me that it was an honor to him, which the Chinese language was too poor to express, that I should have allowed my honorable and dignified person to visit his mean and contemptible abode. He commenced this compliment to me as he was showing me the well-equipped hospital in connection with the prison—containing eight separate wards in charge of a Chinese doctor.

I smiled in return a smile of deepest gratitude, and waving a fond farewell, left him in a happy mood.

## The Schools

One would scarce dream of a university for the province of Yuen-nan. Yet such is the case.

In former days—and it is true, too, to a great extent to-day—the prominent place given to education in China rendered the village schools an object of more than common interest, where the educated men of the Empire received their first intellectual training. Probably in no other country was there such uniformity in the standards of instruction. Every educated man was then a potential school master—this was certainly true of Yuen-nan. But all is now changing, as the infusion of the spirit of the phrase "China for the Chinese" gains forceful meaning among the people.

The highest hill within the city precincts has been chosen as the site for a university, which is truly a remarkable building for Western China. One of the students of the late. Dr. Mateer (Shantung) was the architect—a man who came originally to the school as a teacher of mathematics—and it cannot be said that the huge oblong building, with a long narrow wing on either side of a central dome, is the acme of beauty from a purely architectural standpoint.

Of red-faced brick, this university, which cost over two hundred thousand taels to build, is most imposing, and possesses conveniences and improvements quite comparable to the ordinary college of the West. For instance, as I passed through the many admirably-equipped schoolrooms, well ventilated and airy, I saw an Italian who was laying in the electric light,[32] the power for which was generated by an immense dynamo at the basement, upon which alone twenty thousand taels were spent. Thirty professors have the control of thirty-two classrooms, teaching among other subjects mathematics, music, languages (chiefly English and Japanese), geography, chemistry, astronomy, geology, botany, and so on. The museum, situated in the center of the building, does not contain as many specimens as one would imagine quite easily obtainable, but there are certainly some capital selections of things natural to this part of the Empire.

The authorities probably thought I was rather a queer foreigner, wanting to see everything there was to see inside the official barriers in the city. Day after day I was making visits to places where foreigners seldom have entered, and I do not doubt that the officials, whilst treating me with the utmost deference and extreme punctiliousness, thought I was a sort of British spy.

When I went to the Agricultural School, probably the most interesting visit I made, I was met by the Secretary for Foreign Affairs, a keen fellow, who spoke English well, and who, having been trained at Shanghai, and therefore understanding the idiosyncrasies of the foreigner's character, was invited to entertain. And this he did, but he was careful that he did not give away much information regarding the progress that the Yuen-nanese, essentially sons of the soil, are making in agriculture. For this School of Agriculture is an important adjunct.

---

32    Soon afterwards a disturbance occurred among the students, and had it not been for the promptitude of the inspector, some of them might have lost their heads.

The electric light had just been laid in, and was working so well that the authorities found it imperative to charge each of the 400 resident students one dollar per month for the upkeep. This simple edict was the cause of the riot In a body the boys rolled up their pukais, and marched down to the main entrance, declaring that they were determined to resign if the order was not rescinded. The inspector, however, had had all the doors locked. The frenzied students broke these open, and incidentally thrashed some of the caretakers for interfering in matters which were not considered to be strictly their business.

Subsequently the Chancellor of Education visited the college in person, but no heed was paid to his exhortations, and it was only when the dollar charge for lighting was reduced that peace was restored.

The Chancellor, as a last word, told them that if they vacated their schoolrooms a fine of about a hundred taels would be imposed upon each man.

The occasion was marked by all the foolish ardor one finds among college boys at home, and it seems that, despite the enormous amount of money the college is costing to run, the students are somewhat out of hand.—E.J.D.

Scholars are taken on an agreement for three years, during which time they are fed and housed at the expense of the school; if they leave during the specified period they are fined heavily. No less than 180 boys, ranging from sixteen to twenty-three, are being trained here, with about 120 paid apprentices. Three Japanese professors are employed—one at a salary of two hundred dollars a month, and two others at three hundred, the latter having charge of the fruit and forest trees and the former of vegetables.

In years to come the silk industry of Yuen-nan will rank among the chief, and the productions will rank among the best of all the eighteen provinces. There are no less than ten thousand mulberry trees in the school grounds for feeding the worms; four thousand catties of leaves are used every day for their food; five hundred immense trays of silkworms are constantly at work here. The worms are in the charge of scholars, whose names appear on the various racks under their charge, and the fact that feeding takes place every two hours, day and night, is sufficient testimony that the boys go into their work with commendable energy. As I was being escorted around the building, through shed after shed filled with these trays of silkworms, several of the scholars made up a sort of procession, and waited for the eulogy that I freely bestowed. In another building small boys were spinning the silk, and farther down the weavers were busy with their primitive machinery, with which, however, they were turning out silk that could be sold in London at a very big price. The colorings were specially beautiful, and the figuring quite good, although the head-master of the school told me that he hoped for improvements in that direction. And I, looking wise, although knowing little about silk and its manufacture, heartily agreed with the little fat man.

There is a department for women also, and contrary to custom, I had a look around here, too. The girls were particularly smart at spinning.

# Second Journey: Yuen-Nan-Fu to Tali-fu (Via Ch'u-hsiong-fu)

## CHAPTER XV

*Stages to Tali-fu. Worst roads yet experienced. Stampede among ponies. Hybrid crowd at Anning-cheo. Simplicity of life of common people. Does China want the foreigner? Straits Settlements and China Proper compared. China's aspect of her own position. Renaissance of Chinese military power. Europeans NOT wanted in the Empire. Emptiness of the lives of the common people. Author erects a printing machine in Inland China. National conceit. Differences in make-up of the Hua Miao and the Han Ren. The Hua Miao and what they are doing. Emancipation of their women. Tribute to Protestant missionaries. Betrothal and marriage in China. Miao women lead a life of shame and misery. Crude ideas among Chinese regarding age of foreigners. Musty man and dusty traveller at Lao-ya-kwan. Intense cold. Salt trade. Parklike scenery, pleasant travel, solitude.*

From the figures of heights appearing below, one would imagine that between the capital and Tali-fu hard climbing is absent. But during each stage, with the exception of the journey from Sei-tze to Sha-chiao-kai, there is considerable fatiguing uphill and downhill work, each evening bringing one to approximately the same level as that from which he started his morning tramp. I went by the following route:—

| | LENGTH OF STAGE | HEIGHT ABOVE SEA LEVEL |
|---|---|---|
| 1st day—Anning-cheo | 70 li | 6,300 ft. |
| 2nd day—Lao-ya-kwan | 70 li | 6,800 ft. |
| 3rd day—Lu-feng-hsien | 75 li | 5,500 ft. |
| 4th day—Sei-tze | 80 li | 6,100 ft. |
| 5th day—Kwang-tung-hsien | 60 li | 6,300 ft. |
| 6th day—Rest day. | | |

165

| | LENGTH OF STAGE | HEIGHT ABOVE SEA LEVEL |
|---|---|---|
| 7th day—Ch'u-hsiong-fu | 70 li | 6,150 ft. |
| 8th day—Luho-kai | 60 li | 6,000 ft. |
| 9th day—Sha-chiao-kai | 65 li | 6,400 ft. |
| 10th day—Pu-peng | 90 li | 7,200 ft. |
| 11th day—Yuen-nan-i | 65 li | 6,800 ft. |
| 12th day—Hungay | 80 li | 6,000 ft. |
| 14th day—Chao-chow | 60 li | 6,750 ft.[33] |
| 15th day—Tali-fu | 60 li | 6,700 ft. |

A long, winding and physically-exhausting road took me from Sha-chiao-kai to Yin-wa-kwan, the most elevated pass between Yuen-nan-fu and Tali-fu, and continued over barren mountains, bereft of shelter, and void of vegetation and people, to Pupeng. A rough climb of an hour and a half then took me to the top of the next mountain, where roads and ruts followed a high plateau for about thirty li, and with a precipitous descent I entered the plain of Yuen-nan-i. Then over and between barren hills, passing a small lake and plain with the considerable town of Yuen-nan-hsien ten li to the right, I continued in a narrow valley and over mountains in the same uncultivated condition to Hungay, situated in a swampy valley. Having crossed this valley, another rough climb brings the traveler to the top of the next pass, Ting-chi-ling, whence the road descends, and leads by a well-cultivated valley to Chao-chow. After an easy thirty li we reached Hsiakwan,[34] one of the largest commercial cities in the province, lying at the foot of the most magnificent mountain range in Yuen-nan, and by the side of the most famous lake. A paved road takes one in to his destination at Tali-fu, where I was welcomed by Dr. and Mrs. Clark, of the China Inland Mission, and hospitably entertained for a couple of days.

The roads in general from Yuen-nan-fu to Tali-fu were worse than any I have met from Chung-king onwards, partly owing to the mountainous condition of the country, and partly to neglect of maintenance.

Where the road is paved, it is in most places worse than if it had not been paved at all, as neither skill nor common sense seems to have been exercised in the work. It is probably safe to say that there are no ancient roads in Yuen-nan, in the sense of the constructed highways which have lasted through the centuries, for the civilization of the early Yuen-nanese was not

33  The 13th day is missing in the original book. —*publishers*

34  Hsiakwan would be supplied by a branch line of the main railway in the Kunlong scheme advocated by Major H.R. Davies, leaving at Mi-tu, to the south of Hungay.— E.J.D.

equal to such works. As a matter of fact, the condition of the roads is all but intolerable. Many were never made, and are seldom mended—one may say that with very few exceptions they are never repaired, except when utterly impassable, and then in the most make-shift manner.

My highly-strung Rusty received a shock to his nervous system as I led him leisurely from the incline leading into Anning-cheo (6,300 feet), through the arched gateway in a pagoda-like entrance, which when new would have been a credit to any city. The stones of the main street were so slippery that I could hardly keep on my legs. Frightened by one of their number dragging its empty wooden carrying frame along the ground behind it, a drove of unruly-pack-ponies lashed and bucked and tossed themselves out of order, and an instant afterwards came helter-skelter towards my ten-inch pathway by the side of the road. All of my men caught the panic, and in their mad rush several were knocked down and trampled upon by the torrent of frightened creatures. I thought I was being charged by cavalry, but beyond a good deal of bruising I escaped unhurt. Closer and closer came the hubbub and the din of the town—the market was not yet over. As I approached the big street, throngs of blue-cottoned yokels, quite out of hand, created a nerve-racking uproar, as they thriftily drove their bargains. I shrugged my shoulders, gazed long and earnestly at the motley mob, and putting on a bold front, pushed through in a careless manner. Ponies with salt came in from the other end of the town, and in their waddling the little brutes gave me more knocks.

It was an awful crowd—Chinese, Minchia, Lolo, and other specimens of hybridism unknown to me. Yet I suppose the majority of them may be called happy. Certainly the simplicity of the life of the common people, their freedom from fastidious tastes, which are only a fetter in our own Western social life, their absolute independence of furniture in their homes, their few wants and perhaps fewer necessities, when contrasted with the demands of the Englishman, is to them a state of high civilization. Here were farmers, mechanics, shopkeepers, and retired people living a simple, unsophisticated life. All the strength of the world and all its beauties, all true joy, everything that consoles, that feeds hope, or throws a ray of light along our dark paths, everything that enables us to discern across our poor lives a splendid goal and a boundless future, comes to us from true simplicity. I do not say that we get all this from the Chinese, but in many ways they can teach us how to live in the *spirit of simplicity*. They were living from hand to mouth, with seemingly no anxieties at all—and yet, too, they were living without God, and with very little hope.

And here the foreigner re-appeared to disturb them. Even in Anning-cheo, only a day from the capital, I was regarded as a being of another species, and was treated with little respect. I was not wanted.

No international question has become more hackneyed than "Does China want the foreigner?" Columns of utter nonsense have from time to time been printed in the English press, purporting to have come from men supposed to know, to the effect that this Empire is crying out, waiting with open arms to welcome the European and the American with all his advanced methods of Christendom and civilization. It has by general assent come to be understood that China *does* want the foreigner. But those who know the Chinese, and who have lived with them, and know their inherent insincerity in all that they do, still wonder on, and still ask, "Does she?"

To the European in Hong-Kong, or any of the China ports, having trustworthy Chinese on his commercial staff—without whom few businesses in the Far East can make progress—my argument may seem to have no *raison d'etre*. He will be inclined to blurt out vehemently the absurdity of the idea that the Chinese do not want the foreigner. First, they cannot do without him if China is to come into line as a great nation among Eastern and Western powers. And then, again, could anyone doubt the sincerity of the desire on the part of the Celestial for closer and downright friendly intercourse if he has had nothing more than mere superficial dealings with them?

Thus thought the writer at one time in his life. He has had in a large commercial firm some of the best Chinese assistants living, in China or out of it, and has nothing but praise for their assiduous perseverance and remarkable business acumen and integrity.

As a business man, I admire them far and away above any other race of people in the East and Far East. Is there any business man in the Straits Settlements who has not the same opinion of the Straits-born Chinese? But as one who has traveled in China, living among the Chinese and with them, seeing them under all natural conditions, at home in their own country, I say unhesitatingly that at the present time only an infinitesimal percentage of the population of the vast Interior entertain genuine respect for the white man, and, in centers where Western influence has done so much to break down the old-time hatred towards us, the real, unveneered attitude of the ordinary Chinese is one not calculated to foster between the Occident and the Orient the brotherhood of man. Difficult is it for the foreigner in civilized parts of China—and impossible for the great preponderance of the European peoples at home—to grasp the fact that in huge tracts of Interior

China the populace have never seen a foreigner, save for the ubiquitous missionary, who takes on more often than not the dress of the native.

Although the Chinese Government recognizes the dangerous situation of the nation *vis-a-vis* with nations of Europe, and has ratified one treaty after another with us, the nation itself does not, so far as the traveler can see, appreciate the fact that she cannot possibly resist the white man, and hold herself in seclusion as formerly from the Western world. China is discovering—has discovered officially, although that does not necessarily mean nationally—as Japan did so admirably when her progress was most marked, that steam and machinery have made the world too small for any part thereof to separate itself entirely from the broadening current of the world's life.

Whilst not for a moment failing to admire the aggressive character of Occidentals, and the resultant necessity of thwarting them—we see this especially in official circles in Yuen-nan—Chinese leaders of thought and activity are recognizing that in international relations the final appeal can be only to a superior power, and that power, to be superior, must be thorough, and thorough throughout. So different to what has held good in China for countless ages. That is why China is making sure of her army, and why she will have ready in 1912—ten years before the period originally intended—no less than thirty-six divisions, each division formed of ten thousand units.[35] China is now endeavoring to walk the ground which led Japan to greatness among the nations—she takes Japan as her pattern, and thinks that what Japan has done she can do—and, officially abandoning her long course of self-sufficient isolation, is plunging into the flood of international progress, determined to acquire all the knowledge she can, and thus win for herself a place among the Powers.

But I am in Yuen-nan, and things move slowly here.

All this does not mean that my presence is desired, or that fear of me, the foreigner, has ceased. On the contrary, it signifies that I am more greatly to be feared. The European is *not* wanted in China, no matter how absurd

35    A most important factor in the altering circumstances is the renaissance of the Chinese military power. Japanese instructors swarm in China and are swiftly building up a mighty military engine as their ally. The original plan of the Chinese Government was to form thirty-six divisions, each of ten thousand men, and to have this entire force ready to take the field before the year 1922, but it is perfectly evident from the reports which have filtered through to Europe, that this huge army will be ready by 1912, or ten years earlier than was originally intended. The Review of Reviews for January 1910, in referring to an article written by General von der Boeck, one of Germany's most brilliant infantry commanders, says: "The General is inclined to believe that in 1912 China will possess a well-equipped army of half a million men, the greater part armed with modern weapons, and with a discipline and organization infinitely superior to anything which China has yet produced." —E.J.D

it may seem to the student of international politics, who sits and devours all the newspaper copy—good, bad and indifferent—which filters through regarding China becoming the El Dorado of the Westerner. He is wanted for no other reason than that of teaching the Chinese to foreignize as much as he can, teaching the leaders of the people to strive to modify national life, and to raise public conduct and administration to the best standards of the West.

When China is capable of looking after herself, and able to maintain the position she is securing by the aid of the foreigner in her provinces, following her present mode of thought and action, the foreigner may go back again. But it is to be hoped that the evolution of the country will be different.

Another feature impressed upon me was the emptiness of the lives of the people. Education was rare, and any education they had was confined to the Chinese classics.

Neither of the three men I had with me could read or write. The thoughts of these people are circumscribed by the narrow world in which they live, and only a chance traveler such as myself allows them a glimpse of other places. Each man, with rare exception, lives and labors and dies where he is born—that is his ambition; and in the midst of a people whose whole out-look of life is so contracted, I find difficulty in believing that progress such as Japan made in her memorable fifty-year forward movement will be made by the Chinese of Yuen-nan in two hundred years. Everything one can see around him here, at this town of Anning-cheo, seems to make against it. In my dealings with Chinese in their own country—I speak broadly—I have found that they "know everything." I erected a printing-press in Tong-ch'uan-fu some months ago—a type of the old flat handpress not unlike that first used by Caxton. It was a part of the equipment of the Ai Kueh Hsieh Tang (Love of Country School), and I was invited by the gentry to erect it. Now the thing had not been up an hour before all the old fossils in the place knew all about it. Printing to them was easy—a child could do it. It is always, "O ren teh, o ren teh" ("I know, I know"). These men, dressed in their best, stood with arms behind them, and smiled stupidly as I labored with my coat off fixing their primitive machinery. Yet they did *not* know, and now, within a few months, not a sheet has been printed, and the whole plant is going to rack and ruin.

This is the difference between the Chinese and the tribespeople of Yuen-nan. Here we see the god of the missionary again, quite apart from any religious basis. The tribesman comes and lays himself at the feet of the missionary, and says at once, "I do not know. Tell me, and I will follow you. I want to learn." That is why it is that the Chinese stand open-eyed and open-mouthed when they see the Miao making strides altogether impossible to themselves, in proportion to their standard of civilization, and this position of things will not be altered, unless they cease to deceive themselves. I have seen a Miao boy of nine who never in his life had seen a Chinese character, who did not know that school existed and, whose only tutoring depended on the week's visit of the missionary twice a year. I have seen this young-ster read off a sheet of Chinese characters no Chinese boy of his age in the whole city would succeed in. I have not been brought into contact with any other tribe as I have with the Hua Miao.[36]

But if the progress this once-despised people are making is maintained, the Yuen-nanese will very soon be left behind in the matter of practical scholarship. These Miao live the simplest of simple lives, but they wish to become better—to live purer lives, to become civilized, to be uplifted; and therefore they are most humble, most approachable, and are slowly evolv-ing into a happy position of proud independence. Education among the Hua Miao is not lost: among the Chinese much of the labor put forward in endeavors to educate them is lost, or seems to bear no immediate fruit. The Miao are living by confidence and hope that turns towards the future; the Yuen-nanese are content with their confidence in the past. The Miao, however, were not like this always—but a few years ago they were not heard of outside China.

The coming emancipation of their women, demands some attention. The few Europeans who have lived among the multitudes in Central China would not associate beds of roses with the lives of the women anywhere.

The daughter is seldom happy, and unless the wife present her husband with sons, who will perpetuate the father's name and burn incense at his tablet after his death, her life is more often than not made absolutely un-bearable—a fact more than any other one thing responsible for the numer-ous suicides. She is the drudge, the slave of the man. And the popular belief is that all the women of the Middle Kingdom are essentially Chinese; but little is heard of the tribespeople—more numerous probably than in any other given area in all the world—whose womankind are as far removed from the Chinese in language, habits and customs as English ladies of to-day are removed from Grecians. A decade or so ago no one heard of the Miao women: they were the lowest of the low, having no *status*. They were far worse off than their Chinese sisters, who, no matter what they had to endure after marriage, were certainly safeguarded by law and etiquette al-

36    In many parts of China at the present day many Chinese imagine that the Miao tribes are monkeys, and that they have tails in the natural order of things (for more infor-mation see Chapters IX and X.)

lowing them to enter the married state with respectability; but no social laws, no social ties protect the Miao women.

Until a few years ago their "club" was a common brothel, too horrible to describe in the English language. As soon as a girl gave birth to her first child she came down on the father to keep her. In many cases, it is only fair to say, they lived together faithfully as man and wife, although such cases were not by any means in the majority. The poor creatures herded together in their unspeakable vice and infamy, with no shame or common modesty, fighting for the wherewithal to live, and only by chance living regularly with one man, and then only just so long as he wished. Little girls of ten and over regularly attended these awful hovels, and children grew out of their childhood with no other vision than that of entering into the disgraceful life as early as Nature would allow them. It meant little less than that practically the whole of the population was illegitimate, viewed from a Western standpoint. No such thing as marriage existed. Men and women cohabited in this horrible orgy of existence, with the result that murder, disease and pestilence were rife among them. It was only a battle of the survival of the fittest to pursue so terrible a life. Nearly all the people were diseased by the transgression of Nature's laws.

After a time, however, through the instrumentality of Protestant missionaries, these wretched people began to see the light of civilization. Gradually, and of their own free will, the girls gave up their accursed dens of misery and shame, and the men lived more in accord with social law and order.

The Miao, too, had hitherto been dependent for their literature upon the Chinese character, which only a few could understand. Soon they had literature in their own language,[37] and a great social reform set in. They showed a desire for Western learning such as has seldom been seen among any people in China—these were people lowest down in the social scale; and now the latest phase is the establishment of bethrothal and marriage laws, calculated to revolutionize the community and to introduce what in China is the equivalent for home life.

Betrothal among the Chinese is a matter with which the parties most deeply concerned have little to do. Their parents engage a go-between or match-maker, and another point is that there is no age limit. Not so now with the Christian Miao. No paid go-between is engaged, and brides are to be at a minimum age of eighteen years, and bridegrooms twenty. The establishment of these laws will, it is hoped, make for the emancipation

---

37 The written language was framed and instituted by the Rev. Sam. Pollard, of the Bible Christian Mission (now merged into the United Methodist Mission).—E.J.D.

from a life of the most dreadful misery of thousands of women in one of the darkest countries of the earth.[38]

But now the Miao is pressing forward under his burdens, to guide himself in the struggle, to retrieve his falls and his failures; and in the future lies his hope—the indomitable hope upon which the interest of humanity is based—and he has in addition the grand expectation of escaping despair even in death. It is all the praiseworthy work of our fellow-countrymen, living isolated lives among the people, building up a worthy Christian structure upon Miao simplicity and humble fidelity to the foreigner.

But I digress from my travel.

Little out of the ordinary marked my travels to Lao-ya-kwan (6,800 feet), an easy stage. My meager tiffin at an insignificant mountain village was, as usual, an educational lesson to the natives. Each tin that came from my food basket—one's servant delighted to lay out the whole business—underwent the severest criticism tempered with unmeaning eulogy, picked up and put down by perhaps a score of people, who did not mean to be rude. When I used their chopsticks—dirty little pieces of bamboo—in a manner very far removed from their natural method, they were proud of me. Outrageously panegyric references were made when an old man, scratching at his disagreeable itch-sores under my nose, clipped a youngster's ear for hazarding my age to be less than that of any of the bystanders, the length of my moustache and a three-day growth on my chin giving them the opinion that I was certainly over sixty.[39]

I entered Lao-ya-kwan under an inauspicious star. No accommodation was to be had, all the inns were literally overrun with sedan chairs and filled with well-dressed officials, already busy with the "hsi-lien" (wash basin). In my dirty khaki clothes, out at knee and elbow, looking musty and mean and dusty, with my topee botched and battered, I presented a most unhappy contrast as I led my pony down the street under the sarcastic stare of bystanding scrutineers. The nights were cold, and in the private house where I stayed, mercifully overlooked by a trio of protesting effigies with visages grotesque and gruesome, rats ran fearlessly over the room's mud floor, and

---

38    The marriage laws were instituted by the China Inland Mission at Sa-pu-shan, where a great work is being done among the Hua Miao. A good many more stipulations are embodied in the excellent rules, but I have no room here to detail.—E.J.D.]

39    The Chinese have the crudest ideas of the age of foreigners. Among themselves the general custom is for a man to shave his upper lip so long as his father is alive, so that in the ordinary course a man wearing a moustache is looked upon as an old man. In Tong-ch'uan-fu the rumor got abroad that three "uei kueh ren" ("foreign men") went riding horses—(two young ones and one old one. The "old one" was myself, because I had hair on my top lip, despite the fact that I was considerably the junior. And the fact that one was a lady was not deemed worthy of the slightest consideration.—E.J.D.

EDWIN JOHN DINGLE

at night I buried my head in my rugs to prevent total disappearance of my
ears by nibbling. Not so my men. They slept a few feet from me, three on
one bench, two on another. Bedding was not to be had, and so among the
dirty straw they huddled together as closely as possible to preserve what
bodily heat they had. Snow fell heavily. In the early morning sunlight on
January 13th the undulating valley, with its grand untrodden carpet of white,
looked magnificently beautiful as I picked out the road shown me by a poor
fellow whose ears had got frost-nipped.

No easy work was it climbing tediously up the narrow footway in a sharp
spur rising some 1,000 feet in a ribbed ascent, overlooking a fearful drop.
Over to the left I saw an unhappy little urchin, hardly a rag covering his
shivering, bleeding body, grovelling piteously in the snow, while his blind
and goitrous mother did her best at gathering firewood with a hatchet. The
pass leading over this range, through which the white crystalline flakes
were driven wildly in one's face, was a half-moon of smooth rock actually
worn away by the endless tramping of myriads of pack-ponies, who then
were plodding through ruts of steps almost as high as their haunches.

A man with a diseased hip joined me thirty li farther on, dismounting
from his pile of earthly belongings which these men fix on the backs of
their ponies. It is a creditable trapeze act to effect a mount after the pony is
ready for the journey. He had, he said, met me before. He knew that I was a
missionary, and had heard me preach. He remembered my wife and myself
and children passing the night in the same inn in which he stayed on one of
his pilgrimages from his native town somewhere to the east of the province.
I had never seen him before! I had no wife; I have never preached a sermon
in my life. I should be pained ever again to have to suffer his unmannerly
presence anywhere.

Ponies were being loaded near my table. The rapscallion in question
explained that the black blocks were salt, taking a pinch from my salt-cel-
lar with his grimy fingers to add point to his remarks. I kicked at a couple
of mongrels under the rude form on which I sat—they fought for the skins
of those potato-like pears which grow here so prolifically. The person announced that they were dogs, and that an idiosyncrasy of Chinese dogs was
to fight. Several wags joined in, and all appeared, through the traveling
nincompoop, to know all about my past and present, lapsing into a desultory harangue upon all men and things foreign. The street reminded me of
Clovelly—rugged and ragged—and the people were wrinkled and wretched; and, indeed, being a Devonian myself by birth, I should be excused of
wantonly intending to hurt the delicate feelings of the lusty sons of Devon

174

were I to declare that I thought the life not of a very terrible dissimilarity from that port of antiquity in the West.

Salt was everywhere, much more like coal than salt, certainly as black. The blocks were stacked up by the sides of inns ready for transport, carried on the backs of a multitude of poor wretches who work like oxen from dawn to dusk for the merest pittance, on the backs of droves and droves of ponies, scrambling and spluttering along over the slippery once-paved streets.

All day long, with the exception of two or three easy ascents, we were travelling in pleasantly undulating country of park-like magnificence. My men dallied. I tramped on alone; and sitting down to rest on the rocks, I realized that I was in one of the strangest, loneliest, wildest corners of the world. Great mountain-peaks towered around me, white and sparkling diadems of wondrous beauty, and at my feet, black and stirless, lay a silent pool, reflecting the weird shadows of my coolies flitting like specters among the jagged rocks of these most solitary hills.

# CHAPTER XVI

*Lu-feng-hsien and its bridge. Magnificence of mountains towards the capital. Opportunity for Dublin Fusiliers. Characteristic climbing. Crockery crash and its sequel. Mountain forest. Changeableness of climate. Wayside scene and some reflections. Is your master drunk? Babies of the poor. Loess roads. Travelers, and how they should travel. Wrangling about payment at the tea-shop. The lying art among the Chinese. Difference of the West and East. Strange Chinese characteristic. Eastern and Western civilization, and how it is working. Remarks on the written character and Romanisation. Will China lose her national characteristics? "Ih dien mien, ih dien mien." A nasty experience of the impotently dumb. Rescued in the nick of time.*

*W*hen the day shall come for its history to be told, the historian will have little to say of Lu-feng-hsien, that is—if he is a decent sort of fellow.

He may refer to its wonderful bridge, to its beggars and its ruins. The stone bridge, one of the best of its kind in the whole empire, and I should think better than any other in Yuen-nan, stands to-day conspicuously emblematic of ill-departed prosperity. So far as I remember, it was the only public ornament in a condition of passable repair in any way creditable to the ratepayers of the hsien. The wall is decayed, the people are decayed, and in every nook and cranny are painful evidences of preventable decay, marked by a conservatism among the inhabitants and unpardonable indolence.

The bridge, however, has stood the test of time, and bids fair to last through eternity. Other travelers have passed over it since the days of Marco Polo, but I should like to say a word about it. Twelve yards or so wide, and no less than 150 yards long, it is built entirely of grey stone; with its massive piers, its excellent masonry, its good (although crude) carving, its old-time sculpturing of dreadful-looking animals at either end, its decorative triumphal arches, its masses of memorial tablets (which I could not read), its seven arches of beautiful simplicity and symmetry and perfect proportion, it would have been a credit to any civilized country in the world. I noticed that, in addition to cementing, the stones and pillars forming the sides of the roadway were also dovetailed. Among the works of public interest with which successive emperors have covered China, the bridges are not the least remarkable; and in them one is able to realize the perseverance of the Chinese in the enormous difficulties of construction they have had to overcome.

Passing over the stream—the Hsiang-shui Ho, I believe—I stepped out across the plain with one foot soaked, a pony having pulled me into the water as he drank. Peas and beans covered with snow adjoined a heart-breaking road which led up to a long, winding ascent through a glade overhung by frost-covered hedgerows, where the sun came gently through and breathed the sweet coming of the spring. From midway up the mountain the view of the plain below and the fine range of hills separating me from the capital was one of exceeding loveliness, the undisturbed white of the snow and frost sparkling in the sunshine contrasting most strikingly with the darkened waves of billowy green opposite, with a background of sharp-edged mountains, whose summits were only now and again discernible in the waning morning mist. Snow lay deep in the crevices. My frozen path was treacherous for walking, but the dry, crisp air gave me a gusto and energy known only in high latitudes. In a pass cleared out from the rock we halted and gained breath for the second ascent, surmounted by a dismantled watch-tower. It has long since fallen into disuse, the sound tiles from the roof having been appropriated for covering other habitable dwellings near by, where one may rest for tea. The road, paved in some places, worn from the side of the mountain in others, was suspended above narrow gorges, an entrance to a part of the country which had the aspect of northern regions. The sun, tearing open the curtain of blue mist, inundated with brightness one of the most beautiful landscapes it is possible to conceive. A handful of Dublin Fusiliers with quick-firing rifles concealed in the hollows of the heights might have stopped a whole army struggling up the hill-sides. But no one appeared to stop me, so I went on.

Climbing was characteristic of the day. Lu-feng-hsien is about 5,500 feet; Sei-tze (where we were to sleep) 6,100 feet. Not much of a difference in height; but during the whole distance one is either dropping much lower than Lu-feng or much higher than Sei-tze. For thirty li up to Ta-tsue-si

(6,900 feet) there is little to revel in, but after that, right on to the terrific drop to our destination for the night, we were going through mountain forests than which there are none better in the whole of the province, unless it be on the extreme edge of the Tibetan border, where accompanying scenery is altogether different.

From a height of 7,850 feet we dropped abruptly, through clouds of thick red dust which blinded my eyes and filled my throat, down to the city of Sei-tze. I went down behind some ponies. Upwards came a fellow struggling with two loads of crockery, and in the narrow pathway he stood in an elevated position to let the animals pass. Irony of fate! One of the horses—it seemed most intentional—gave his load a tilt: man and crockery all went together in one heap to a crevice thirty yards down the incline, and as I proceeded I heard the choice rhetoric of the victim and the muleteer arguing as to who should pay.

Just before that, I dipped into the very bosom of the earth, with rugged hills rising to bewildering heights all around, base to summit clad luxuriously in thick greenery of mountain firs, a few cedars, and the Chinese ash. Black patches of rock to the right were the death-bed of many a swaying giant, and in contrast, running away sunwards, a silver shimmer on the unmoving ocean of delicious green was caused by the slantwise sun reflections, while in the ravines on the other side a dark blue haze gave no invitation. Smoothly-curving fringes stood out softly against the eternal blue of the heavens. Farther on, eloquent of their own strength and imperturbability, were deep rocks, black and defiant; but even here firs grew on the projecting ledges which now and again hung menacingly above the red path, shading away the sunlight and giving to the dark crevices an atmosphere of damp and cold, where men's voices echoed and re-echoed like weird greetings from the grave. Onwards again, and from the cool ravines, adorned with overhang branches, forming cosy retreats from the now blazing sun, one emerged to a road leading up once more to undiscovered vastnesses. Yonder narrowed a gorge, fine and delicately covered, pleasing to one's aesthetic sense. The center was a dome, all full of life and waving leafage, ethereal and sweet; and running down, like children to their mother, were numerous little hills densely clothed in a green lighter and more dainty than that of the parent hill, throwing graceful curtsies to the murmuring river at the foot. As I write here, bathed in the beauty of spring sunlight, it is difficult to believe that a few hours since the thermometer was at zero. Little spots of habitation, with foodstuffs growing alongside, looking most lonely in their patches of green in the forest, added a human and sentimental picturesqueness to a scene so strongly impressive.

A thatched, barn-like place gave us rest, the woman producing for me a huge chunk of palatable rice sponge-cake sprinkled with brown sugar. Little naked children, offspring of parents themselves covered with merest hanging rags, groped round me and treated me with courteous curiosity; goats smelt round the coolie-loads of men who rested on low forms and smoked their rank tobacco; smoke from the green wood fires issued from the mud grates, where receptacles were filled with boiling water ready for the traveler, constantly re-filled by a woman whose child, hung over her back, moaned piteously for the milk its mother was too busy to give to it. Near by a young girl gave suck to a deformed infant, lucky to have survived its birth; her neck was as big as her breasts—merely a case of goitre. Coolies passed, panting and puffing, all casting a curious glance at him to whose beneficence all were willing to pander.

At tiffin I counted thirty-three wretched people, who turned out to see the barbarian. They desired, and desired importunately, to touch me and the clothes which covered me. And I submitted.

This half-way place was interesting owing to the fact that the lady in charge of the buffet could speak two words of French—she had, I believe, acted as washerwoman to a man who at one time had been in the Customs at Mengtsz. Great excitement ensued among the perspiring laborers of the road and the dumb-struck yokels of the district. The lady was so goitrous that it would have been extremely risky to hazard a guess as to the exact spot where her face began or ended; and here, in a place where with all her neighbors she had lived through a period noted for famine, for rebellion, for wholesale death and murder of an entire village, she endured such terrible poverty that one would have thought her spirit would have waned and the light of her youth burned out. But no! The lusty dame was still sprightly. She had been three times divorced. The person at present connected with her in the bonds of wedded life—also goitrous and morally repulsive—stood by and gazed down upon her like a proud bridegroom. He resented the levity of Shanks and his companion, but, owing to the detail of a sightless eye, he could not see all that transpired. However, we were all happy enough. Charges were not excessive. My men had a good feed of rice and cabbage, with the usual cabbage stump, two raw rice biscuits (which they threw into the ashes to cook, and when cooked picked the dirt off with their long finger-nails), and as much tea as they could drink—all for less than a penny.

There is something in traveling in Yuen-nan, where the people away from the cities exhibit such painful apathy as to whether dissolution of this life comes to them soon or late, which breeds drowsiness. After a tramp over mountains for five or six hours on end, one naturally needed rest. To-day, as I sat after lunch and wrote up my journal, I nearly fell asleep. As I watched the reflections of all these ill-clad figures on the stony roadway, and dozed meanwhile, one rude fellow asked my man whether I was drunk!

I was not left long to my reverie.

Entering into a conversation intended for the whole village to hear, my bulky coolie sublet his contract for two tsien for the eighty li—we had already done fifty. The man hired was a weak, thin, half-baked fellow, whose body and soul seemed hardly to hang together. He was the first to arrive. As soon as he got in; this same man took a needle from the inside of his great straw hat and commenced ridding his pants of somewhat outrageous perforations. Such is the Chinese coolie, although in Yuen-nan he would be an exception. Late at night he offered to put a shoe on my pony. I consented. He did the job, providing a new shoe and tools and nails, for 110 cash—just about twopence.

I could not help, thinking of the children I had seen to-day, "Sad for the dirt-begrimed babies that they were born." These children were all a family of eternal Topsies—they merely grew, and few knew how. They are rather dragged up than brought up, to live or die, as time might appoint. Babies in Yuen-nan, for the great majority, are not coaxed, not tossed up and down and petted, not soothed, not humored. There are none to kiss away their tears, they never have toys, and dream no young dreams, but are brought straight into the iron realities of life. They are reared in smoke and physical and moral filth, and become men and women when they should be children: they haggle and envy, and swear and murmur. When in Yuen-nan—or even in the whole of China—will there be the innocence and beauty of childhood as we of the West are blessed with?

Roads here were in many cases of a light loess, and some of red limestone rock, with a few li of paved roads. Many of the main roads over the loess are altered by the rains. Two days of heavy rain will produce in some places seas of mud, often knee-deep, and this will again dry up quite as rapidly with the next sunshine. They become undermined, and crumble away from the action of even a trickling stream, so as to become always unsafe and sometimes quite impassable.

Delays are very dear to the heart of every Chinese. The traveler, if he is desirous of getting his caravan to move on speedily, has little chance of success unless he assumes an attitude of profoundest indifference to all men and things around him—never *appear* to be in a hurry.

We are accompanied to-day to Kwang-tung-hsien by the coolie who carried the load yesterday. He sits by staring enviously at his compatriots in the employ of the foreign magnate, who rests on a stone behind and listens to the conversation. They invite him to carry again; he refuses. Now the argument—natural and right and proper—is ensuing with warmth. Lao Chang, with the air of a hsien "gwan," sits in judgment upon them, bringing to bear his long experience of coolies and the amount of "heart-money" they receive, and has decided that the fellow should receive a tenth of a dollar and twenty cash in addition for carrying the heavier of the loads the remaining thirty li, as against ten cents offered by the men. He is now extending philosophic advice to them all, based on a knowledge of the coolie's life; the little meeting breaks up, good feeling prevails, and the loads carried on merrily. I still linger, sipping my tea. Lao Chang has grumbled because he has had to shell out seven cash, and I have already drunk ten cups (he generally uses the tea leaves afterwards for his personal use).

But wrangling about payment prevails always where Chinese congregate. In China, by high and low, lies are told without the slightest apparent compunction. One of the men in the above-mentioned dispute had an irrepressible volubility of assertion. He at once flew into a temper, adopting the style of the stage actor, proclaiming his virtue so that it might have been heard at Yuen-nan-fu. He was preserving his "face." For in this country temper is often, what it is not in the West, a test of truth. Among Westerners nothing is more insulting sometimes than a philosophic temper; but in China you must, as a first law unto yourself, protect yourself at all costs and against all comers, and it generally requires a good deal of noise. Here the bully is not the coward. In respect of prevarication, it seems to be absolutely universal; the poor copy the vice from the rich. It seems to be in the very nature of the people, and although it is hard to write, my experience convinces me that my statement is not exaggeration. I have found the Chinese—I speak of the common people, for in my travels I have not mixed much with the rich—the greatest romancer on earth. I question whether the great preponderance of the Chinese people speak six consecutive sentences without misrepresentation or exaggeration, tantamount to prevarication. Regretting that I have to write it, I give it as my opinion that the Chinese is a liar by nature. And when he is confronted with the charge of lying, the culprit seems seldom to feel any sense of guilt.

And yet in business—above the petty bargaining business—we have as the antithesis that the spoken word is his bond. I would rather trust the Chinese merely on his word than the Jap with a signed contract.

The Chinese knows that the Englishman is not a liar, and he respects him for it; and it is to be hoped that in Yuen-nan there will soon be seen the two streams of civilization which now flow in comparative harmony in other more enlightened provinces flowing here also in a single channel. These two streams—of the East and the West—represent ideas in social structure, in Government, in standards of morality, in religion and in almost every human conception as diverse as the peoples are racially apart. They cannot, it is evident, live together. The one is bound to drive out the other, or there must be such a modification of both as will allow them to live together, and be linked in sympathies which go farther than exploiting the country for initial greed. The Chinese will never lose all the traces of their inherited customs of daily life, of habits of thought and language, products which have been borne down the ages since a time contemporary with that of Solomon. No fair-minded man would wish it. And it is at once impossible.

The language, for instance. Who is there, who knows anything about it, who would wish to see the Chinese character drop out of the national life? Yet it is bound to come to some extent, and in future ages the written language will develop into pretty well the same as Latin among ourselves. Romanization, although as yet far from being accomplished, must sooner or later come into vogue, as is patent at the first glance at business. If commerce in the Interior is to grow to any great extent in succeeding generations, warranting direct correspondence with the ports at the coast and with the outside world, the Chinese hieroglyph will not continue to suffice as a satisfactory means of communication. No correspondence in Chinese will ever be written on a machine such as I am now using to type this manuscript, and this valuable adjunct of the office must surely force its way into Chinese commercial life. But only when Romanization becomes more or less universal.

This, however, by the way.

My point is, that no matter how Occidentalized he may become, the Chinese will never lose his national characteristics—not so much probably as the Japanese has done. What the youth has been at home, in his habits of thought, in his purpose and spirit, in his manifestation of action, will largely determine his after life. Chinese mental and moral history has so stamped certain ineffaceable marks on the language, and the thought and character of her people, that China will never—even were she so inclined—obliterate her Oriental features, and must always and inevitably remain Chinese. The conflict, however, is not racial, it is a question of civilization. Were it racial only, to my way of thinking we should be beaten hopelessly.

And as I write this in a Chinese inn, in the heart of Yuen-nan—the "backward province"—surrounded by the common people in their common, dirty, daily doings, a far stretch of vivid imagining is needed to see these people in any way approaching the Westernization already current in eastern provinces of this dark Empire.

This is what I wrote sitting on the top of a mountain during my tour across China. But it will be seen in other parts of this book that Western ideas and methods of progress in accord more with European standards are being adopted—and in some places with considerable energy—even in the "backward province." In travel anywhere in the world, one becomes absorbed more or less with one's own immediate surroundings, and there is a tendency to form opinions on the limitations of those surroundings. In many countries this would not lead one far astray, but in China it is different. Most of my opinion of the real Chinese is formed in Yuen-nan, and it is not to be denied that in all the other seventeen provinces, although a good many of them may be more forward in the trend of national evolution and progress, the same squalidness among the people, and every condition antagonistic to the Westerner's education so often referred to, are to be found. But China has four hundred and thirty millions of people, so that what one writes of one particular province—in the main right, perhaps—may not necessarily hold good in another province, separated by thousands of miles, where climatic conditions have been responsible for differences in general life. With its great area and its great population, it does not need the mind of a Spencer to see that it will take generations before every acre and every man will be gathered into the stream of national progress.

The European traveler in China cannot perhaps deny himself the pleasure of dwelling upon the absurdities and oddities of the life as they strike him, but there is also another side to the question. Our own civilization, presenting so many features so extremely removed from his own ancient ideas and preconceived notion of things in general, probably looks quite as ridiculous from the standpoint of the Chinese. The East and the West each have lessons to offer the other. The West is offering them to the East, and they are being absorbed. And perhaps were we to learn the lessons to which we now close our eyes and ears, but which are being put before us in the characteristics of Oriental civilization, we may in years to come, sooner than we expect, rejoice to think that we have something in return for what we have given; it may save us a rude awakening. It does not strike the average European, who has never been to China, and who knows no more about the country than the telegrams which filter through when massacres of our own compatriots occur, that Europe and America are not the only territories on this little round ball where the inhabitants have been left with a glorious heritage.

But I was speaking of my men delaying on the road to Kwang-tung-hsien, when they laughed at my impatience.

"Ih dien mien, ih dien mien," shouted one, as he held out a huge blue bowl of white wormlike strings and a couple of chopsticks. "Mien," it should be said, is something like vermicelli. A tremendous amount of it is eaten; and in Singapore, without exception, it is dried over the city's drains, hung from pole to pole after the rope-maker's fashion. Its slipperiness renders the long boneless strings most difficult of efficient adjustment, and the recollection of the entertainment my comrades received as I struggled to get a decent mouthful sticks to me still.

After that I hurried on, got off the "ta lu," and suffered a nasty experience for my foolishness. When nearing the city, inquiring whether my men had gone on inside the walls, a manure coolie, liar that he was, told me that they had. I strode on again, encountering the crowds who blocked the roadway as market progressed, who stared in a suspicious manner at the generally disreputable, tired, and dirty foreigner. Each moment I expected the escort to arrive. I could not sit down and drink tea, for I had not a single cash on my person. I could speak none of the language, and could merely push on, with ragtags at my heels, becoming more and more embarrassed by the pointing and staring public. I turned, but could see none of my men. I managed to get to the outer gate, and there sat down on the grass, with five score of gaping idiots in front of me. Seeing this vulgar-looking intruder among them, who would not answer their simplest queries, or give any reason for being there, suspicion grew worse; they naturally wanted to know what it was, and what it wanted. Some thought I might be deaf, and raved questions in my ear at the top of their voices. Even then I remained impotently dumb. Two policemen came and said something. At their invitation I followed them, and found myself later in a small police box, the street lined with people, facing an officer.

The man hailed me in speech uncivil. He was huge as the hyperborean bear, and cruel looking, and with a sort of apologetic petitionary growl I sidled off; but it was anything but comfortable, and I should not have been surprised had I found myself being led off to the yamen. After a nerve-trying half-hour, I was thankful to see the form of my men appearing at the moment when I was vehemently expressing indignation at not being understood.

# Chapter XVII

*A bumptious official. Ignominious contrasts of two travelers. Diminishing respect for foreigners in the Far East. Where the European fails. His maltreatment of Orientals. Convicts on the way to death. At Ch'u-hsiony-fu. Buffaloes and children. Exasperating repetition met in Chinese home life. Unaesthetic womanhood. Quarrymen and careless tactics. Scope for the physiologist. Interesting unit of the city's humanity. Signs of decay in the countryside. Carrying the dead to eternal rest. At Chennan-chou. Public kotowing ceremony and its aftermath. Chinese ignorance of distance.*

*A*ll-round idyllic peace did not reign at Kwang-tung-hsien, where I rested over Sunday. Contacts in social conditions gave rise inevitably to causes for conflicts.

Arriving early, my men were able to secure the best room and soon after, with much imposing pomp and show, a "gwan"[40] arrived, disgusted that he had to take a lower room. I bowed politely to him as he came in. He did not return it, however, but stood with a contemptuous grin upon his face as he took in the situation. I do not know who the person was, neither have a wish to trace his ancestry, but his bumptiousness and general misbehavior, utterly in antagonism to national etiquette, made me hate the sight of the fellow. Pride has been said to make a man a hedgehog. I do not say that this man was a hedgehog altogether, but he certainly seemed to wound everyone he touched. He had with him a great retinue, an extravagant equipage, fine clothes, and presumably a great fortune; but none of this offended me—it

---

40   "Gwan" is the Chinese for "official."

was his contempt which hurt. He seemed to splash me with mud as he passed, and was altogether badly disposed. In his every act he heaped humiliation upon me, and insulted me silently and gratuitously with unbearable disdain. Luckily, be it said to the credit of the Chinese Government, one does not often meet officials of this kind; such an atmosphere would nurture the worst feeling. It is, of course, possible that had I been traveling with many men and in a style necessary for representatives of foreign Governments, this hog might have been more polite; but the fact that I had little with me, and made a poor sort of a show, allowed him to come out in his true colors and display his unveneered feeling towards the foreigner. That he had no knowledge of the man crossing China on foot was evident. He was great and rich—that was the sentiment he breathed out to everyone—and the foreigner was humble. There is no wrong in enjoying a large superfluity, but it was not indispensable to have displayed it, to have wounded the eyes of him who lacked it, to have flaunted his magnificence at the door of my commonplace.

Had I been able to speak, I should have pointed out to this fellow that to know how to be rich is an art difficult to master, and that he had not mastered it; that as an official his first duty in exercising power was to learn that of humility; and that it is the irritating authority of such very lofty and imperious beings as himself, who say, "I am the law," that provokes insurrection. However, I was dumb, and could only return his contemptuous glance now and again.

To him I could have said, as I would here say also to every foreigner in the employ of the Chinese Government, "The only true distinction is superior worth." If foreigners in China are to have social and official rank respected, they must begin to be worthy of their rank, otherwise they help to bring it into hatred and contempt. It is a pity some native officials have to learn the same lesson.

In several years of residence in the Far East I have noticed respect for the foreigner unhappily diminishing. The root of the evil is in the mistaken idea that high station exempts him who holds it from observing the common obligations of life. It comes about—so often have I seen it in the Straits Settlements and in various parts of India—that those who demand the most homage make the least effort to merit that homage they demand. That is chiefly why respect for the foreigner in the Orient is diminishing, and I have no hesitancy in asserting that the average European in the East and Far East does not treat the Oriental with respect. He considers that the Chinese, the Malay, the Burman, the Indian is there to do the donkey work only. The newcomer generally discovers in himself an astounding personal omnipotence, and even before he can talk the language is so obsessed with it that as he grows older, his sense of it broadens and deepens. And in China—of the Chinese this is true to-day as in other spheres of the Far East—the native is there to do the donkey work, and does it contentedly and for the most part cheerfully. But he will not always be so content and so cheerful. He will not always suffer a leathering from a man whom he knows he dare not now hit back.[41] Some day he may hit back. We have seen it before, how at some moment, by some interior force making a way to the light, an explosion takes place: there is an upheaval, all sorts of grave disorders, and because some Europeans are killed the Celestial Government is called upon to pay, and to pay heavily. Indemnities are given, but the Chinese pride still feels the smart.

Pulling away up the sides of barren, sandy hills in my lonely pilgrimage, I could see wide, fertile plains sheltered in the undulating hollows of mountains, over which in arduous toil I vanished and re-appeared, how or where I could hardly calculate. Suddenly, rounding an awkward corner, a magnificent panorama broke upon the view in a rolling valley watered by many streams below, all green with growing wheat. A high spur about midway up the rolling mountain forms a capital spot for wayfarers to stop and exchange travelers' notes. A couple of convicts were here, their feet manacled and their white cotton clothing branded with the seal of death; by the side were the crude wooden cages in which they were carried by four men, with whom they mixed freely and manufactured coarse jokes. In six days bang would fall the knife, and their heads would roll at the feet of the executioners at Yuen-nan-fu.

Coming into Ch'u-hsiong-fu[42]—the stage is what the men call 90 li, but it is not more than 70—I was brought to an insignificant wayside place where the innkeeper upbraided my boy for endeavoring to allow me to pass without wetting a cup at his bonny hostelry. Had I done so, I should have avouched myself utterly indifferent to reputation as a traveler.

But I did not stay the night here. I passed on through the town to a new building, an inn, into which I peered inquiringly. A well-dressed lad came courteously forward, in his bowing and scraping seeming to say, "Good sir, we most willingly embrace the opportunity of being honored with your noble self and your retinue under our poor roof. Long since have we known

---

41    I have seen a European, with an imperfect hold of an eastern language, knock an Asiatic down because he thought the man was a fool, whereas he himself was ignorant of what was going on. The message the coolie was bringing was misunderstood by the conceited assistant, and as a result of having just this smattering of the vernacular, he ran his firm in for a loss of fifty thousand dollars.—E.J.D.

42    Ts'u-hsiong-fu, as it is pronounced locally, with a strong "ts" initial sound.

your excellent qualities; long have we wished to have you with us. We can have no reserve towards a person of your open and noble nature. The frankness of your humor delights us. Disburden yourself, O great brother, here and at once of your paraphernalia."

I stayed, and was charged more for lodging than at any other place in all my wanderings in China. My experience was different from that of Major Davies when he visited this city in 1899. He writes:—

"The people of this town are particularly conservative and exclusive. They have such an objection to strangers that no inn is allowed within the city walls, and no one from any other town is allowed to establish a shop.... When the telegraph line was first taken through here there was much commotion, and so determined was the opposition of the townspeople to this new-fangled means of communication that the telegraph office had to be put inside the colonel's yamen, the only place where it would be safe from destruction."

The proprietor of the inn in which I stayed was a man of about fifty, of goodly person and somewhat corpulent, comely presence, good humor, and privileged freedom. He had a pretty daughter. He was an exception to the ordinary father in China, in the fact that he was proud of her, as he was of his house and his faring. But in all conscience he should have been abundantly ashamed of his charges, for my boy said I was charged three times too much, and I have no cause for doubting his word either, for he was fairly honest. I once had a boy in Singapore who acted for three weeks as a "ganti"[43] whilst my own boy underwent a surgical operation, and between misreckonings, miscarriages, misdealings, mistakes and misdemeanors, had he remained with me another month I should have had to pack up lock, stock and barrel and clear.

I stayed here a day in the hope of getting my mail, but had the pleasure of seeing only the bag containing it. It was sealed, and the postmaster had no authority to break that seal.

There were no telegraph poles in the district through which I was passing; the connections were affixed to the trunks of trees. The telegraph runs right across the Ch'u-hsiong-fu plain, on entering which one crosses a rustic bridge just below a rather fine pagoda, from which an excellent view is obtained of the old city. The wall up towards the north gate, where there is another pagoda, is built over a high knoll. Inside the wall half the town is uncultivated ground. Four youngsters here were having a great time on the back of a lazy buffalo, who, turning his head swiftly to get rid of some

43    Meaning a relief hand (Malay).

irritating bee, dislodged the quartet to the ground, where they fought and cursed each other over the business.

Everything that one sees around here is particularly "Chinesey." It may be supposed that I am not the first person who has gone through town after town and found in all that he looks at, particularly the houses, certain forms identical, inevitable, exasperating by common repetition. It has been said that poetry is not in things, it is in us; but in China very little poetry comes into the homes and lives of the common millions: they are all dead dwelling-houses, even the best, bare homes without life or brightness. Among the working-classes of the West there is to be found a kind of ministering beauty which makes its way everywhere, springing from the hands of woman. When the dwelling is cramped, the purse limited, the table modest, a woman who has the gift finds a way to make order and puts care and art into everything in her house, puts a soul into the inanimate, and gives those subtle and winsome touches to which the most brutish of human beings is sensible. But in China woman does nothing of this. Her life is unaesthetic to the last degree. No happy improvisations or touches of the stamp of personality enter her home; one cannot trace the touches of witchery in the tying of a ribbon. Everywhere you find the same class of furniture and garniture, the same shape of table, of stool, of form, of bed, of cooking utensils, of picture, of everything; and all the details of her housekeeping are so apathetically uninteresting. The Chinese woman has no charming art, rather is it a common, horrid, daily grind. She is not, as the woman should be, the interpreter in her home of her own grace, and she differs from her Western sister in that it is impossible for her to express in her dress also the little personalities of character—all is eternally the same. But I know so very little of ladies' clothing, and therefore cease.

Quarrying was going on high up among the hills as I left the city. Men were out of sight, but their hammering was heard distinctly. As each boulder was freed these wielders of the hammer yelled to passers-by to look out for their heads, gave the stone a push to start it rolling, and if it rolled upon you it was your own fault and not theirs—you should have seen to it that you were somewhere else at the time. If it blocked the pathway, another had to be made by those who made the traffic. Directly under the quarry I was accosted by a beggar. "Old foreign man! Old foreign man!" he yelled. Stones were falling fast; it is possible that he does not sit there now.

Physiognomists do not swarm in China. There is grand scope for someone. There would be ample material for research for the student in the soldiers alone who would be sent to guard him from place to place. He would not need to go farther afield; for he would be given fat men and lean men, brave men and cowards, some blessed with brains and some not one whit brainy, civil and surly, stubby and lanky, but rogues and liars all. Travelers are always interested in their chairmen; oftentimes my interest in them was greater than theirs in me, until the time came for us to part. Then the "Ch'a ts'ien,"[44] always in view from the outset of their duty, brought us in a manner nearer to each other.

As I came out of the inn at Ch'u-hsiong-fu somewhat hurriedly, for my men lingered long over the rice, I stumbled over the yamen fellow who crouched by the doorside. He laughed heartily. Had I fallen on him his tune might have been changed; but no matter. This unit of the city humanity was not bewilderingly beautiful. He was profoundly ill-proportioned, very goitrous, and ravages of small-pox had bequeathed to him a wonderful facial ugliness. He had, however, be it written to his honor, learnt that life was no theory. One could see that at a glance as he walked along at the head of the procession, with a stride like an ox, manfully shouldering his absurd weapon of office, which in the place of a gun was an immense carved wooden mace, not unlike a leg of the old-time wooden bedstead of antiquity. His ugliness was embittered somewhat by sunken, toothless jaws and an enigmatical stare from a cross-eye; he was also knock-kneed, and as an erstwhile gunpowder worker, had lost two fingers and a large part of one ear. But he had learnt the secret of simple duty: he had no dreams, no ambition embracing vast limits, did not appear to wish to achieve great things, unless it were that in his fidelity to small things he laid the base of great achievements. He waited upon me hand and foot; he burned with ardor for my personal comfort and well-being; he did not complicate life by being engrossed in anything which to him was of no concern—his only concern was the foreigner, and towards me he carried out his duty faithfully and to the letter. I would wager that that man, ugly of face and form, but most kindly disposed to one who could communicate little but dumb approval, was an excellent citizen, an excellent father, an excellent son.

So very different was another traveler who unceremoniously forced himself upon me with the inevitable "Ching fan, ching fan," although he had no food to offer. He commenced with a far-fetched eulogium of my ambling palfrey Rusty, who limped along leisurely behind me. So far as he could remember, poor ignorant ass, he had never seen a pony like it in his extensive travels—probably from Yuen-nan-fu to Tali-fu, if so far; but as a matter of fact, Rusty had wrenched his right fore fetlock between a gully in the rocks the day before and was now going lame. Dressed fairly respectably in the universal blue, my unsought companion was of middle stature,

---

44    Literally, "tea money."

strongly built, but so clumsily as to border almost on deformity, and to give all his movements the ungainly awkwardness of a left-handed, left-legged man. He walked with a limp, was suffering (like myself) with sore feet; if not that, it was something incomparably worse. Not for a moment throughout the day did he leave my side, the only good point about him being that when we drank—tea, of course—he vainly begged to be allowed to pay. In that he was the shadow of some of my friends of younger days.

But of men enough.

From Ch'u-hsiong-fu on to Tali-fu the whole country bears lamentable signs of gradual ruin and decay, a falling off from better times. The former city is probably the most important point on the route, and is mentioned as a likely point for the proposed Yuen-nan Railway.

The country has never recovered from the terrible effects of the great Mohammendan Rebellion of 1857. Foundations of once imposing buildings still stand out in fearful significance, and ruins everywhere over the barren country tell plain tales all too sad of the good days gone. Temples, originally fit for the largest city in the Empire, with elaborate wood and stone carving and costly, weird images sculptured in stone, with particularly fine specimens of those blood-curdling Buddhistic hells and their presiding monsters, with miniature ornamental pagodas and intricate archways, are all now unused; and when the people need material for any new building (seldom erected now in this district), the temple grounds are robbed still more. In the days of its prosperity Yuen-nan must have been a fair land indeed, bright, smiling, seductive; now it is the exact antithesis, and the people live sad, flat, colorless existences.

For three days my caravan was preceded by twelve men, headed by a sort of gaffer with a gong, carrying a corpse in a massive black coffin, elaborate in red and blue silk drapings and with the inevitable white cock presiding, one leg tied with a couple of strands of straw to the cover, on which it crowed lustily. Their mission was an honorable one, carrying the honored dead to its last bed of rest eternal; for this dead man had secured the fulfillment of the highest in human destiny—to have his bones buried near the scene of his youth, near his home. This is a simple custom the Chinese cherish and reverence, of highest honor to the dead and of no mean value to the living. To the dead, because buried near the home of his fathers he would not be subject to those delusive temptations in the future state of that confused and complex life; to the living, because it gave work to a dozen men for several days, and enabled them to have a good time at the expense of the departed. A perpetual and excruciatingly unmusical chant, in keeping with the occasion's sadness, rent the mountain air, interrupted only when the bearers lowered the coffin and left the remains of the great dead on a pair of trestles in the roadway, whilst they drank to his happiness above and smoked tobacco which the relatives had given them. Once this heaper-up of Chinese merit[45] was dumped unceremoniously on the turf while the headman entered into a blackguarding contest with one of the fellows who was alleged to be constantly out of step with his brethren, because he was a much smaller man. The gaffer gave him a bit of a drubbing for his insolence.

Rain came on at Chennan-chou, a small town of about three hundred houses, where I sought shelter in the last house of the street. The householder, a shrivelled, goitrous humpback, received me kindly, removed his pot of cabbage from the fire to brew tea for his uninvited guest, and showed great gratitude (to such an extent that he nearly fell into the fire as he moved to push the children forward towards me) when I gave a few cash to three kiddies, who gaped open-mouthed at the apparition thus found unexpectedly before their parent's hearth. More came in, my beneficent attention being modestly directed towards them; others followed, and still more, and more, whilst the man, removing from his mouth his four-foot pipe, and wiping the mouthpiece with his soiled coat-sleeve before offering it to me to smoke, smiled as I distributed more cash.

"They are all mine," he said cutely.

Poor fellow! There must have been a dozen nippers there, and I sighed at the thought of what some men come to as the last of half a string of cash slipped through my fingers.[46]

45 "Heaping up merit" is one of the elementary practices of Chinese religious life.

46 Chennan-chou, which stands at a height of 6,500 feet, has been visited again since by myself. My caravan consisted on this occasion of two ponies (one I was riding), two coolies, a servant, and myself. As we got to the archway in the middle of the street leading to the busy part of the town, my animal nearly landed me into the gutter, and the other horse ran into a neighboring house, both frightened by crackers which were being fired around a man who was bumping his head on the ground in front of an ancestral tablet, brought into the street for the purpose. A horrid din made the air turbulent. I sought refuge in the nearest house, tying my ponies up to the windows, and was most hospitably received as a returned prodigal by a well-disposed old man and his courtly helpmate. The genuineness of the hospitality of the Chinese is as strong as their unfriendliness can be when they are disposed to show a hostile spirit to foreigners. Just as I had laid up for dinner the din stopped, we breathed gunpowder smoke instead of air, everyone from the head-bumping ceremony came around me, and there lingered in silent admiration. My boy came and whispered, quite aloud enough for all to hear, that in that part of the town cooked rice could not be bought, and that I was going to be left to look after the horses and the loads whilst the men went away to feed. He advised the assembled crowd that if they valued sound physique they had better keep their hands off my gear and depart. My friendly host shut the doors and windows, with the exception of that through which I watched our impedimenta, and at once commenced good-natured inquiry into my past, and concerning vicissitudes of life in general. Luckily, I was able to give the old man good reason for

Outside the town, on the lee side of a triumphal arch—erected, maybe, to the memory of one of the virtuous widows of the district—I untied my pukai and donned my mackintosh and wind-cap. A gale blew, my fingers ached with the cold, breathing was rendered difficult by the rarefied air. As we were thus engaged and discussing the prospects of the storm, yelling from under a gigantic straw hat, a fellow said—

"Suan liao" ("not worth reckoning") "only five more li to Sha-chiao-kai."

We had thirty li to do. Such is the idea of distance in Yuen-nan.[47]

The storm did not come, however, and my men ever after reminded me to keep out my wind-cap and my mackintosh, partly to lighten their loads, of course, and partly on account of the good omen it seemed to them to be.

---

congratulating me upon my ancestral line, my own great age, the number of my wives and offshoots—mostly "little puppies"—and as each curious caller dropped in to sip tea, so did one after another of the patriarchal dignitaries who were responsible for the human product then entertaining the crowd come vividly before the imagination of the company, and they were graced with every token of age and honor. (Chinese speak of sons as "little puppies.")

47    In crossing a river here I slipped, and from ray pocket there rolled a box of photographic films, and in reaching over to re-capture it, I let my loaded camera fall into the water. I was disappointed, as most of my best pictures were thus (as I imagined) spoilt. But when I developed at Bhamo, I found not a single film damaged by water, and every picture was a success from both the roll in the tin and the roll in the camera. It is a tribute to the Eastman-Kodak Company Ltd. that their non-curling films will stand being dipped into rivers and remain unaffected. The films in question should have been developed six months prior to the date of my exposure.—E.J.D.

# CHAPTER XVIII

*Stampede of frightened women. To the Eagle Nest. An acrobatic performance,
and some retaliation at the author's expense. Over the mountains to Pu-peng
A magnificent storm, and a description. In a "rock of ages." Hardiness of my
comrades. Early morning routine and some impressions. Unspeakable filth of
the Chinese. Lolo people of the district. Physique of the women. Aspirations
towards Chinese customs. Skilless building. Mythological, anthropological,
craniological and antediluvian disquisitions. At Yuen-nan-i. Flat country.
Thriftless humanity. To Hungay. A day of days. Traveler in bitter cold unable to procure food. Fright in middle night. A timely rescue. Murder of a
bullock on my doorstep. Callous disposition of fellow-travelers. Leaving the
capital of an old-time kingdom. Bad roads and good men. National virtue
of unfailing patience. Human consumption of diseased animals. Minchia
at Hungay. Major Davies and the Minchia. Author's differences of opinion.
Increasing popularity of the small foot.*

*B*ut the storm came the next day, as we were on our way to Pu-peng,
during the ninety li when we passed the highest point on this journey. By name The Eagle Nest Barrier (Ting-wu-kwan), this elevated
pass, 8,600 feet above the level, reached after a gradual ascent between two
mountain ranges, was surmounted after a couple of hours' steep climbing,
where rain and snow had made the paths irritatingly slippery and the task
most laborious. Although the condition of the road was enough to take all
the wind out of one's sails, the sublimity of the scenery of the dense woods
which clothed the mountains, exquisitely pretty ravines, tumbling waterfalls, running rivulets and sparkling brooks, with little patches of snow hidden away in the maze of greens of every hue, all rendered it a climb less
tiring than the narrow pathways over which we were then to travel. Half-

way up we met a string of ponies, and I underwent a few nervous moments until they had passed in the twenty-inch road—a slight tilt, a slip, a splutter, probably a yell, and I should have dropped 500 feet without a bump.

As we went along together, just before reaching this hill, we saw women carrying bags of rice. They saw us, too. One passed me safely, but with fear. The others carelessly dropping their burdens, scampered off, afraid of their lives; and when one of my soldiers (whose sense of humor was on a par with my own when as a boy I used to stick butterscotch drops on the bald head of my Sunday School teacher, and bend pins for small boys to sit on and rise from) shouted to them, they dived straight as a die over the hedge into a submerged rice-field, and made a sorry spectacle with their "lily" feet and pale blue trousers, covered with the thin mud. In struggling to get away, one of them, the silly creature, went sprawling on all fours in the slime, and with only the imperfect footing possible to her with her little stumps, she would have been submerged, had not the man who had frightened her, at my bidding, gone to drag her out. As it was, they looked anything but beautiful with their wet and muddy garments clinging tightly to their bodies, and betraying every curve of their not unbeautiful figures. One of the women, a comely damsel of some twenty summers, did not jump into the field, but lay flat on the ground behind some bushes, thereby hoping to get out of sight, and now came forward with amorous glances. We, however, sent them on their way, and I will lay my life that they will not "scoot" at the sight of the next foreigner.

And now we are at the "Nest." Many travelers have made remarks upon this place, where I was waited upon by a shrivelled, shambling specimen of manhood, whose wife—in contrast to her kind in China—seemed to rule house and home, bed and board. Whilst we were there, a Chinese, bound on the downward journey, endeavored to mount his mule at the very moment the animal was reaching out for a blade of straw. As he swung his leg across the mule took another step forward, and the rider fell bodily with an enormous bump into the lap of one of my coolies, upsetting him and his bowl of tea over his trousers and my own. I could not suppress hearty approval of this acrobatic incident.

But the end was not yet.

I sat on one end of one of those narrow forms, and this same coolie sat on the other. He rose up suddenly, reached over for the common salt-pot, and I came off—with the multitude of alfresco diners laughing at this smart retaliation until their chock-full mouths emitted the grains of rice they chewed.

After that I cleared off. Descending through a fertile valley, from the bottom there loomed upwards higher mountains, looking black and dismal, with clouds black and dismal keeping them company. We had now to cross the undulating ground still separating us from Pu-peng. The early portion of the ground was something like Clifton Downs, something like Dartmoor. The country was poor, and the people barely put themselves out to boil water for chance travelers.

The storm broke suddenly. From the shelter of a hollowed rock I watched it all.

Over the submerged plain and the bare hills the blackness was as of night. Red earth without the sun looked brown, brown looked black, and the trees, swaying helplessly before the raging fury of the gale, seemed struck by death. Lightning continued its electrical vividity of fork-like greenish white among the heavy clouds, drooping threateningly from the hill-tops to the darkened valleys below, laden still with their waiting, unshed deluge. Through a narrow incision in the cruel clouds the sun peeped out with a nervous timidity, and a tiny patch over yonder, in a flash illuminated with gold and purple, across which the lightning danced in heavenly rivalry, displayed the magic touch of the Artist of the skies. Then came a rainbow of sweetest multi-color, of a splendor glorious and exquisite, delicate as the breath from paradise, stretching its majestic archbow athwart the waning gloom from range to range. As one drank in the glimpses of that dark corner in this peculiar fairyland, a mighty peal of magnificent, stentorian clashing broke finally upon me, and heaven's electricity again flitted fearfully over the earth, aslant, upwards, downwards again, upwards again, disappearing over the unmoved hills like a thousand tortured souls fleeing from Dante's Hades. And here I sit on, in that veritable "rock of ages" cleft for me, glad that no human touch save that of my own mean clay, that no human voice came between me and the voice of that Infinite beyond. I seemed to have been standing on the verge of another world, another great unknown. The heavens raged and the thunders thereof roared, and the wild wind hissed and moaned and wailed the hopeless wail of a lonely, tormented soul. The cold was intense, and through it all I sat drenched to the skin.

On the bleak mountain thus I was the pitifulest atom of loneliest humanity, yet felt no loneliness. The face of the earth frowned in angry fury, the awfulness of the raging elements dwarfed all else to utter annihilation. But even at such a time, coming all too seldom in the lives of most of us, when standing in some remote spot which still tells forth the story of the world's youth, one's inmost nature thrills with a sense of unison with it all beyond human expression. All was so grand, inspiring one with an awe beyond one's comprehension, a peculiar, dread of one's own earthly insignificance. These pictures, graven in one's memory with the strong pencil of our common mother, are indelible, yet quite beyond expression. As in our own souls we cannot frame in words our deepest life emotions, so as we penetrate into the depths of that kindly common mother of us all we find human words the same utterly futile channel of expression. To have our souls tuned to this silent eloquence of Nature, to catch the sweetness of those wind-swept, heaven-directed mountains, to understand the unspoken messages of those rushing rivers and those gigantic gorges, to feel the heart-beat of Nature and her beauty in perfect harmony with all that is best within us, we must be silent, undisturbed, preferably alone. This is not flowery sentiment—it is what every true lover of old and lovely Nature would feel in Western China, yet still unspoiled by the taint of man's absorbing stream of civilization. And in the stress of modern life, and the progress of man's monopolization of the earth on which he lives, it is beautiful to some of us, of whom it may be said the highest state of inward happiness comes from solitary meditation in unperturbed loneliness under the broad expanse of heaven, to know that there are still some spots of isolation where human foot has never turned the clay, and where, out of sight and sound of fellow mortals, we may even for a time shake off the violating, unnatural fetters of a harassing Western life.

Soon it seemed as if a silken cord had suddenly been severed, and I had been dragged from a world of sweet infinitude down to a sphere mundane and everyday, to something I had known before.... "....Or what is Nature? Ha! why do I not name thee God? Art thou not the 'Living Garment of God'? O Heaven, is it in very deed, He, then, that ever speaks through thee; that lives and loves in thee, that lives and loves in me?"[48]

I heard the crack of the bamboo and the patter of feet in the sodden, slippery pathway, and I knew my men were come. Crawling out from my rock, I descended again to common things, having to listen to the disgusting talk of my Chinese followers, though a very slender vocabulary saved me from losing entirely the memory of that great picture then passing away. The sun shone through the clouds, which had given place again to blue, the pervading blackness of a few moments before had disappeared, and with the sinking sun we descended thoughtfully to the town. The hill is solid sandstone, and the uneven ruts made by the daily procession of ponies were transformed into a network of tiny streams.

That my comrades were drenched to the skin gave them no thought; they turned to immediately, while I dived hurriedly to the bottom of my box and

---

48    Carlyle, Sartor Resartus.

gulped down quinine. They sat around and drank hot water, holding forth with eloquence beyond their wont on the general advantages, naturally and supernaturally, of their native city of Tong-ch'uan-fu. And well they might, for I know no prettier spot in the whole of Western China.

Fifty men—coolies who were carrying general merchandise in all directions, and who had taken shelter in the large inn I stayed at—rose with me the next morning. As I ate my morning meal, spluttering the rice over the floor as I tried vainly to control my chopsticks with frost-nipped fingers, they went through the filthy round of early morning routine. Squatting about with their dirty face-rags, and a half-pint of greasy water in their brass receptacle shaped like the soup-plate of civilization, and leaving upon their necks the traces of their swills, they wiped the dirt into their hair, and considered they had washed themselves. Men would emerge from their rooms, fully dressed, with the dishclout in one hand and the hand-basin in the other—on the way to their morning tub. Oh, the filth, the unspeakable filth of these people! Would that the Chinese would emulate the cleanliness of the Japs, though even that I would question. In several years in the Orient I have not yet come across the cleanliness in any race of people to be compared with that cleanliness which in England is next to godliness.

The people of Pu-peng were pleased to see me. They hurried about obligingly to get food for man and beast, and the womankind, poor but light-hearted, cracked suggestive jokes with my men with the utmost freedom.

In this town there are many Lolo—it might be said that the entire population is of Lolo origin, although had I suggested to any particular inhabitant that this was a fact he would probably have taken keen offense, and things might have gone badly with me. With the men it is most difficult to tell—there is little difference between the *Han ren* and the tribesman. But the difference is often most marked in respect to the women. The Chinese woman has a considerably fairer skin than the female of Lolo descent, and her customs and manners, apart from the distinct colloquial accent, are quite evident as pretty sure proof of distinction of race. After the Lolo have mingled with the Chinese for a few years, however, it is quite difficult to differentiate between them, as most of the Lolo women now speak Chinese (in this town I did not hear any language foreign to the Chinese language), and a good many of the men are sufficiently educated to read the Chinese character even if they do not write it. The forward racial condition of the Lolo people in this district is far greater than that of the people of the same tribe to the west of Tali-fu, and in latitudes where their language and customs of life and dress are more or less maintained. The women are generally of better physique than the Chinese, principally on account of the fact that their work is almost exclusively outdoor; but as they begin to copy the Chinese, and live a more sedentary life, this fine physique will probably gradually disappear. A good many already bind their feet.

When I came out in the early morning the thermometer was twenty degrees below zero, and my nose was red and without feeling. *Feng-mao*[49] and great coat were required, but I was totally oblivious of the hour's stiff climbing awaiting me immediately outside the town, to reach the highest point in which bathed me in perspiration as if I had played three sets of tennis in the tropics.

Mountains were wild and barren, with nothing in them to enable one to forget in natural beauty the fatigues of a toilsome ascent. Villages came now and again in sight, stretched out at the extremity of the plain before my eyes, with their white gables, red walls, and black tiled roofs, but during the day we passed through two only. The first was a little place where decay would have been absolute had it not been for the likin[50] flag, which enables "squeezes" to be extorted ruthlessly from the muleteer and conveyed to the pockets of the prospering customs agent. It boasted only ten or twelve tumbling lean-to tenements, where my sympathy went out to the half-dozen physical wrecks of men who came slowly and stared long, and wondered at the commonest article of my meager impedimenta. They seemed poorer and lower down the human scale than any I had yet seen. On one of the ragged garments worn by a man of about twenty-five I counted no less than thirty-four patches of different shapes, sizes and materials, hieroglyphically and skillessly thrown together to hide his sore-strewn back; but still his brown unwashed flesh was visible in many places.

Looking upon them, one did not like to think that these beings were men, men with passions like to one's own, for all the interests, real and imaginary, all the topics which should expand the mind of man, and connect him in sympathy with general existence, were crushed in the absorbing considerations of how rice was to be procured for their families of diseaseful brats. They had no brains, these men; or if Heaven had thus o'erblessed them, they did not exercise them in their industry—their coarse, rough hands alone gained food for the day's feeding. And these mud-roofed, mud-sided dwellings—these were their homes, to me worse homes than none at all. In their architecture not even a single idea could be traced—the Chinese here had proceeded as if by merest accident. All I could think as

49    Wind-cap, a long Chinese wadded hat which reaches over one's head and down over the shoulders, tied under the chin with ribbons.—E.J.D.

50    Likin, as everyone knows, is custom duty. All along the main roads of China one meets likin stations, distinguished by the flag at the entrance.—E.J.D.

I returned their wondering glances was that their world must be very, very old. But I have no time or space to talk of them here. To throw more than a cursory glance at them Would lead me into interminable disquisitions of a mythological, anthropological, craniological, and antediluvian nature for which one would not find universal approval among his readers. To those who would study such questions I say, "Fall to!" There is enough scope for a lifetime to bring into light the primeval element so strangely woven into the lives of these people.

At Yuen-nan-i bunting and weird street decoration made the place hideous in my eyes. The crowded town was making considerable ado about some expected official. I saw none, more than a courteous youth—to whom, of course, I was quite unknown and deaf and dumb—who graciously shifted goods and chattels from the inn's best room to hand it over to me for my occupation. With due tact and some excitability, I protested vigorously against his coming out. He insisted. Smiling upon him with grave benignity, I said that I would take a smaller room, and gave orders to that effect to my man, adding that my whole sense of right and justice towards fellow-travelers revolted against such self-sacrifice on his part. He still insisted. Smiling again, this time the timid smile of the commoner looking up into the face of the great, I allowed myself reluctantly to be pushed bodily into the best apartment.

This was my intention from the first. Although not too familiar with it, I allowed the Chinese to imagine that I was well grounded in the absurdities of his national etiquette; whilst he, observing, too, the outrageous routine of common politeness, probably went away swearing that he had been turned out. He had cut off his nose to spite his face.

I cannot truthfully deny, however, that the fellow was very kind, but he would persist in the belief that it was an impossibility for me to tell the truth. Later, pointing at me and eyeing me up and down as I shaved in the twilight, he sneered, "Engleeshman! Engleeshman!" and scooting with an armful of clothing, small pots of eatables, official documents and other sundries, told me point-blank that he did not believe that such a noble person could not speak such a contemptible language as Chinese.

Seeing no official, then, I presumed I was their man. Whilst I fed slowly on my rice and cabbage in a small earth-floor room, with my nose as near as convenient to my oil lamp to get a little warmth, the discomfort of Chinese life was forced upon me, and I imagined I was having a good time. I was the best off in the inn by far; the others must have been colder, certainly had worse food to eat, and yet to me it was all the height of utmost cheerlessness.

From a hamlet opposite the town, where I sat down by the fire exhausted in an old woman's shaky dwelling, and fed on aged sardines and hot rice (atrocious mixture), there is a plain extending for twenty li to Yuen-nan-i—flat as country in the Fen district. The road was good (in wet weather, however, it must be terrible), and I would drive a motor-car across, were it not for the 15-in. ruts which disfigure the surface. And I know a man who would do this even, despite the ruts: he takes a delight in running over dogs and small boys, damaging rickshaws, bumping into bullock-carts, and so on—he would have done it with liveliest freedom.

But what poverty there was! What women! What Children! With barely an exception, the women had faces ground by want and bare necessity, in which every cheerful and sympathetic lineament had been effaced by life-long slavery and misery. In the bitter cold they, women and children, crouched round a scanty fir-wood firing, not enough even to keep alive their natural heat. One long pitiful sight of thriftless poverty.

To Hungay was a fearful day. Little to eat could I procure, and the cold gave me a lusty ox's appetite. To me a bellyful came as a windfall.

At last we sat down by the roadside at one small table, hearing the test of age, rickety and worm-eaten. We gathered like hogs at their troughs, with the household hog scratching at our feet. I grew impatient and querulous over constant culinary disappointment. I longed not for the heaped-up board of the pampered and luxurious, I wanted food. Indigent man was I, whose dietetical elegancies had been forgotten, a man with ravenous desires seeking sustenance, not relishes; the means of life, not the means of pampering the carcass; I wanted food.

And here I had it. The hungry were to be fed.

It was a foul orgy, a gruesome spectacle, a horrible picture of the gluttony of famished men. This meal conjured up visions of the "most unlovely of the functions." We fed on *mien*, that long, greasy, grimy, slippery, slimy string of boneless white—I see it now! And the half-done tin of sardines set before me, too, the broken stools in the thatch-worn shed, the dismantled hearth, the muddy earthen floor, the haggard, hungry villains—I see them all again.[51]

---

51    I passed this spot a month or so afterwards, and am convinced that at the time I wrote the above there must have been something radically wrong with my liver. Had it been in Killarney in summer, nothing could have been more entrancing than the two lakes midway between Yuen-nan-i and Hungay. Patches of light green vegetation, interspersed with brown-red houses, skirting the lake-shore in pleasant contrast to the green of the water, which, bathed in soft sunshine, lapped their walls in endless restlessness. Of that delicate blue which is indescribably beautiful, the morning sky looked down tranquilly upon the undulating hills of grey and brown, which seemed to hem in and guard a very fairyland. Geomancers of the place did not go wrong when they suggested the overlook-

ing hill-sides as suitable resting-places for the departed. All was ancient and primitive, yet simple and glorious, and as one of my followers called my attention to the telegraph wires, I was struck by the fact that this alone stood as the solitary element of what we in the West call civilization. Yet nothing bore traces of gross uncivilization; the people, hard workers albeit, were happy and quite content, with their slow-moving caravan, which we would, if we could, soon displace for the railway engine. Ploughmen with their buffaloes and their biblical ploughshare, raked over the red ground; women, with babies on their backs, picked produce already ripe; children played roundabout, and those old enough helped their fathers in the fields; coolies bustled along with exchanges of merchandise with neighboring villages, quite content if but a couple of meals each day were earned and eaten; the official, the ruler of these peaceful people, passed with old-time pomp—not in a modern carriage, not in a modern saloon, but in the same way as did his ancestors back in the dim ages, in a sedan-chair carried by men. There was plenty of everything—enough for all—but all had to contribute to its getting. There was no greed, their few wants were easily satisfied, and here, as everywhere in my journeyings, I have noticed it to be the case among the common people, there was no desire to get rich and absorb wealth. They wanted to live, to learn to labor as little as the growth of food supplies demanded, to become fathers and mothers, and, to their minds, to get the most out of life. And who will contradict it? They do not see with the eyes of the West; we do not, we cannot, see with their eyes. But surely the living of this simple life, the same as it was in the beginning, has a good deal in it; it is not uncivilization, not barbarism, and the fair-minded traveler in China can come to but one opinion, even in the midst of all the conflicting emotions which result from his own upbringing, that we could, if we would, learn many a good lesson from the old-time life of the Celestial in his own country.

Yet these are the very people who may jostle us harshly later on in the racial struggle.

I am not suggesting that when the Chinese adopts the cult of the West, and comes into general contact with it—and I believe that I am right in saying that this is the desire, generally speaking, of the whole of the enlightened classes—he continues with his few wants. As a matter of fact, he does not. He is as extravagant, and perhaps more so, than the most of us. I have seen Straits Chinese waste at the gaming tables in their gorgeous clubs as much in one night as some European residents handle in one year, and he is quick to get his motor-car, his horses and carriages, and endless other ornaments of wealth. So that if progress in the course of the evolution of nations means that the Chinese too will demand all that the European now demands, and will cease to find satisfaction in the existing conditions of his life in the new goal towards which he is moving, and if he, in course of time, should increase the cost of living per head to equal that of the Westerner, then he will lose a good deal of the advantage he now undoubtedly has in the struggle for racial supremacy. But if, gradually taking advantage of all in religion, in science, in literature, in art, in modern naval and military equipment and skill, and all that has made nations great and made for real progress in the West, he were also to continue his present hardy frugality in living—which is not a tenth as costly in proportion to that of the Occident—then his advantage in entering upon the conflict among the nations for ultimate supremacy would be undoubted, immeasurable.

The question is, will he?

If he will, then the Occident has much to fear. China, going ahead throughout the Empire as she is at the present moment in certain parts, will in course of time (as is only fair and natural to expect) have an army greater in numbers than is possible to any European power, and her food-bill will be two-thirds lower per head per fighting man. Subsequently, granting that China fulfils our fears, and becomes as great a fighting power as military experts declare she will, even in our generation, by virtue of her numbers alone, apart from phenomenal powers of endurance, which as every writer on China and her people is agreed,

It should, however, be said that I went away from the main road over a range of hills where nobody lives. Had I kept to the "ta lu" food would have been quite easy to get.

To Hungay was given the honor of entertaining me over the Sunday, a pleasant rest after a week of arduous and exhausting walking. I arrived late at night, and the old town's rough streets were bathed in a silver shower of moonbeams, the air was cold and frosty, little groups of the curious came to the doors of their dwellings, laughing sarcastically, despite their own poverty, at the distinguished traveler thus coming upon them.

In marked contrast to this outside animation were the happenings at the inn which gave me shelter. Business was bad. Three undistinguished travelers—coolies with loads—and myself and men made up the meager total of paying guests. This was the reason why it was chosen for me, for peace and quiet. Quiet had been forced upon the household, so I was told, by the death by fits of a haughty and resolute lady; and now that the night had fallen and we had all had our rice, the deep hush—or its equivalent in Cathay, at all events—seemed likely to be unbroken until a new day should dawn. My room here had a verandah overlooking a back court, and here I sat at midnight, unseen by anyone, looking up to the changeless stars in an unpitying sky; and as I stood thus there blew from the gates of night and across the mountains a wind that made me shiver less with physical cold than with a sense of loneliness and captivity. For on to my verandah came four soldiers, and it seemed as if the hour of death drew nigh; and as I looked again, first upon the cloudswept sky and upon the cold and steely glitter of the stars, and then again at the soldiers with their guns, I turned giddy, shuddering at the darkness and the loneliness, and with a nameless fear lying at the center of life like a lurking shadow of an unknown, unseen foe.

---

is excelled by no other race on earth, she would be able to dictate terms to the West. But, again, will she? Will the people continue to live as they are living?

I personally believe that the Chinese will not. I believe that as the nation progresses, more in accordance with lines of progress laid down by the West, so will her wants increase, and consequent expenses of life become greater. The Yuen-nanese even are beginning to acknowledge that they have no ordinary comforts. In other parts of the empire the people are already beginning to learn what comfort, sanitation, lighting, and general organization means—in the home, in the city, in the country, in the nation.

And they are learning too that it all costs money, and means, perhaps, a higher state of social life. For this they do not mind the money. They are not going half-way—they are going to be whole-hoggers. And when in the future, near or far, we shall find them, as is almost inevitable, able to compete in everything with other nations, we shall find that they have not been successful in learning the source of strength without having absorbed also some of the weaknesses; they will not escape the vices, even if they learn some of the virtues of the West.—E.J.D.

They addressed me, but I cared not what they said. I pretended I could not speak Chinese, watched the quartet form a circle, and talk slowly and low, and it did not need the mind of a prophet to see that they were discussing how best they could capture me. Were they going to kill me? My boy and the other friends I had in the place were sleeping blissfully, ignorant that their master was in such trying straits. I was asked my name, and the inquirers, not over civil, were told. They again asked me for something, I knew not what, probably for my passport. I had none, and cursed my luck that I had forgotten to pack it when I had left Tong-ch'uan-fu.

To me it was quite evident that they were deciding my destiny, or so it seemed in the stillness of the night. Looking upwards, I wondered whether I was soon to learn the secret of the stars and sky, and those men seemed to watch the secret workings of my soul. Outside the wind made moan continuously.

Suddenly my door opened noisily, a light was flashed upon us, and I saw the bulky form of the landlord. Then all was well. Soon one of my men appeared, and explained that the soldiers were on their way to meet an official who was coming from Tali-fu, that their instructions were that they would meet him at Hungay. They took me for the "gwan."

So my end was not yet. But now, months afterwards, when I stand and listen to the wind at midnight, there seems borne to me in every sob and wail a memory of that hateful night and the four soldiers with their guns.

It seemed not long afterwards that I was awakened by noises on the doorstep. Looking out, I found a bullock, its four feet tied together with a straw rope, writhing in its last agonies; the butcher, in his hand a cruel 24-inch bladed knife still red with blood, smiling the smile of ironic torture as he looked down upon his struggling victim. He straightway skinned the animal and cut up the carcass immediately in front of my door, where Lao Chang waited to get the best cut for my dinner. My three fellow-lodgers squatted alongside, going through their apologetic ablutions as if naught were happening. Their dirty face-rags were wrung and rewrung; they got to work with that universal tooth-brush (the forefinger!), and that the dead body of a bullock was being dissected two feet from the table at which they ate their steaming rice was a detail of not the slightest consequence in the world.

Hungay is an old-time capital of one of the original kingdoms, destroyed in the year A.D. 749. The road leading out towards Chao-chow was built some considerable time before that year, and has never been subject to any repairs whatever (for this fact I have drawn upon my imagination, but should be very much surprised to know that I am far out in my reckoning).

Villagers have appropriated the public slabs and small boulders which comprised the wretched thoroughfare; reminiscent puddles tell you the tale, and the badness of the road renders it necessary for the traveler to be out of bed a little earlier than usual to face the ordeal. The road to-day has been practically as bad as walking along the sides of the Yangtze. But as I studied the patience and physical vitality of my three men, laughing and joking with the light-heartedness of children, with nearly seventy catties dangling from their shoulder-pole, without a word of murmuring, I felt a little ashamed of myself that I, whose duty it was merely to *walk*, should have made such a fuss. These men were prepared to work a very long time for very little reward, as no matter how small the rewards for the terribly exhausting labor, it were better than none at all,—so they philosophized.

That quiet persistence and unfailing patience form a national virtue among the Chinese—the capacity to wait without complaint and to bear all with silent endurance. This virtue is seen more clearly in great national disasters which occasionally befall the country. The terrible famine of 1877-8 was the cause of the death of millions of people, and left scores of millions without house, food or clothing; they were driven forth as wanderers on the face of the earth without home, without hope. The Government does nothing whatever in these cases. The people who wish to live must find the means to live, and what impressed me all through my wanderings was the absolute science to which poverty is reduced. In such calamities the Chinese, of all men on the earth's surface, will battle along if there is any chance at all. If he is blessed, he once more becomes a farmer; but if not, he accepts the position as inevitable and irremediable. The Chinese race has the finest power in the world to withstand with fortitude the ills of life and the miseries which follow inability to procure the wherewithal to live. Their nerves are somehow different from our Western nerves.

In China nothing is wasted, not only in food, but in everything affecting the common life.

That a beast dies of disease is of no concern. It is eaten all the same from head to hoof, from skin to entrail, and the remarkable fact is that they do not seem to suffer from it, either. At Kiang-ti (mentioned in a previous chapter) I saw a horse being pushed down the hillside to the river. It was not yet dead, but was dying, so far as I could see, of inflammation of the bowels. Its body was cut up, and there were several people waiting to buy it at forty cash the catty.

From Hungay onwards I met a class of people I had not seen before. They were the Minchia (Pe-tso).

Major H.R. Davies, whose treatise on the tribes of Yuen-nan at the end of his excellent work on travel in the province, is probably the best yet written, writes that he met Minchia people only on the plains of Tali-fu and Chao-chow, and never east of the latter place. This was in travel some ten or twelve years ago, and the fact that there are now many Minchia families living in Hungay is a testimony to their enterprise as a tribe in going farther afield in search of the means to live. There is little doubt that the Minchia originally came from country lying between the border of the province and round Li-chiang-fu and the Tali-fu plain and lake. Most of them wear Chinese dress; many of the women bind their feet (and the practice is growing in popularity), although those who have not small feet are still in the majority. In a small city lying some few li from the city of Tali all the inhabitants are Minchia, and I found no difficulty in spotting a Chinese man or woman—there is a distinct facial difference. Minchia have bigger noses, generally the eyes are set farther apart, and the skin is darker. Pink trousers are in fashion among the ladies—trace of base feminine weakness!—but are not by any means the distinguishing features of race.

# Chapter XIX

This morning, from the foot of a high spur, I saw a couple of gawky fellows shambling along in an imitation European dress, and I pricked up my ears—it seemed as if Europeans were about. One of the fellows had on a pair of long-legged khaki trousers ludicrously patched with Chinese blue, a tweed coat of London cut also patched with Chinese blue, and a battered Elswood topee. I saw this through my field-glasses. Soon after, coming out from a cup in the winding pathway, emerged a four-man chair, and I had no doubt then that it was a European on the road, and I began to get as curious as anyone naturally would in a country where in interior travel his own foreign kind are met with but seldom. Hurrying on, I managed to pass the chair in a place where overhanging foliage shut out the light, so that I could not see through the windows, and as the front curtain was down I concluded that it must be a lady, probably a missionary lady. I pushed on to the nearest tavern—a tea tavern, of course—buttoned up my coat so that she should not see my dirty shirt, and waited for the presence to approach. From an inner apartment, through a window, I could see all that went on outside, but could not be seen. What is it that makes a man's heart go pit-a-pat when he is about to meet a European lady in mid-China?

Presently the chair approached. From it came a person covered in a huge fur-lined, fur-collared coat many sizes too large for his small body—it was a Chinese. Several men were pushed out of his way as he strode towards me, extending his hand in a cordial "shake, old fellow" style, and yelling in purest accent, "Good morning, sir; *good* morning, sir!"

"Oh, good morning. You speak English well. I congratulate you. Have you had a good journey? How far are you going? Very warm?" I waited. "It is so interesting when one meets a gentleman who can speak English; it is a pleasant change." I waited again. "Will you—"

"Good morning, morning, morn—he, he, he."

"But pardon me, will—"

"Morning, morning—he, h-e-e."

"Yes, you silly ass, I know it is morning, but—"

"Yes, yes; morning, morning—he-e-e-e-e."

He then made for the door, not the least abashed. Later he came back, and invited me to speak Chinese, probably thinking that I was wondering why he had made such an absolute fool of himself. I learned that this august gentleman possessed a name in happy correspondence with a fowl ("Chi"). He pointed contemptuously to a member of that feather tribe as he told me. Whether he could speak Chinese when he was or was not at Chen-tu, or whether he had a son whose knowledge of my language was vast, and who was at that moment at Chen-tu, I could not quite fathom, and he could not explain. He had a look at my caravan generally, and then turned his scrutiny upon my common tweeds, informing me that the quality bore no comparison with his own. He could travel in a four-man chair; I had to *walk*. It was all very "pub hao."

After some time he cleared out with much empty swagger, and I followed leisurely on behind, feeling—yes, why not publish it?—pleased that this bolt from the blue had not been a lady.

This young fellow—a mere slip of a boy—wore every indication of perfect self-confidence, borne out in a multitude of ways common to his class. He, I presumed, was one of the fledglings who undertake responsibilities far beyond them, or I should not be surprised if he had been one of the army of young men who, having the merest smattering of English, wholly unable to converse, set up as teachers of English. I have found this quite common among the rising classes in Yuen-nan. The cool assumption of unblushing superiority evinced in discussing intellectual and philosophic problems is remarkable. The Chinese, in the area I speak of, are little people with little brain: this was a specimen. Yet, to be fair, in China to-day the work of reform is mainly the work of young men, who although but only partly equipped for their work, approach it with perfect confidence and considerable energy, not knowing sufficient to realize the difficulties they are undertaking. In Japan the same thing was done. The young men there undertook to dispute and doubt everything which came in the way of national reorganization, setting aside—as China must do if she is to take her place alongside the ideal she has set up for herself, Japan—parental teaching, ancestral authority, the customs of centuries. A large proportion of the population of China has a passion for reform and progress. This young fellow was a typical example. In the west of China, however, to conform with the spirit of reform and real progress—not the make-believe, which is satisfying them at the present moment—they must needs change their ways.

Seventeen memorial plates were passed at the entrance to Chao-chow, a particularly modern-looking place, as one approaches it from the hill.

A remarkably ungainly individual, with a hole in the top of his skull and his body one mass of sores, came to me here, addressed me as "Sien seng," and then commenced an oration to the effect that he was a Szech'wanese, that he had known the missionaries down by the Yangtze, and that he knew he would be welcome to accompany me to Hsiakwan.[52] He switched himself on the main line of my caravan. Here was a man who had been brought in contact with the missionary away down in another province, and he knew he was welcome. I liked that. In all my journeyings in Yuen-nan I was increasingly impressed with the value of the missionary, that man who of all men in the Far East is the most subject to malicious criticism, and generally, be it said, from those persons who know little or nothing about his work. You cannot measure the missionary's work by conversions, by mere statistics. I venture to assert that it is through the missionary that the West applied pressure and supplied China with political ideas, and put within her reach the material and instruments which would enable her to carry such ideas into practice—this apart from religious teaching. More particularly is this the case in respect to popular education, perhaps, by means of which the transformation of Old China into New China will be a less long and difficult process. The people may not want the missionary—I do not for a moment say that they do—but they need to know the secret of his power and the power of his kind, and they must study his language, his science, his machinery, his steamboats, his army, his *Dreadnaughts*. They realize

---

52    The commercial center of Tali-fu, the official city is 30 li further on—E.J.D

that the foreigner is useful not for what he can do, but for what he can teach—therefore they tolerate the missionary. This is virtually the national policy of China towards foreigners, a policy gaining the acceptance of the people with remarkable quickness.

After having set aside all considerations of national prejudice and patriotism, it is interesting to ask whether it is actually a fact that the Chinese, as a race, are inferior to the peoples of the West? Much has been said on the subject. I give my opinion flatly that the Chinese is *not* inferior, and the longer I live with him the more numerous become the lessons which he teaches me.

"The question, when we examine it closely, has really very little to do with political strength or military efficiency, or (*pace* Mr. Benjamin Kidd) relative standards of living, or even the usual material accompaniments of what we call an advanced civilization; it is a question for the trained anthropologist and the craniologist rather than for the casual observer of men and manners. The Japanese people are now much more highly civilized—according to western notions—than they were half a century ago, but it would be ludicrously erroneous to say that they are now a higher race, from the evolutionary point of view, than they were then. Evolution does not work quite so rapidly as that even in these days of 'hustle.' The Japanese have advanced, not because their brains have suddenly become larger, or their moral and intellectual capabilities have all at once made a leap forward, but because their intercourse with Western nations, after centuries of isolated seclusion, showed them that certain characteristic features of European civilization would be of great use in strengthening and enriching their own country, developing its resources, and giving it the power to resist aggression. If the Japanese were as members of the *homo sapiens* inferior to us fifty years ago, they are inferior to us now. If they are our equals to-day—and the burden of proof certainly now rests on him who wishes to show that they are not—our knowledge of the origin and history of Eastern peoples, scanty though it is, should certainly tend to assure us that the Chinese are our equals, too. There is no valid reason for supposing that the Chinese people are ethnically inferior to the Japanese. They have preserved their isolated seclusion longer than the Japanese, because until very recently it was less urgently necessary for them to come out of it. They have taken a longer time to appreciate the value of Western science and certain features of Western civilization, because new ideas take longer to permeate a very large country than a small one, and because China was rich within her own borders of all the necessaries of life."[53]

And the West, too, must learn that the peace of Europe depends upon the integrity of China. For the time is coming—not in the lives of any who read these lines, but coming inevitably—when China will, by her might, by her immense numbers of trained men, by her developed naval and military strength, be able to say to the nations of the earth, "There must be no more war." And she will be strong enough to be able to enforce it.

As with individuals, so with nations, and a people who are marked by such rare physical vitality, such remarkable powers of endurance against great odds, are surely designed for some nobler purpose than merely to bear with fortitude the ills of life and the misery of starvation. It is the easiest thing in the world to criticise—the West criticises the Chinese because he is a heathen, because they do not understand him. Hundreds of millions of the Chinese race hate and fear the man of the West for exactly the same reason as would cause us to hate the Chinese were the situation reversed.

I do not need to go into history from the days when the Chinese first began to show their suspicion, contempt, and fear of foreigners, and their interpretation of the motives and purposes which took them to the Celestial Empire; it would take too much space. But if we of the West did our part to-day, as we rub up against the Chinese everywhere, in charitably taking him at his best, things would alter much more speedily that they are doing. Because the Chinese bristles with contradictions and seemingly unanswerable conundrums, we immediately dub him a barbarian, do not endeavor to understand him, do not understand enough of his language to listen to him and learn his point of view. However, it is all slowly passing—so very slowly, too. But still China is progressing, and now this oldest man in the world is becoming again the youngest, but has all the accumulations and advantages of age in all countries to lean upon and learn from.

Chao-chow gave me a very decent inn, the top room in front of which was provided with a well-paved courtyard, with every convenience for the traveler—that is, for China.

The inn cook and water-carrier was out playing on the street when we put in an early appearance. My men lost their temper, ground their teeth, foamed at the mouth, and got desperate. The only man on the premises was a poor old fellow, who foolishly bumped his uncovered head on the ground on which I stood, as an act of great servility and a secret sign that I should throw him a few cash, and then resumed his occupation in the sun of wip-

53    From Peking to Mandalay, by R.F. Johnston, London, John Murray. I am indebted to this racily-written work for other ideas in this chapter.—E.J.D.]

ing his already inflamed eyes with the one unwashed garment which covered him. I pitied him; he knew it, and traded upon my pity until I invoked a few choice words from Lao Chang to fall upon him. When the cook did put in an appearance, he and everybody dead and living placed anywhere near his genealogical tree underwent a rough quarter of an hour from the anathematical tongues of my companions. The Old Man—by virtue of the growth on my chin, this epithet of respect was commonly used towards me—wanted to wash his face and drink his tea. He was tired with walking. He was a foreign mandarin. Did the blank, blank, blank cook, the worm and no man, not know that a foreigner was among them? And then they fell to piling up the ignominy again and placing to the cook's dishonor various degrees of lowliest origin common among the Chinese proletariat, which, thank Heaven, I did not quite understand.

That evening all Chao-chow came to honor me in my room, and to admire and ask to be given all I had in my boxes. That it was all a huge revelation to many who came and inquired who I might be, and whence I might have come, was quite evident. One fellow, dressed gaudily in expensive silks and satins—probably borrowed—came with pomp and pride; and disappointment was writ large upon his ugly face when he learned that I could not, or would not, speak with him. He mentioned that he was one of the cultured of the city. But the Chinese are all more or less cultured. My own coolies, although not knowing a character, are really "cultured"—they are the most polite men I have ever traveled with. The culture, at any rate, although more apparent than real, has a universality in China which the foreigner must observe in moving among the people, and which as a sort of lubrication, makes the wheels of society run smoother. This man was not cultured in the matter of taste in the choice of colors. He was altogether frightfully lacking in sense of harmony, and when one saw the little boy who trotted along with him, one might have thought that Joseph's coat had been revived for my especial edification. He was a peculiar being, this highly-colored man. He would persist in sitting down on his haunches, despite frequent invitations to use a chair—how is it all Orientals can do this, and not one European out of fifty?

Lao Chang afterwards informed me that this man's wife had just presented him with a second son, and great jubilation was taking place. The birth of a child, especially of a boy, is a great event in any Chinese household, and considerable anxiety is felt lest demons should be lurking about the house and cause trouble. A sorcerer is called in just before the birth, to exorcise all evil influences from the house and secure peace. This is the "Exorcism of Great Peace." Simultaneously comes the midwife. Should the birth be attended with great pain and difficulty, recourse is had to crackers, the firing of guns, or whatever similar device can be thought of to scare off the demons. Solicitude is often felt that the first visit to the house after the birth of the child should be made by a "lucky" person, for the child's whole future career may be blighted by meeting with an "ill-starred" person. No outsider will enter the room where the birth took place for forty days. On the anniversary of a boy's birth the relatives and friends bring presents of clothes, hats, ornaments, playthings, and red eggs. The baby is placed on the floor—the earth, which is the first place he touches; he is born into a hole in the ground—and around him are placed various articles, such as a book, pencil, chopsticks, money, and so on. He will follow the profession which has to do with the articles he first touches.[54]

This was the fortieth day, and so my visitant honored me by thrusting his contemptible presence upon me, and he would not go until late at night, when a man with a diseased hip and one eye—and a ghastly thing at that—called to see whether I could treat him with medicine.

Hsiakwan in days to come will probably have a big industry in brick and tile making. Fifteen li from the town, on the Chao-chow side, many people now get their living at the business, and one could easily dream of a "Hsiakwan Brick and Tile Company Limited," with the children's children of the present pioneers running for the morning papers to have a look at the share market reports, with light railways connected up with the main line, which has not yet been built, and so on, and so on.

Hsiakwan is perhaps the busiest town on the main trade route from Yuen-nan-fu to Burma. Tali-fu, although growing, is only the official town, of which Hsiakwan is the commercial entrepot. It was here that I stayed one Sunday some time after this, at one of the biggest inns I have ever been into in China. It had no less than four buildings, each with a paved rectangular courtyard which all the rooms overlooked. A military official, who was on his way to Chao-t'ong to deal with the rebellion, of which the reader has already learnt a good deal, was expected soon after I arrived. My room was already arranged, however, when the landlord came to me and said—

"Yang gwan, you must please go out!"

Now the yang gwan, as was expected, stayed where he was, smiled in magnanimous acquiescence, invited the proprietor—a stout, jolly person with one eye—to be seated, and remained quiet. Again and again was I told that I should be required to clear out, and give up the best room to the official and his aide-de-camp, but unfortunately the inquirer did not im-

---

54    From inquiries I find this custom is not general in some parts of Western China—E.J.D.

prove the situation by persisting in the foolish belief that the foreigner was hard of hearing. He shouted his request into my ear in a stentorian basso, he waved his hands, he pointed, he made signs. The Chinese langage and manner, however, are difficult to an addle-pated foreigner. I, poor foolish fellow, endeavoring to treat the Chinese in a manner identical to that which he would have employed had conditions been reversed, stared vacantly and woodenly into a seemingly bewildering infinite, and timidly remarked, "O t'ing puh lai." Knowing then that my "hearing had not come," he requisitioned my boy, for the aide-de-camp by this time was glumly peering into my doorway; but to his disgust Lao Chang also was equally unsuccessful in making me tumble to their meaning. The best room, therefore, continued to be mine.

Soon after the official came, and my dog began by mauling his canine guardian, tearing away half his ear; and in the middle of the night one of my horses got loose and had a stand-up fight with a mule attached to the official party, laming him seriously; and as the foreigner emerged in his night attire to prevent further damage, he encountered the mandarin himself, and pinned him dead against the wall in the dark, after having stepped on his corn. My pony had pulled several morsels of flesh from the mule's carcase. The yang gwan certainly came off best, and the following morning, as the Chinese gwan with his retinue of six chairs and about one hundred and fifty men departed, the yang gwan smiled a happy farewell which was not effusively reciprocated.

As I came out of the inn I met a Buddhist priest, worn with general dilapidation and old age, with a huge festering wound in the calf of his leg, so that he could hardly hobble along with a stick—he was probably on his way to the medical missionary at Tali-fu for treatment. This spiritual guide was certainly on his last legs, and has probably by this time handed over the priestly robes and official perquisites to more vigorous young blood.

Hsiakwan's High Street reminded me of the main street of Totnes, with its arch over the roadway, and the scenery might have deluded one into the belief that he was in Switzerland in spring, as he gazed upon the glorious spectacle of snow-covered mountains with the world-famed lake at the foot. Tali-fu deserves its name of the Geneva of West China.

In the chapter devoted to Yuen-nan-fu I have referred to the military of Tali-fu, but here I saw the men actually at drill, and a finer set of men I have rarely seen in Europe. The military Tao-tai lives here. Progress is phenomenal. At Yung-chang, the westernmost prefecture of the Empire, the commanding officer could even speak English.

In the famous temple ten li from Tali-fu is an effigy to the Yang Daren who figured conspicuously during the Mohammedan Rebellion. My men somehow got the false information that he was a native of Tong-ch'uan-fu, so they all went down on their knees and bumped their heads on the ground before the image. This Yang, however, was such a brute of a man that no young girl was safe where he was; however, as a soldier he was indomitable. The temple in which he is deified is called the Kwan-in-tang,[55] and there is no place in all China where Kwan-in is worshipped with such relentless vigor. Some years ago, so the wags say, when Tali-fu was threatened by rebels, Kwan-in saved the city by transforming herself into a Herculean creature, and carrying upon her back a stone of several tons weight, presumably to block the path. The amazement of the rebels at the sight of a woman performing such a feat made them wonder what the men could be like, so they turned tail and fled. The story is believed implicitly by the residents of the city, and the priests, with an open eye to the main chance, work upon the public imagination with capital tact. I saw the stone in the center of a lotus pond, over which is the structure in which the Kwan-in sits, not as a weight-lifting woman, but as a tender mother, with a tiny babe in her arms, and none in the whole of the Empire enjoys such favor for being able to direct the birth of male children into those families which give most money to the priests. Women desiring sons come and implore her by throwing cash, one by one, at the effigy, the one who hits being successful,

---

55 Temple to the Goddess of Mercy.

"Kwan-in was the third daughter of a king, beautiful and talented, and when young loved to meditate as a priest. Her father, mother and sisters beseech her not to pass the 'green spring,' but to marry, and the king offers the man of her choice the throne. But no, she must take the veil. She enters the 'White Sparrow Nunnery,' and the nuns put her to the most menial offices; the dragons open a well for the young maidservant, and the wild beasts bring her wood. The king sends his troops to burn the nunnery, Kwan-in prays, rain falls, and extinguishes the conflagration. She is brought to the palace in chains, and the alternative of marriage or death is placed before her. In the room above where the court of the inquisition is held there is music, dancing, and feasting, sounds and sights to allure a young girl; the queen also urges her to leave the convent, and accede to the royal father's wish. Kwan-in declares that she would rather die than marry, so the fairy princess is strangled, and a tiger takes her body into the forest. She descends into hell, and hell becomes a paradise, with gardens of lilies. King Yama is terrified when he sees the prison of the lost becoming an enchanted garden, and begs her to leave, in order that the good and the evil may have their distinctive rewards. One of the genii gives her the 'peach of immortality.' On her return to the terrestrial regions she hears that her father is sick, and sends him word that if he will dispatch a messenger to the 'Fragrant Mountain,' an eye and a hand will be given him for medicine; this hand and eye are Kwan-in's own, and produce instant recovery.

"She is the patron goddess of mothers, and when we remember the value of sons, we can understand the heartiness of worship."—The Three Religions of China, by H.G. Du Bose.

going away with the belief that a son will be born to her. When the deluded females are cleared out, the priest, divesting himself of his shoes, and rolling up his trousers, goes into the water, scoops up the money and uses it for his personal convenience—sometimes as much as thirty thousand cash.

# Third Journey: Tali-Fu to the Mekong Valley

## CHAPTER XX

*Stages to the Mekong Valley. Hardest part of the walking tour. Author as a medical man. Sunday soliloquy. How adversity is met. Chinese life compared with early European ages. Womens enthusiasm over the European. A good send-off. My coolie Shanks, the songster. Laughter for tears. Pony commits suicide. Houses in the forest district. Little encampments among the hills, and the way the people pass their time. Treacherous travel. To Hwan-lien-p'u. Rest by the river, and a description of my companions. How my men treated the telegraph. Universal lack of privacy. Complaints of the carrying coolies.*

From whichever standpoint you regard the cities and villages of Western China, the views are full of interest. Each forms a new picture of rock, river, wood and temple, crenellated wall, and uplifted roof, crowded with bewildering detail.

I am not the first traveler who has remarked this. Several of Mr. Archibald Little's books speak of it. He says: "In Europe, except where the scenery is purely wild, and more especially in America, the delight of gazing on many of the most beautiful scenes is often alloyed by the crude newness of man's work. This is true now of Japan, since the rage for copying western architecture and dress has fallen upon the Islands of the Rising Sun. But here in Western China little has intervened to mar the accord between nature and man." In the country on which we are now entering the natural grandeur is finer than anything I had seen since I left the Gorges, and incidentally I do not mind confessing to the indulgent reader that when I came again through Hsiakwan, again westward bound, I was tired, my feet were blistered and broken, each day and every day had brought me a hard journey, and here I was now facing the most difficult journey yet met with—literally not a li of level road.

My journey was by the following route:—

| | LENGTH OF STAGE | HEIGHT ABOVE SEA LEVEL |
|---|---|---|
| 1st day Ho-chiang-p'u | 90 li | 5,050 ft. |
| 2nd day Yang-pi | 60 li | 5,150 ft. |
| 3rd day T'ai-p'ing-p'u | 70 li | 7,400 ft. |
| 5th day Hwan-lien-p'u | 50 li | 5,200 ft.[56] |
| 6th day Ch'u-tung | 95 li | 5,250 ft. |
| 7th day Shayung | 75 li | 4,800 ft. |

T'ai-p'ing-p'u (two days from Tali-fu), bleak and perched away up among the clouds, could never be called a town; it is merely a ramshackle place which gives one sleep and food in the difficult stage between Hwan-lien-p'u and Yang-pi.

Like most of the small places which suffered from the ravishings of the Mohammedan destructions of the fifties, it has seen better days. Cottages hang clumsily together on ledges in the mountains, 7,400 feet above the sea, standing in their own vast uncultivated grounds. People are of the Lolo origin, but all speak Chinese; their ways of life, however, are aboriginal, and still far from the ideal to which they aspire. They are poor, poor as church mice, dirty and diseased and decrepit, and their existence as a consequence is dreary and dull and void of all enlightenment. The women—sad, lowly females—bind their feet after a fashion, but as they work in the fields, climb hills, and battle in negotiations against Nature where she is overcome only with extreme effort, the real "lily" is a thing possible with them only in their dreams. By binding, however, be it never so bad an imitation, they give themselves the greater chance of getting a Chinese husband.

I stayed here the Sunday, and as I went through my evening ablutions, among my admirers in the doorway was an old woman, who in gentlest confidences with my boy, explained awkwardly that her little daughter lay sick of a fever, and could he prevail upon his foreign master, in whom she placed implicit faith, to come with her and minister? Lao Chang advised that I should go, and I went. My shins got mutilated as I fell down the slippery stone steps in the dark into a pail of hog's wash at the bottom. Having wiped the worst of the grease and slime onto the mud wall, by the aid of a flickering rushlight I saw the "child," who lay on a mattress on the floor in the darkest corner of the room. I reckoned her age to be thirty-five, her

---

56    The 4th day is missing in the original book. —*publishers*

black hair hung in tangled masses, the very bed on which she lay stank with vermin, two feet away was the fire where all the cooking was gone through, and everywhere around was filth. When she saw me the "child" raised her solitary garment, whispered that pains in her stomach were well-nigh unendurable, that her head ached, that her joints were stiff, that she was generally wrong, and—"Did I think she would recover?" I thought she might not.

Rushing back to my medicine chest, I brought along and administered a maximum dose of the oil called castor, and later dosed her with quinine. In the morning she was out and about her work, while the old mother was great in her praises for the passing European who had cured her child. After that came the deluge! They wanted more medicine—fever elixir, toothache cure, and so on, and so on—but I stood firm.

The tedium of the Sunday in that draughty inn gave me an insight into their common lives which I had not before, causing me to meditate upon their simple lives and their simple needs. They did not raise the forests in order to get gold; they did not squander their patrimony in youth, destroying in a day the fruit of long years. They held to simple needs; they had a simplicity of taste, which was also a peculiar source of independence and safety. The more simple they lived the more secure their future, because they were less at the mercy of surprises and reverses. In adversity these people would not act like nurslings deprived of their bottles and their rattles, but would, by virtue of their common simplicity, probably be better armed for any struggles. I do not desire the life for myself, but the ethics of their simple living cannot but be recommended. Multitudes possess in China what multitudes in the West pursue amid characteristic hampering futilities of European life. We would aspire to simple living, and the simplicity of olden times in manners, art and ideas is still cherished and reverenced; but we cannot be simple or return to the simplicity of our forefathers unless we return to the spirit which animated them. They possessed the spirit of real simplicity. And this same spirit the Chinese possess to-day; but they are minus the incomparable features of healthful civilization, inward and outward, of which our forebears were masters. Our ways to-day are not their ways, and their ways not our ways; but one cannot but realize as he moves among them that with a happy infusion of the spirit of their simplicity into the restlessness of our modern life our wearied minds would dream less and realize more of the true simplicity of simple living.

To a man the village of T'ai-p'ing-p'u turned out early on the Monday morning to express regrets that my departure was at hand. When, in parting with this people who had done all in their power to make my comfort complete, I threw a handful of cash to some little children standing wonderingly near by, general approval was expressed, and elaborate felicities anent my beneficence exchanged by the ear-ringed Lolo women. A short apron hung down over their blue trousers, and as I passed out of their sight, they admired me and gossiped about me, with their hands under their aprons, in much the same manner as their more enlightened sisters of the wash-tub gossip sometimes in the West.

It was a beautiful spring morning; the sweet song of the birds pierced through the noise of the rolling river below, the air was fragrant and bracing, and as I left and commenced the rocky ascent leading again to the mountains, the barks of some fierce-disposed canines, who alone objected to my presence among the hill-folk, died away with the rustle of the leafage in a keen north wind.

One of my men was poorly, the solitary element to disturb the equanimity of our camp.

It was Shanks. He had been suffering from toothache, and unfortunately I had no gum-balm with me; without my knowledge Lao Chang had rubbed in some strong embrocation to the fellow's cheek, so that now, in addition to toothache, he had also a badly blistered face, swollen up like a pudding. Upon learning that I had no means of curing him or of alleviating the pain, Shanks bellowed into my ear, loud enough to bring the dead out of the grave-mounds on the surrounding hill-sides, "Puh p'a teh, pub p'a teh"; then, raising his carrying-pole to the correct angle on the hump on his back, went merrily forward, warbling some squealing Chinese ditty. But Shanks was the songster of the party. He often madly disturbed the silence of middle night by a sudden outburst inte song, and when shouted down by others who lay around, or kicked by the man who shared his bed, and whose choral propensities were less in proportion, he would laugh wildly at them all. Poor Shanks; he was a peculiar mortal. He would laugh at men in pain, and think it sympathy. If we could get no food or drink on the march, after having wearily toiled away for hours, he would not be disposed to grumble—he would laugh. Such tragic incidents as the pony jumping over the precipice provoked him to extreme laughter.[57]

---

57    The day before, whilst we were passing along the edge of a cliff, we saw a deliberate suicide on the part of a pony. Getting away from its companions, it first jumped against a tree, then turned its head sharply on the side of a cliff, finally taking a leap into mid-air over the precipice. It touched ground at about two hundred and fifty feet below this point, and then rolled out of sight. My men exhibited no concern, and laughed me down because I did. It was, as they said, merely diseased, and the muleteers went on their way, leaving horse and loads to Providence. This sort of thing is not uncommon.—E.J.D.

And when I caught him sewing up an open wound in the sole of his foot with common colored Chinese thread and a rusty needle, and told him that he might thereby get blood poisoning, and lose his life or leg, he cared not a little. As a matter of fact, he laughed in my face. Not at me, not at all, but because he thought his laughter might probably delude the devil who was president over the ills of that particular portion of human anatomy. He came to me just outside Pu-peng, where we saw a coffin containing a corpse resting in the roadway whilst the bearers refreshed near by and, pointing thereto, told me that the man was "muh tsai" (not here)—the Chinese never on any account mention the word death—and his sides shook with laughter, so much so that he dropped his loads alongside the corpse, and startled the cock on top of the coffin guarding the spirit of the dead into a vigorous fit of crowing for fear of disaster.

We enjoyed fairly level road, although rough, for ten li after leaving T'ai-p'ing-p'u. It rose gradually from 7,400 feet to 8,500 feet, and then dipped suddenly, and continued at a fearful down gradient. I might describe it as a member of a British infantry regiment once described to me a slope on the Himalayas. It was about eight years ago, and a few fellows were at a smoker given to some Tommies returning from India, when a bottle-nosed individual, talking about a long march his battalion had made up the Himalayas, in excellent descriptive exclaimed, "'Twasn't a 'ill, 'twasn't a graydyent, 'twas a blooming precipice, guvnor." The Himalayas and the country I am now describing have therefore something in common.

Just before this the beautiful mountains, behind which was the Tali-fu Lake, made a sight worth coming a long way to see.

Midway down the steep hill we happened on some lonely log cottages, twenty-five li from T'ai-p'ing-p'u (it is reckoned as thirty-five li traveling in the opposite direction). In the forest district I found the houses all built of timber—wood piles placed horizontally and dovetailed at the ends, the roofs being thatched. You have merely to step aside from the road, and you are in dense mountain forest; it is manifestly easier and less costly than the mud-built habitation, although for their part the people are worse off because of the lack of available ground for growing their crops. Here the people were still essentially Lolo, and the big-footed women who boiled water under a shed had difficulty in getting to understand what my men were talking about.

The second descent is begun after a pleasant walk along level ground resembling a well-laid-out estate, and a treacherously rough mile brought us down to an iron chain bridge swung over the Shui-pi Ho, at the far end of which, hidden behind bamboo matting, are a few idols in an old hut;

they act in the dual capacity of gods of the river and the mountain. Tea and some palatable baked persimmon—very like figs when baked—were brought me by an awful-looking biped who was still in mourning, his un-shaven skull sadly betokening the fact. As I sipped my tea and cracked jokes with some Szech'wan men who declared they had met me in Chung-king (I must resemble in appearance a European resident in that city; it was the fourth time I had been accused of living there), I admired the grand scenery farther along. Especially did I notice one peak, towering perpendicularly away up past woods of closely-planted pine and fir trees, the crystal sum-mit glistening with sunlit snow; as soon as I started again on my journey, I was pulling up towards it. Soon I was gazing down upon the tiny patches of light green and a few solitary cottages, resembling a little beehive, and one could imagine the metaphorical wax-laying and honey-making of the inhabitants. These people were away from all mankind, living in life-long loneliness, and all unconscious of the distinguished foreigner away up yon-der, who wondered at their patient toiling, but who, like them, had his Yes-terday, To-day and To-morrow. There they were, perched high up on the bleak mountain sides, with their joys and sorrows, their pains and penalties, struggling along in domestic squalor, and rearing young rusticity and raw produce.

On these mountains in Yuen-nan one sees hundreds of such little en-campments of a few families, passing their existence far from the road of the traveler, who often wished he could descend to them and quench his thirst, and eat with them their rice and maize. Most of them here were isolated families of tribespeople, who, out of contact with their kind, have little left of racial resemblance, and yet are not fully Chinese, so that it is difficult to tell what they really are. Most were Lolo.

Walking here was treacherous. A foot pathway was the main road, wind-ing in and out high along the surface of the hills, in many places washed away, and in others overgrown with grass and shrubbery. "Across China on Foot" would have met an untimely end had I made a false step or slipped on the loose stones in a momentary overbalance. I should have rolled down seven hundred feet into the Shui-pi Ho. Once during the morning I saw my coolies high up on a ledge opposite to me, and on practically the same level, a three-li gully dividing us. They were very small men, under very big hats, bustling along like busy Lilliputians, and my loads looked like match-boxes. I probably looked to them not less grotesque. But we had to watch our footsteps, and not each other.

We were rounding a corner, when I was surprised to see Hwan-lien-p'u a couple of li away. The *fu-song* were making considerable hue and cry because Rusty had rolled thirty feet down the incline, and as I looked I saw the animal get up and commence neighing because he had lost sight of us. He was in the habit of wandering on, nibbling a little here and a little there, and rarely gave trouble unless in chasing an occasional horse caravan, when he gave my men some fun in getting him again into line.

It was not yet midday, and we had four hours' good going. So I calculated. Not so my men. They could not be prevailed upon to budge, and knowing the Chinese just a little, I reluctantly kept quiet. It was entirely unreasonable to expect them to go on to Ch'u-tung, ninety li away—it was impossible. And I learnt that the reason they would not go on was that no house this side of that place was good enough to put a horse into, even a Chinese horse, and they would not dream of taking me on under those conditions. There was not even a hut available for the traveler, so they said. I had come over difficult country, plodding upwards on tiptoe and then downwards with a lazy swing from stone to stone for miles. Throughout the day we had been going through fine mountain forest, everywhere peaceful and beautiful, but it had been hard going. In the morning a heavy frost lay thick and white about us, and by 10:30 a.m. the sun was playing down upon us with a merciless heat as we tramped over that little red line through the green of the hill-sides. Often in this march was I tempted to stay and sit down on the sward, but I had proved this to be fatal to walking. In traveling in Yuennan one's practice should be: start early, have as few stops as possible, when a stop *is* made let it be long enough for a real rest. In Szech'wan, where the tea houses are much more frequent, men will pull up every ten li, and generally make ten minutes of it. In Yuen-nan these welcome refreshment houses are not met with so often, and little inducement is held out for the coolies to stop, but upon the slightest provocation they will stop for a smoke. On this walking trip I made it a rule to be off by seven o'clock, stop twice for a quarter of an hour up to tiffin (my men stopped oftener), when our rest was often for an hour, so that we were all refreshed and ready to push on for the fag-end of the stage. We generally were done by four or five o'clock. And I should be the last in the world to deny that by this time I had had enough for one day.

Upon arrival I immediately washed my feet, an excellent practice of the Chinese, changed my footgear, drank many cups of tea, and often went straight to my p'ukai. The roads of China take it out of the strongest man. There are no Marathon runners here; progress is a tedious toil, often on all fours.

My room at Hwan-lien-p'u was near a telegraph pole; there was a telegraph station there, where my men showed their admiration for the Governmental organization by at once hammering nails into the pole. It was close to their laundry, and served admirably for the clothes-line, a bamboo tied at one end with a string to a nail in the pole and the other end stuck through the paper in the window of the telegraph operator's apartment. But this is nothing. Years ago, when the telegraph was first laid down, the people took turns to displace the wires and sell them for their trouble, and to chop the poles up for firewood. It continued for a considerable period, until an offender—or one whom it was surmised had done this or would have done it if he could—had his ears cut off, and was led over the main road to the capital, to be admired by any compatriot contemplating a deal in wiring or timber used for telegraphic communication purposes.

Just below the town the river ran peacefully down a gradual incline. I decided that a comfortable seat under a tree, spending an hour in preparing this copy, would be more pleasant than moping about a noisome and stench-ridden inn, providing precious little in the way of entertainment for the foreigner. Next door a wedding party was making the afternoon hideous with their gongs and drums and crackers, and everywhere the usual hue and cry went abroad because a European was spending the day there.

I imparted to my man my intentions for the afternoon. Immediately preparations were set on foot to get me down by the river, and it was publicly announced to the townspeople. The news ran throughout the town, that is Hwan-lien-p'u's one little narrow street, a sad mixture of a military trench and a West of England cobbled court. And instead of going alone to my shady nook by that silvery stream, i was accompanied by nine adult members of the unemployed band, three boys, and sundry stark-naked urchins who seemed to be without home or habitation. One of these specimens of fleeting friendship was one-eyed, and a diseased hip rendered it difficult for him to keep pace with us; one was club-footed, one hair-lipped fellow had only half a nose, and they were nearly all goitrous. As I write now these people, curious but not uncouth, are crouched around me on their haunches, after the fashion of the ape, their more Darwinian-evolved companion and his shorthand notes being admired by an open-mouthed crowd. Down below my horse is entertaining the more hilarious of the party in his tantrums with the man who is trying to wash him—

# Chapter XXI

*The mountains of Yuen-nan. Wonderful scenery. Among the Mohammedans. Sorry scene at Ch'u-tung. A hero of a horrid past. Infinite depth of Chinese character. Mule falls one hundred and fifty yards, and escapes unhurt. Advice to future travelers. To Shayung. We meet Tibetans on the mountains. Chinese cruelty. Opium smoker as a companion. Opium refugees. One opinion only on the subject. Mission work among smokers and eaters.*

Mere words are a feeble means to employ to describe the mountains of Yuen-nan.

As I start from Hwan-lien-p'u this morning, to the left high hills are picturesquely darkened in the soft and unruffled solemnity of their own still unbroken shade. Opposite, rising in pretty wavy undulation, with occasional abruptions of jagged rock and sunken hollow, the steep hill-sides are brought out in the brightest coloring of delicate light and shade by the golden orb of early morn; towering majestically sunwards, sheer up in front of me, high above all else, still more sombre heights stand out powerfully in solemn contrast against the pale blue of the spring sky, the effect in the distance being antithetical and weird, with the magnificent Ts'ang Shan[58] standing up as a beautiful background of perpendicular white, from whence range upon range of dark lines loom out in the hazy atmosphere. From the extreme summit of one snow-laden peak, whose white steeple seems truly

---

58    The range of mountains which I had skirted since leaving Tali-fu.—E.J.D.

a heavenward-directed finger, I gaze abstractedly all around upon nothing but dark masses of gently-waving hills, steep, weary ascents and descents, green and gold, and yellow and brown, and one's eyes rest upon a maze of thin white lines intertwining them all. These are the main roads. I am alone. My men are far behind. I am awed with an unnatural sense of bewildered wonderment in the midst of all this glory of the earth.

Everything is so vast, so grand, so overpowering. Murmurings of the birds alone break the sense of sadness and loneliness. Away yonder full-grown pine trees, if discernible at all, are dwarfed so as to appear like long coarse grass. For some thirty li the road runs through beautiful woods, high above the valleys and the noise of the river; and now we are running down swiftly to a point where two ranges meet, only to toil on again, slowly and wearily, up an awful gradient for two hours or more. But the labor and all its fatiguing arduousness are nothing when one gets to the top, for one beholds here one of the most magnificent mountain panoramas in all West China. Far away, just peeping prettily from the silvered edges of the bursting clouds, are the giant peaks which separate Tali-fu from Yang-pi—white giants with rugged, cruel edges pointing upwards, piercing the clouds asunder as a ship's bow pierces the billows of the deep; and then, gradually coming from out the mist, are no less than eight distinct ranges of mountains from 14,000 feet to 16,000 feet high, besides innumerable minor heights, which we have traversed with much labor during the past four days, all rich with coloring and natural grandeur seen but seldom in all the world. Switzerland could offer nothing finer, nothing more sweeping, nothing more beautiful, nothing more awe-inspiring. With the glorious grandeur of these wondrous hills, rising and falling playfully around the main ranges, the marvellous tree growth, the delicate contrasts of the formidable peaks and the dainty, cultivated valleys, and the face of Nature everywhere absolutely unmarred, Switzerland could in no way compare.

Is it then surprising that I look upon these stupendous masses with wonder, which seem to breathe only eternity and immensity?

The air is pure as the breath of heaven, all is still and peaceful, and the fact that in the very nature of things one cannot rush through this pervading beauty of the earth, but has to plod onwards step by step along a toilsome roadway, enables the scenery to be so impressed upon one's mind as to be focussed for life in one's memory. One is held spellbound; these are the pictures never forgotten. Here I sit in a corner of the earth as old as the world itself. These mountains are as they were in the great beginning, when the Creator and Sustainer of all things pure and beautiful looked upon His handiwork and saw that it was good.

The country here seems so vast as to render Nature unconquerable by man: man is insignificant, Nature is triumphant. Railways are defied; and these mountains, running mostly at right angles, will probably never—not in our time, at least—be made unsightly by the puffing and the reeking of the modern railway engine. They present so many natural obstacles to the opening-up of the country, according to the standard we Westerners lay down, that one would hesitate to prophesy any mode of traffic here other than that of the horse caravan and human beast of burden. Nature seems to look down upon man and his earth-scouring contrivances, and assert, "Man, begone! I will have none of thee." And the mountains turn upwards to the sky in silent reverence to their Maker, whose work must in the main remain unchanged until eternity.

It is now 12:30, and we have fifty li to cover before reaching Ch'u-tung. We sit here to feed at a place called Siao-shui-tsing, a sorry antediluvian make-shift of a building, where in subsequent travel I was hung up in bitter weather and had to pass the night. The people, courteous and civil as always, show a simple trustfulness with which is associated some little suspicion. I gave a cake to a little child, but its mother would not allow it to be eaten until she was again and again assured and reassured that it was quite fit to eat. This home life of the very poor Chinese, if indeed it may be called home life, has a listlessness about it in marked contrast to that of the West. There is little housework, no furniture more than a table and chair or two, and the simplicity of the cooking arrangements does not tend to increase the work of the housewife.

People here to-day are going about their work with a restful deliberation very trying to one in a hurry. The women, with infants tied to their backs, do not work hard but very long. A mud-house is being built near by, and between the cooking and attending to passing travelers, two women are digging the earth and filling up the baskets, while the men are mixing the mud, filling in the oblong wooden trough, and thus building the wall. At my elbow a man—old and grizzled and dirty—is turning back roll upon roll of his wadded garments, and ridding it of as many as he can find of the insects with which it is infested. A slobbering, boss-eyed cretin chops wood at my side, and when I rise to try a snap on the women and the children they hide behind the walls. Thus my time passes away, as I wait for the coolies who sit on a log in the open road feeding on common basins of dry rice.

After that we had to cross the face of a steep hill. We could, however, find no road, no pathway even, but could merely see the scratchings of coolies and ponies already crossed. It was an achievement not unrisky, but we managed to reach the other side without mishap. My horse, owing to the stupidity of the man who hung on to his mouth to steady himself, put his foot in a hole and dragged the fool of a fellow some twenty yards downwards in the mud. My coolies, themselves in a spot most dangerous to their own necks, stuck the outside leg deep in the mud to rest themselves, and set to assiduously in blackguarding the man in their richest vein, then, extricating themselves, again continued their journey, satisfied that they had shown the proper front, and saved the face of the foreigner who could not save it for himself. Then we all went down through a narrow ravine into a lovely shady glade, all green and refreshing, with a brook gurgling sweetly at the foot and birds singing in the foliage. There was something very quaint in this cosy corner, with the hideous echoes and weird re-echoes of my men's squealing. Then we went on again from hill to hill, in a ten-inch footway, broken and washed away, so that in places it was necessary to hang on to the evergrowing grass to keep one's footing in the slopes. One needs to have no nerves in China.

Down in the valley were a number of muleteers from Burma, cooking their rice in copper pans, whilst their ponies, most of them in horrid condition, and backs rubbed in some places to the extent of twelve inches square, grazed on the hill-sides. In most places the foot of this ravine would have been a river; here it was like a park, with pretty green sward intersected by a narrow path leading down into a lane so thick with virgin growth as to exclude the sunlight. As we entered a man came out with his p'ukai and himself on the back of a ten-hand pony; the animal shied, and his manservant got behind and laid on mighty blows with the butt-end of a gun he was carrying. The pony ceased shying.

To Ch'u-tung was a tedious journey, rising and falling across the wooded hills, and when we arrived at some cottages by the riverside, the *fu-song* had a rough time of it from my men for having brought us by a long road instead of by the "new" road (so called, although I do not doubt that it has been in use for many generations). Some Szech'wan coolies and myself had rice together on a low form away from the smoke, and the while listened to some tales of old, told by some half-witted, goitrous monster who seemed sadly out at elbow. The soldier meantime smelt round for a smoke. As he and my men had decided a few moments ago that each party was of a very low order of humanity, their pipes for him were not available. So he took pipe and dried leaf tobacco from this half-witted skunk, who, having wiped the stem in his eight-inch-long pants, handed it over in a manner befitting a monarch. It measured some sixty or seventy inches from stem to bowl.

From Hwan-lien-p'u to Ch'u-tung is reckoned as eighty li; it is quite one hundred and ten, and the last part of the journey, over barren, wind-swept hills, most fatiguing.

In contrast to the beauty of the morning's scenery, the country was black and bare, and a gale blew in our faces. My spirits were raised, how-ever, by a coolie who joined us and who had a remarkable knowledge of the whole of the West of China, from Chung-king to Singai, from Mengtsz to Tachien-lu. Plied with questions, he willingly gave his an-swers, but he would persist in leading the way. As soon as a man endeav-ored to pass him, he would trot off at a wonderful speed, making no ado of the 120 pounds of China pots on his back, yelling his explanations all the time to the man behind. Yung-p'ing-hsien lay over to the right, fifteen li from Ch'u-tung, which is protected from the elements by a bell-shaped hill at the foot of a mountain lit up with gold from the sinking sun, which dipped as I trudged along the uneven zigzag road leading across the plain of peas and beans and winter crops. Four eight-inch planks, placed at vari-ous dangerous angles on three wood trestles, form the bridge across the fifty-foot stream dividing Ch'u-tung from the world on the opposite side. Across this I saw men wander with their loads, and then I led Rusty in. Whilst the stream washed his legs, I sat dangling mine until called upon to make way for another party of travelers. Remarkable is the agility of these men. They swing along over eight inches of wood as if they were in the middle of a well-paved road.

Ch'u-tung is a Mohammedan town. There are a few Chinese only—Buddhists, Taoists and other ragtags; although when the follower of the Prophet has his pigtail attached to the inside of his hat, as it not unusual when he goes out fully dressed, there is little difference between him and the Chinese.

Pigs here are conspicuously absent. People feed on poultry and beef. I rested in this city some month or so after my first overland trip whilst my man went to convert silver into cash, a trying ordeal always. Whilst I sipped my tea and ate a couple of rice cakes, I was impressed, as I seldom have been in my wanderings, with the remarkable number of people, from the six hundred odd houses the town possesses, who during that half-hour found nothing whatever to do to benefit themselves or the community, as members of which they passed monotonous lives, but to stare aimlessly at the resting foreigner. The report spread like wildfire, and they ran to the scene with haste, pulling on their coats, wiping food from their mouths, scratching their heads *en route*, one trouser-leg up and the other down, all anxious to get a seat near the stage. A river flows down the center of the street, and into this a sleepy fellow got tipped bodily in the crush, sat down in the water, seemingly in no hurry to move until he had finished his vigorous bullying of the man who pushed him in. Those who could not get standing room near my table went out into the street and shaded the sun from their eyes, in order that they might catch even a glimpse of the traveler who sat on in uncompromising indifference.

Several old wags were there who had witnessed the Rebellion—at the moment, had I not become callous, another might have seemed imminent—and were looked up to by the crowd as heroes of a horrid past, being listened to with rapt attention as they described what it was the crowd looked at and whence it came. Had I been a wild animal let loose from its cage, mingled curiosity and a peculiar foreboding among the people of something terrible about to happen could not have been more intense.

But I had by this time got used to their crowding, so that I could write, sleep, eat, drink, and be merry, and go through personal and private routine with no embarrassment. If I turned for the purpose, I could easily stare out of face a member of the crowd whose inquisitive propensities had become annoying, but as soon as he left another filled the gap. Quite pitiful was it to see how trivial articles of foreign manufacture—such, for instance, as the cover of an ordinary tin or the fabric of one's clothing—brought a regular deluge of childish interest and inane questioning; and if I happened to make a few shorthand notes upon anything making a particular impression, a look half surprised, half amused, went from one to another like an electric current. Had I been scheming out celestial hieroglyphics their mouths could not have opened wider. As I write now I am asked by a respectable person how many ounces of silver a Johann Faber's B.B. costs. I have told him, and he has retired smiling, evidently thinking that I am romancing.

That I impress the crowd everywhere is evident. But with all their questioning, they are rarely rude; their stare is simply the stare of little children seeing a thing for the first time in their lives. It is all so hard to understand. My silver and my gold they solicit not; they merely desire to see me and to feel me. A certain faction of the crowd, however, do solicit my silver.

Lao Chang has been buying vegetables, and has brought all the vegetable gardeners and greengrocers around me. The poultry rearers are here too, and the forage dealers and the grass cutters and the basket makers, and other thrifty members of the commercial order of Ch'u-tung humankind. When I came away the people dropped into line and strained their necks to get a parting smile. I was sped on my way with a public curiosity as if I were a penal servitor released from prison, a general home from a war, or something of that kind. And so this wonderful wonder of wonders was glad when he emerged from the labyrinthic, brain-confusing bewilderment of Chinese interior life of this town into somewhat clearer regions. I could not understand. And to the wisest man, wide as may be his vision, the Chinese mind and character remain of a depth as infinite as is its possibility of expansion. The volume of Chinese nature is one of which as yet but the alphabet is known to us.

My own men had got quite used to me, and their minds were directed more to working than to wondering. In China, as in other Asiatic countries, one's companions soon accustom themselves to one's little peculiarities of character, and what was miraculous to the crowd had by simple repetition ceased to be miraculous to them.

As I put away my notebook after writing the last sentence, I saw a mule slip, fall, roll for one hundred and fifty yards, losing its load on the down journey, and then walk up to the stream for a drink.[59]

We started for Shayung on February 2nd, 1910, going over a road literally uncared for, full of loose-jointed stones and sinking sand, down which ponies scrambled, while the Tibetans in charge covered themselves close in the uncured skins they wore. This was the first time I had ever seen Tibetans. They had huge ear-rings in their ears, and their antiquated topboots—much better, however, than the Yuen-nan topboot—gave them a peculiar appearance as they tramped downward in the frost.

---

59    On my return journey into Yuen-nan, I again called at Ch'u-tung, traveling not by the main road, but by a steep path intertwisting through almost impossible places, and requiring four times the amount of physical exertion. I was led over what was called a new road. It was quite impossible to horses carrying loads, and only by tremendous effort could I climb up. How my coolies managed it remains a mystery. And then, as is almost inevitable with these "new" roads and the "short" cuts, they invariably lose their way. Mine did. Hopeless was our obscurity, unspeakable our confusion. Men kept vanishing and reappearing among the rocks, and it was very difficult to fix our position geographically. Up and up we went, in and out, twisting and turning in an endless climb. A gale blew, but at times we pulled ourselves up by the dried grass in semi-tropical heat. After several hours, standing on the very summit of this bleak and lofty mountain, I could just discern Ch'u-tung and Yung-p'ing-hsien far away down in the mists. There lay the "ta lu" also, like a piece of white ribbon stretched across black velvet—the white road on the burnt hillsides. We were opposite the highest peaks in the mountains beyond the plain, far towards Tengyueh—they are 12,000 feet, we were at least 10,500 feet, and as Ch'u-tung is only 5,500 feet, our hours of toil may be imagined. When we reached the top we found nothing to eat, nothing to drink (not even a mountain stream at which we could moisten our parched lips), simply two memorial stones on the graves of two dead men, who had merited such an outrageous resting-place. I donned a sweater and lay flat on the ground, exhausted. It must have been a stiff job to bring up both stones and men.

I strongly advise future travelers to keep to the main road in this district.—E.J.D.

Going up with us was a Chinese, on the back of a pony not more than eleven hands high, sitting as usual with his paraphernalia lashed to the back of the animal. He laughed at me because I was not riding, whilst I tried to solve the problem of that indefinable trait of Chinese nature which leads able-bodied men with sound feet to sit on these little brutes up those terrible mountain sides. Some parts of this spur were much steeper than the roof of a house—as perpendicular as can be imagined—but still this man held on all the way. And the Chinese do it continuously, whether the pony is lame or not, at least the majority. But the cruelty of the Chinese is probably not regarded as cruelty, certainly not in the sense of cruelty in the West. Being Chinese, with customs and laws of life such as they are, their instinct of cruelty is excusable to some degree. Not only is it with animals, however, but among themselves the Chinese have no mercy, no sympathy. In Christian England within the last century men where hanged for petty theft; but in Yuen-nan—I do not know whether it is still current in other provinces—men have been known to be burnt to death for stealing maize. A case was reported from Ch'u-tsing-fu quite recently, but it is a custom which used to be quite common. A document is signed by the man's relatives, a stick is brought by every villager, the man lashed to a stake, and his own people are compelled to light the fire. It seems incredible, but this horrible practice has not been entirely extirpated by the authorities, although since the Yuen-nan Rebellion it has not been by any means so frequent. I have no space nor inclination to deal with the ghastly tortures inflicted upon prisoners in the name of that great equivalent to justice, but the more one knows of them the more can he appreciate the common adage urging *dead men to keep out of hell and the living out of the yamens!*

Hua-chow is thirty li from here at the head of an abominable hill, and here women, overlooking one of the worst paved roads in the Empire, were beating out corn. Then we climbed for another twenty-five li, rising from 5,900 feet to 8,200 feet, till we came to a little place called Tien-chieng-p'u. It took us three hours. Looking backwards, towards Tali-fu, I saw my 14,000 feet friends, and as we went down the other side over a splendid stone road we could see, far down below, a valley which seemed a veritable oasis, smiling and sweet. A temple here contained a battered image of the Goddess of Mercy, who controls the births of children. A poor woman was depositing a few cash in front of the besmeared idol, imploring that she might be delivered of a son. How pitiable it is to see these poor creatures doing this sort of thing all over the West of China!

For two days we had been accompanied by a man who was an opium smoker and eater. Now I am not going to draw a horrible description of a shrivelled, wasted bogey in man's form, with creaking bones and shivering limbs and all the rest of it; but I must say that this man, towards the time when his craving came upon him, was a wreck in every worst sense—he crept away to the wayside and smoked, and arrived always late at night at the end of the stage. This was the effect of the drug which has been described "as harmless as milk." I do not exaggerate. In the course of Eastern journalistic experience I have written much in defence of opium, have paralleled it to the alcohol of my own country. This was in the Straits Settlements, where the deadly effects of opium are less prominent. But no language of mine can exaggerate the evil, and if I would be honest, I cannot describe it as anything but China's most awful curse. It cannot be compared to alcohol, because its grip is more speedy and more deadly. It is more deadly than arsenic, because by arsenic the suicide dies at once, while the opium victim suffers untold agonies and horrors and dies by inches. It is all very well for the men who know nothing about the effect of opium to do all the talking about the harmlessness of this pernicious drug; but they should come through this once fair land of Yuen-nan and see everywhere—not in isolated districts, but everywhere—the ravaging effects in the poverty and dwarfed constitutions of the people before they advocate the continuance of the opium trade. I have seen men transformed to beasts through its use; I have seen more suicides from the effect of opium since I have been in China than from any other cause in the course of my life. As I write I have around me painfullest evidence of the crudest ravishings of opium among a people who have fallen victims to the craving. There is only one opinion to be formed if to himself one would be true. I give the following quotation from a work from the pen of one of the most fair-minded diplomatists who have ever held office in China:—

"The writer has seen an able-bodied and apparently rugged laboring Chinese tumble all in a heap upon the ground, utterly nerveless and unable to stand, because the time for his dose of opium had come, and until the craving was supplied he was no longer a man, but the merest heap of bones and flesh. In the majority of cases death is the sure result of any determined reform. The poison has rotted the whole system, and no power to resist the simplest disease remains. In many years' residence in China the writer knew of but four men who finally abandoned the habit. (Where opium refuges have been conducted by missionaries, reports more favorable have been given concerning those who have become Christians.)

237

Three of them lived but a few months thereafter; the fourth survived his reformation, but was a life-long invalid."[60]

Much good work is now being done by the missionaries, and the number of those who have given up the habit has probably increased since Mr. Holcombe wrote the above. In point of fact, helping opium victims is one of the most important branches of mission work.

---

60    China's Past and Future (p. 165) by Chester Holcombe.

# Fourth Journey: The Mekong Valley to Tengyueh

## CHAPTER XXII

*The Valley of the Shadow of Death. Stages to Tengyueh. The River Mekong, Bridge described. An awful ascent. On-the-spot conclusions. Roads needed more than railways. At Shui-chai. A noisy domestic scene at the place where I fed. Disregard of the value of female life. Remarkable hospitality of the gentry of the city. Hard going. Lodging at a private house on the mountains. Waif of the world entertains the stranger. From Ban-chiao to Yung-ch'ang. Buffaloes and journalistic ignorance. Excited scene at Pu-piao. Chinese barbers. A refractory coolie. Military interest.*

*T*he journey which I was about to undertake was the most memorable of my travels in China, with the exception of those in the unexplored Miao Lands; for I was to pass through the Valley of the Shadow of Death, the dreaded Salwen Valley. I had made up my mind that I would stay here for a night to see the effects of the climate, but postponed my sojourn intead to a later period, when I stayed two days, and went up the low-lying country towards the source of the river; I am, so far as I know, the only European who has ever traveled here. Not that my journeyings will convey any great benefit upon anyone but myself, as I had no instruments for surveying or taking accurate levels, and might not have been able to use them had I had them with me. However, I came in contact with Li-su, and saw in my two marches a good deal of new life, which only acts as an incentive to see more. My plan on the present occasion was to travel onwards by the following stages:—

| | LENGTH OF STAGE | HEIGHT ABOVE SEA LEVEL |
|---|---|---|
| 1st day—Tali-shao | 65 li. | 7,200 ft. |
| 2nd day—Yung-ch'ang-fu | 75 li. | 5,500 ft. |
| 5th day—Fang-ma-ch'ang | 90 li. | 7,300 ft.[61] |
| 6th day—Ta-hao-ti | 120 li. | 8,200 ft. |
| 7th day—Tengyueh (Momien) | 85 li. | 5,370 ft. |

On Friday, February 26th, 1909, I steamed up the muddy mouth of the Mekong to Saigon in Indo-China in a French mail steamer. To-day, February 3rd, 1910, I cross the same river many hundreds of miles from where it empties into the China Sea. I cross by a magnificent suspension bridge.

A cruel road, almost vertical and negotiated by a twining zigzag path, has brought me down, after infinite labor, from the mountains over 4,000 feet below my highest point reached yesterday, and I now stand in the middle of the bridge gazing at the silent green stream flowing between cliffs of wall-like steepness. I am resting, for I have to climb again immediately to over 8,000 feet. This bridge has a wooden base swinging on iron chains, and is connected with the cliffs by bulwarks of solid masonry. It is hard to believe that I am 4,000 feet above the mouth of the river. To my left, as I look down the torrent, there are tea-shops and a temple alongside a most decorative buttress on which the carving is elaborate. At the far end, just before entering the miniature tunnel branching out to a paved roadway leading upwards, my coolies are sitting in truly Asiatic style admiring huge Chinese characters hacked into the side of the natural rock, descriptive of the whole business, and under a sheltering roof are also two age-worn memorial tablets in gilt. My men's patriotic thermometer has risen almost to bursting-point, and in admiring the work of the ancients they feel that they have a legitimate excuse for a long delay.

At a temple called P'ing-p'o-t'ang we drank tea, and prepared ourselves for the worst climb experienced in our long overland tramp.

The Mekong is at this point just 4,000 feet above sea level, as has been said; the point in front of us, running up perpendicularly to a narrow pass in the mountains, leads on to Shui-chai (6,700 feet), and on again to Tali-shao, itself 7,800 feet high, the mountains on which it occupies a ledge being much higher. For slipperiness and general hazards this road baffles description. It leads up step by step, but not regular steps, not even as regularity goes in China.

"There are two small arched bridges in the journey. On the first I sit down and gaze far away down to the shining river below, and must ascend

---

61    The 3rd & 4th days are missing in the original book. —*publishers*

again in the wake of my panting men.... Where the road is not natural rock, it is composed of huge fragments of stone in the rough state, smooth as the face of a mirror, haphazardly placed at such dangerous spots as to show that no idea of building was employed when the road was made. Sometimes one steps twenty inches from one stone to another, and were it not that the pathway is winding, although the turning and twisting makes unending toil, progress in the ascent would be impossible.... Mules are passing me—puffing, panting, perspiring. Poor brutes! One has fallen, and in rolling has dragged another with him, and there the twain lie motionless on those horrid stones while the exhausted muleteers raise their loads to allow them slowly to regain their feet. There are some hundreds of them now on the hill."

This description was made in shorthand notes in my notebook as I ascended. And I find again:—

"I have seen one or two places in Szech'wan like this, but the danger is incomparably less and the road infinitely superior. We pull and pant and puff up, up, up, around each bend, and my men can scarce go forward. Huge pieces of rock have fallen from the cliff, and well-nigh block the way, and just ahead a landslip has carried off part of our course. The road is indescribably difficult because it is so slippery and one can get no foothold. My pony, carrying nothing but the little flesh which bad food has enabled him to keep, has been down on his knees four times, and once he rolled so much that I thought that he must surely go over the ravine.... Rocks overhang me as I pass. If one should drop!... But one does not mind the toil when he looks upon his men. In the midst of their intense labor my men's squeals of songs echo through the mountains as the perspiration runs down their uncovered backs; they chaff each other and utmost good feeling prevails. Poor Shanks is nearly done, but still laughs loudly.... A natural pathway more difficult of progress I cannot conceive anywhere in the world; and yet this is a so-called paved road, the road over which all the trade of the western part of this great province, all the imports from Burma, are regularly carried. Should the road ever be discarded, that is if the railway ever comes over this route, only a long tunnel through the mountain would serve its purpose.... We have just sat down and fraternized with the man carrying the mails to Tali-fu, and now we are working steadily for the top, around corners where the breeze comes with delicious freshness. Here we are on a road now leading through a widening gorge to Shui-chai, and as I cross the narrow pass I see the river down below looking like a snake waiting for its prey."

Roads are needed far more than railways.

Being hungry, we sat down at Shui-chai to feed on rice at a place where a man minded the baby while the woman attended to the food. Over my head hung sausages—my men swore that they were sausages, although for my life I could see no resemblance to that article of food—things of 1 1/2 inches in circumference and from 12 to 60 inches long, doubled up and hung up for sale over a bamboo to dry and harden in the sun. Hams there were, and dried bacon, and dirty brown biscuits, and uninviting pickled cabbage. By the side of the table where I sat was a wooden pun of unwashed rice bowls, against which lay the filthy domestic dog.

Outside, the narrow street was lined to the farthest point of vantage by kindly people, curious to see their own feeding implements in the incapable hands of the barbarian from the Western lands, and the conversation waxed loud and excited in general hazards regarding my presence in their city.

Stenches were rife; they nearly choked one.

A little boy yelled out to his mother in complaint of the food he had been given by a feminine twelve-year-old, his sister. The mother immediately became furious beyond all control. She snatched a bamboo to belabor the girl, and in chasing her knocked over the pun of pots aforesaid. The place became a Bedlam. Men rose from their seats, and with their mouths full of rice expostulated in vainest mediation, waving their chopsticks in the air, and whilst the mother turned upon them in grossest abuse the daughter cleared out at the back of the premises. I left the irate parent brandishing the bamboo; her voice was heard beyond the town.

But I was not allowed to leave the town. All the intellect of the place had assembled in one of the shops, into which I was gently drawn by the coat sleeve by a good-natured, well-dressed humpback, and all of the men assembled began an examination as to who the dignitary was, his honorable age, the number of the wives, sons and daughters he possessed, with inevitable questioning into the concerns of his patriarchal forbears. Accordingly I once again searched the archives of my elastic memory, and there found all information readily accessible, so that in a few moments, by the aid of Bailer's *Primer*, I had explained that I was a stranger within their gates, wafted thither by circumstances extraordinarily auspicious, and had satisfied them concerning my parentage, birthplace, prospects and pursuits, with introspective anecdotal references to various deceased members of my family tree. I did not tell them the truth—that I was a pilgrim from a far country, footsore and travel-soiled, that I had been well-nigh poisoned by their bad cooking and blistered with their bug-bites!

I rose to go. Like automotons, everyone in the company rose with me. The humpback again caught me, this time by both hands, and warmly pressed me to stay and "uan" ("play") a little. "Great Brother," he ejaculated, "why journeyest thou wearisomely towards Yung-ch'ang? Tarry here." And he had pushed me back again into my chair, he had re-filled my teacup, and invited me to tell more tales of antiquarian relationship. And finally I was allowed to go. Greater hospitality could not have been shown me anywhere in the world.

The day had been hard going. We pursued our way unheedingly, as men knowing not whither we went; and at 4:00 p.m., fearing that we should not be able to make Ban-chiao, where we intended stopping, I decided to go no farther than Tali-shao. The evening was one of the happiest I spent in my journeys, although personal comfort was entirely lacking. The place is made up of just a few hovels; people were hostile, and turned a deaf ear to my men's entreaties for shelter. For very helplessness I laughed aloud. I screamed with laughter, and the folk gathered to see me almost in hysterics. They soon began to smile, then to laugh, and seeing the effect, I laughed still louder, and soon had the whole village with tears of laughter making furrows down their unwashed faces, laughing as a pack of hyenas. At last a kind old woman gave way to my boy's persuasions, beckoning us to follow her into a house. Here we found a young girl of about nine summers in charge. It was all rare fun. There was nothing to eat, and so the men went one here and another there buying supplies for the night. Another cleared out the room, and made it a little habitable. The bull-dog coolie cooked the rice, Shanks boiled eggs and cut up the pork into small slices, another fed the pony, and then we fed ourselves.

In the evening a wood fire was kindled in the corner near my bed, and we all sat round on the mud floor—stools there were none—to tell yarns. My confederates were out for a spree. We smoked and drank tea and yarned. Suddenly a stick would be thrust over my shoulder to the fire: it was merely a man's pipe going to the fire for a light. Chinese never use matches; it is a waste when there are so many fires about. If on the road a man wants to light his pipe, he walks into a home and gets it from the fire. No one minds. No notice is taken of the intrusion. Everybody is polite, and the man may not utter a word. At a wayside food-shop a man may go behind to where the cooking is being conducted, poke his pipe into the embers, and walk out pulling at it, all as naturally as if that man were in his own house. An Englishman would have a rough time of it if he had to go down on his hands and knees and pull away at a pipe from a fire on the floor.

No father, no mother, no elder brother had the little girl in charge. She was left without friends entirely, and a man must have been a hard man indeed were he to steel his heart against such a helpless little one. I called her to me, gave her a little present, and comforted her as she cried for the very knowledge that an Englishman would do a kind act to a little waif such as herself. She was in the act of giving back the money to me, when Lao Chang, with pleasant aptitude, interposed, explained that foreigners occasionally develop generous moods, and that she had better stop crying and lock the money away. She did this, but the poor little mite nearly broke her heart.

Ban-chiao, which we reached early the next morning, is a considerable town, where most of the people earn their livelihood at dyeing. Those who do not dye drink tea and pass rude remarks about itinerant magnates, such as the author. I passed over the once fine, rough-planked bridge at the end of the town.

In the evening we are at Yung-ch'ang. Here I saw for the first time in my life a man carrying a *cangue*, and a horrible, sickening feeling seized me as I tramped through the densely-packed street and watched the poor fellow. The mob were evidently clamoring for his death, and were prepared to make sport of his torments. There is nothing more glorious to a brutal populace than the physical agony of a helpless fellow-creature, nothing which produces more mirth than the despair, the pain, the writhing of a miserable, condemned wretch.

Great drops of sweat bathed his brow, and as one, looked on one felt that he might pray that his hot and throbbing blood might rush in merciful full force to a vital center of his brain, so that he might fall into oblivion. The jeers and the mockery of a pitiless multitude seemed too awful, no matter what the man's crime had been.

Yung-ch'ang (5,500 feet) is as well known as any city in Far Western China. I stayed here for two days' rest, the only disturbing element being a wretch of a mother-in-law who made unbearable the life of her son's wife, a girl of about eighteen, who has probably by this time taken opium, if she has been able to get hold of it, and so ended a miserable existence.

On a return visit this mother-in-law, as soon as she caught sight of me, ran to fetch an empty tooth-powder tin, a small black safety pin, and two inches of lead pencil I had left behind me on the previous visit. I have made more than one visit to Yung-ch'ang, and the people have always treated me well.

Along the ten li of level plain from the city, on the road which led up again to the mountains, I counted-no less than 409 bullocks laden with nothing but firewood, and 744 mules and ponies carrying cotton yarn and other general imports coming from Burma. There was a stampede at the foot of the town, and quite against my own will, I assure the reader, I got mixed up in the affair as I stood watching the light and shade effects of the morning sun on the hill-sides. Buffaloes, with a crude hoop collar of wood around their coarse necks, dragged rough-hewn planks along the stone-paved roadway, the timber swerving dangerously from side to side as the heavy animals pursued their painful plodding. To the Chinese the buffalo is the safest of all quadrupeds, if we perhaps except the mule, which, if three legs give way, will save himself on the remaining one. But it is certainly the slowest. I am here reminded that when I was starting on this trip a journalistic friend of mine, who had spent some years in one of the coast ports, tried to dissuade me from coming, and cited the buffalo as the most treacherous animal to be met on the main road in China. He put it in this way:

"Well, old man, you have evidently made up your mind, but I would not take it on at any price. The buffaloes are terrors. They smell you even if they do not see you; they smell you miles off. It may end up by your being chased, and you will probably be gored to death."

The buffalo is the most peaceful animal I know in China. Miniature belfries were attached to the wooden frames on the backs of carrying oxen, and were it not for the huge tenor bell and its gong-like sound keeping the animal in motion, the slow pace would be slower still.

Turning suddenly and abruptly to the left, we commenced a cold journey over the mountains, although the sun was shining brightly. A goitrous man came to me and waxed eloquent about some uncontrollable pig which was dragging him all over the roadway as he vainly tried to get it to market. Some dozen small boys, with hatchets and scythes over their shoulders for the cutting of firewood they were looking for, laughed at me as I ploughed through the mud in my sandals. We had been going for three hours, and when, cold and damp, we got inside a cottage for tea, I found that we had covered only twenty li—so we were told by an old fogey who brushed up the floor with a piece of bamboo. He was dressed in what might have been termed undress, and was most vigorous in his condemnation of foreigners.

Leng-shui-ch'ang we passed at thirty-five li out, and just beyond the aneroid registered 7,000 feet; Yung-ch'ang Plain is 5,500 feet; Pu-piao Plain is 4,500 feet. The range of hills dividing the two plains was bare, the clouds hung low, and the keen wind whistled in our faces and nipped our ears. Ten li from Pu-piao, on a barren upland overlooking the valley, a mere boy had established himself as tea provider for the traveler. A foreign kerosene tin placed on three stones was the general cistern for boiling water, which was dipped out and handed round in a slip of bamboo shaped like a mug with a stick to hold it by. Farther on, sugar-cane grew in a field to the left, and near by a man sat on his haunches on the ground feeding a sugar-grinding machine propelled by a buffalo, who patiently tramped round that small circle all day and every day.

Turning from this, I beheld one of the worst sights I have ever seen in China. Seven dogs were dragging a corpse from a coffin, barely covered with earth, which formed one of the grave mounds which skirt the road. No one was disturbed by the scene; it was not uncommon. But the foreigner suffered an agonizing sickness, for which his companions would have been at a loss to find any possible reason, and was relieved to reach Pu-piao.

Market was at its height. It was warm down here in the valley. The streets were packed with people, many of whom were pushed bodily into the piles of common foreign and native merchandise on sale on either side of the road. A clodhopper of a fellow, jostled by my escort, fell into a stall and broke the huge umbrella which formed a shelter for the vendor and his goods, and my boy was called upon to pay. Fifty cash fixed the matter. I walked into a crowded inn and made majestically for the extreme left-hand corner. Everybody wondered, and softly asked his neighbor what in the sacred name of Confucius had come upon them.

"See his boots! Look at his old hat! What a face! It *is* a monstrosity, and—"

But as I sat down the general of the establishment cruelly forced back the people, and screamingly yelled at the top of his voice that those who wanted to drink tea in the room must pay double rates. His unusual announcement was received with a low grunt of dissatisfaction, but no one left. Every table in the square apartment was soon filled with six or eight men, and the noise was terrific. Curiosity increased. The fun was, as the comic papers say, fast and furious; and despite the ill-favored pleasantries passed by my own men and the inquisitive tea-shop keeper-as to peculiarities of heredity in certain noisy members of the crowd, a riot seemed inevitable. I stationed my two soldiers in the narrow doorway to defend the only entrance and entertain the uninitiated with stories of their prowess with the rifle and of the weapon's deadliness. Boys climbed like monkeys to the overhead beams to get a glimpse of me as I fed, and incidentally shook dust into my food.

Everyone pushed to where there was standing room. Outside a rolling sea of yellow faces surmounted a mass of lively blue cotton, all eager for a look. The din was terrible. All very visibly annoyed were my men at the rudeness of their low-bred fellow countrymen, and especially surprised at the equanimity of Ding Daren in tolerating quietly their pointed and personal remarks. I became more and more the hero of the hour.

Turning to the crowd as I came out, I smiled serenely, and with a quiet wave of the hand pointed out in faultless English that the gulf between my own country and theirs was already wide enough, and that Great Britain might—did not say that she *would*, but might—widen it still more if they persisted in treating her subjects in China as monstrous specimens of the human race. This was rigorously corroborated by my two soldier-men, to whom I appealed, and a parting word on the ordinary politeness of Western nations to a greasy fellow (he was a worker in brass), who felt my clothes with his dirty fingers, ended an interesting break in the day's monotony. In the street the crowd again was at my heels, and evinced more than comfortable curiosity in my straw sandals. They cost me thirty cash, equal to about a halfpenny in our coinage.

Since then I have paid other visits to Pu-piao. On one occasion in subsequent travel I had a public shave there. My arrival at the inn in the nick of time enabled me to buttonhole the barber who was picking up his traps to clear, and I had one of the best shaves I have ever had in my life, in one of the most uncomfortable positions I ever remember. My seat was a low, narrow form with no back or anything for my neck to rest upon, and afterwards I went through the primitive and painful massage process of being bumped all over the back. Between every four or five whacks the barber snapped his fingers and clapped his hands, and right glad was I when he had finished. The yard was full, even to the stable and cook-house alongside each other, the anger of a grizzly old dame, who smoked a reeking pipe and who had charge of the rice-and-cabbage depot, being eclipsed only by my infuriated barber as he gave cruel vent to his anger upon my aching back.

This reminds me of an uncomfortable shave I had some ten years ago in Trinidad, where a black man sat me on the trunk of a tree whilst he got behind and rested my head on one knee and got to work with an implement which might have made a decent putty knife, but was never meant to cut whiskers. However, in the case of the Chinese his knife was in fair condition, but he grunted a good deal over my four-days' growth.

This little story should not convey the impression that I am an advocate of the public shave in China, or anywhere else; but there are times when one is glad of it. I have been shaved by Chinese in many places; and whilst resident at Yuen-nan-fu with a broken arm a man came regularly to me, his shave sometimes being delightful, and—sometimes not.

I had another rather amusing experience at Pu-piao about a month after this. A supplementary coolie had been engaged for me at Tengyueh at a somewhat bigger wage than my other men were getting, and this, known, of course, to them, added to the fact that he was not carrying the heaviest load, did not tend to produce unmarred brotherhood among them. The man had been told that he would go on to Tali-fu with me on my return trip, so that when I took the part of my men (who had come many hundreds of miles with me, and who had engaged another man on the route to fill the gap), in desiring to get rid of him, he certainly had some right on his side. The day before we reached Yung-ch'ang he was told that at that place he would not be required any longer; but he decided then and there to go no farther, and refused point-blank to carry when we were ready to start. I should have recompensed him fully, however, for his disappointment had he not made some detestable reference to my mother, in what Lao Chang assured me was not strictly parliamentary language. As soon as I learnt this—I was standing near the fellow—he somehow fell over, sprawling to the floor over my walnut folding chair, which snapped at the arm. It was my doing. The man said no more, picked up his loads, and was the first to arrive at Yung-ch'ang, so that a little force was not ineffective.

Indiscriminate use of force I do not advocate, however; I believe in the reverse, as a matter of fact. I rarely hit a man; but there have been occasions when, a man having refused to do what he has engaged to do, or in cases of downright insolence, a little push or a slight cut with my stick has brought about a capital feeling and gained for me immediate respect.

Fang-ma-ch'ang, off the main road, was our sleeping-place. Travelers rarely take this road. Gill took it, I believe, but Baber, Davies and other took the main road. This short road was more fatiguing than the main road would have been.

We again turned a dwelling-house upside down. People did not at first wish to take me in, so I pushed past the quarrelsome man in the doorway, took possession, and set to work to get what I wanted. Soon the people calmed down and gave all they could. My bed I spread near the door, and to catch a glimpse of me as I lay resting, the inhabitants, in much the same manner as people at home visit and revisit the cage of jungle-bred tigers at a menagerie, assembled and reassembled with considerable confusion. But I was beneath my curtains. So they came again, and when I ate my food by candlelight many human and tangible products of the past glared in at the doorway. After dark we all foregathered in the middle of the room and round the camp fire, the conversation taking a pleasant turn from ordinary things, such as the varying distances from place to place, how many basins of rice each man could eat, and other Chinese commonplaces, to things military. Everybody warmed to the subject. My military bodyguard were the chief speakers, and cleverly brought round the smoky fire, for the benefit of the thick-headed rustics who made up the fascinated audience, a modern battlefield, and made their description horrible enough.

One carefully brought out his gun, waving it overhead to add to the tragedy, as he weaved a powerful story of shell splinters, blood-filled trenches, common shot, men and horses out of which all life and virtue had been blown by gunpowder. The picture was drawn around the Chinese village, and in the dim glimmer each man's thought ran swiftly to his own homestead and the green fields and the hedgerows and dwellings all blown to atoms—left merely as a place of skulls. They spoke of great and horrible implements of modern warfare, invented, to their minds, by the devilry of the West. Each man chipped in with a little color, and the company broke up in fear of dreaming of the things of which they had heard, afraid to go to their straw to sleep.

As I lay in my draughty corner, my own mind turned to what the next day would bring, for I was to go down to the Valley of the Shadow of Death—the dreaded Salwen. I had read of it as a veritable death-trap.

# CHAPTER XXIII

*To Lu-chiang-pa. Drop from 8,000 feet to 2,000 feet. Shans meet for the first time. Dangers of the Salwen Valley exaggerated. How reports get into print. Start of the climb from 2,000 feet to over 8,000 feet. Scenery in the valley. Queer quintet of soldiers. Semi-tropical temperature. My men fall to the ground exhausted. A fatiguing day. Benighted in the forest. Spend the night in a hut. Strong drink as it affects the Chinese. Embarrassing attentions of a kindly couple. New Year festivities at Kan-lan-chai. The Shweli River and watershed. Magnificent range of mountains. Arrival at Tengyueh.*

No Chinese, I knew, lived in the Valley; but I had yet to learn that so soon as the country drops to say less than 4,000 feet the Chinese consider it too unhealthy a spot for him to pass his days in. The reason why Shans control the Valley is, therefore, not hard to find.

And owing to the probability that what European travelers have written about the unhealthiness of this Salwen Valley has been based on information obtained from Chinese, its bad name may be easily accounted for. The next morning, as I descended, I saw much malarial mist rising; but, after having on a subsequent visit spent two days and two nights at the lowest point, I am in a position to say that conditions have been very much exaggerated, and that places quite as unhealthy are to be found between Lu-chiang-pa (the town at the foot, by the bridge) and the low-lying Shan States leading on to Burma.

A good deal of the country to the north of the Yuen-nan province, towards the Tibetan border, is so high-lying and so cold that the Yuen-nanese Chinese is afraid to live there; and the fact that in the Shan States, so low-lying and sultry, he is so readily liable to fever, prevents him from living there. These places, through reports coming from the Chinese, are, as a matter of course, dubbed as unhealthy. The average inhabitant—that is, Chinese—strikes a medium between 4,000 feet and 10,000 feet to live in, and avoids going into lower country between March and November if he can.

To pass the valley and go to Kan-lan-chi (4,800 feet), passing the highest point at nearly 9,000 feet—140 li distant from Fang-ma-ch'ang—was our ambition for the day.

Starting in the early morning, I had a pleasant walk over an even road leading to a narrowing gorge, through which a heart-breaking road led to the valley beyond. Two and a half hours it took me, in my foreign boots, to cover the twenty li. I fell five times over the smooth stones. The country was bare, desolate, lonely—four people only were met over the entire distance. But in the dreaded Valley several trees were ablaze with blossom, and oranges shone like small balls of gold in the rising sun. Children playing in between the trees ran away and hid as they saw me, although I was fifty yards from them—they did not know what it was, and they had never seen one!

Farther down I caught up my men, Lao Chang and Shanks, and pleasant speculations were entered into as to what Singai (Bhamo) was like. They were particularly interested in Singapore because I had lived there, and after I had given them a general description of the place, and explained how the Chinese had gone ahead there, I pointed out as well as I could with my limited vocabulary that if the people of Yuen-nan only had a conscience, and would only get out of the rut of the ages, they, too, might go ahead, explaining incidentally to them that as lights of the church at Tong-ch'uan-fu, it was their sacred duty to raise the standard of moral living among their countrymen wherever they might wander. Their general acquiescence was astounding, and in the next town, Lu-chiang-pa, these two men put their theory into practice and almost caused a riot by offering 250 cash for a fowl for which the vendor blandly asked 1,000. But they got the chicken—and at their own price, too.

As I was thus gently in soliloquy, I first heard and then caught sight of the river below—the unnavigable Salwen, 2,000 feet lower than either the Mekong or the Shweli (which we were to cross two days later). It is a pity the Salwen was not preserved as the boundary between Burma and China.

Gradually, as we approached the steep stone steps leading down there-to, I saw one of the cleverest pieces of native engineering in Asia—the double suspension bridge which here spans the Salwen, the only one I had seen in my trip across the Empire. The first span, some 240 feet by 36 feet, reaches from the natural rock, down which a vertical path zigzags to the foot, and the second span then runs over to the busy little town of Lu-chiang-pa.

Here, then, were we in the most dreaded spot in Western China! If you stay a night in this Valley, rumor says, you go to bed for the last time; Chinese are afraid of it, Europeans dare not linger in it. Malaria stalks abroad for her victims, and snatches everyone who dallies in his journey to the topside mountain village of Feng-shui-ling. The river is 2,000 feet above the sea; Feng-shui-ling is nearly 9,000 feet.

It was ten o'clock as I pulled over my stool and took tea in the crowded shop at Lu-chiang-pa. I saw Shans here for the first time.

The village now, however, is anything but a Shan village. Of the people in the immediate vicinity I counted only ten typical Shans, and of the company around me in this popular tea-house twenty-one out of twenty-eight were Chinese, including ten Mohammedans. It was, however, easy to see that several of these were of Shan extraction, who, although they had features distinctly un-Chinese, had adopted the Chinese language and custom. A party of Tibetans were here in the charge of a Lama, in an inner court, and scampered off as I rose to snap their photographs.[62] This was a very low altitude for Tibetans to reach.

Whilst I sipped my tea the local horse dealer wanted so very much to sell me a pony cheap. He offered it for forty taels, I offered him five. It was gone in the back, was blind in the left eye, and was at least seventeen years old. The man smiled as I refused to buy, and told me that my knowledge of horse-flesh was wonderful.

The road then led up to a plain, where paths branched in many directions to the hills. Men either going to the market or coming from it leaned on their loads to rest under enormous banyans and to watch me as I passed. Horses browsed on the hill-sides. One of my soldiers had laid in provisions for the day, and ran along with his gun (muzzle forward) over one shoulder and four lengths of sugar-cane over the other. Ploughmen with their buffaloes halted in the muddy fields to gaze admiringly upon me; women ran scared from the path when my pony let out at a casual passer-by who tickled him with a thin bamboo. Maidenhair ferns grew

---

62    The photographs were included in the original hardcover edition of the book but are not included in this edition —publisher

in great profusion, showing that we were getting into warmer climate; streams rushed swiftly under the stone roadway from dyked-up dams to facilitate the irrigation, at which the Chinese are such past-masters. All was smiling and warm and bright, dispelling in one's mind all sense of gloom, and breeding an optimistic outlook.

We were now a party of nine—my own three men, an extra coolie I had engaged to rush Tengyueh in three days from Yung-ch'ang, four soldiers, and the paymaster of the crowd. We still had ninety li to cover, so that when we left the shade of two immense trees which sheltered me and my perspiring men, one of the soldiers agreed that everyone had to clear from our path. We brooked no interception until we reached the entrance to the climb, where I met two Europeans, of the Customs staff at Tengyueh, who had come down here to camp out for the Chinese New Year Holiday. I knew that these men were not Englishmen. I was so thirsty, and the best they could do was to keep a man talking in the sun outside their well-equipped tent. How I *could* have done with a drink!

A tributary of the Salwen flows down the ravine. Too terrible a climb to the top was it for me to take notes. I got too tired. Everything was magnificently green, and Nature's reproduction seemed to be going on whilst one gazed upon her. But the natural glories of this beautiful gorge, with a dainty touch of the tropical mingling with the mighty aspect of jungle forest, with glistening cascades and rippling streams, where all was bountiful and exquisitely beautiful, failed to hold one spellbound. For since I had left Tali-fu I had rarely been out of sight of some of the best scenery on earth. Yet vegetation was very different to that which we had been passing. There were now banyans, palms, plantains, and many ferns, trees and shrubs and other products of warmer climates, which one found in Burma. What impressed me farther up was the marvelous growth of bamboos, some rising 120 feet and 130 feet at the bend, in their various tints of green looking like delicate feathers against the haze of the sky-line, upon which houses built of bamboo from floor to roof seemed temporarily perched whilst others seemed to be tumbling down into the valley. This spot was the nearest approach to real jungle I had seen in China; but Whilst we were climbing laboriously through this densely-covered country, over opposite—it seemed no more than a stone's throw—the hills were almost bare, save for the isolated cultivation of the peasantry at the base. But then came a division, appearing suddenly to view farther along around a bend, and I saw a continuation of the range, rising even higher, and with a tree growth even more magnificent, denser and darker still.

Here I came upon a party of soldiers with foreign military peak caps on their heads, which they wore outside over their Chinese caps. In fact, the only two other garments besides these Chinese caps were the distinguishing marks of the military. Coats they had, but they had been discarded at the foot of the climb, rolled into one bundle, and tied together with a piece of ribbon generally worn by the carrier to keep his trousers tight. We were now in summer heat, and this military quintet made a peculiar sight in dusty trousers, peak caps and straw sandals, with the perspiration streaming freely down their naked backs as they plodded upwards under a pitiless sun. Thus were they clad when I met them; but catching sight of my distinguished person, mistaking me for a "gwan," they immediately made a rush for the man carrying the tunics, to clothe themselves for my presence with seemly respectability. But a word from my boy put their minds at rest (my own military were far in the rear). A couple of them then came forward to me sniggeringly, satisfied that they were not to be reported to Peking or wherever their commander-in-chief may have his residence—they probably had no more idea than I had.

By the side of a roaring waterfall, in a spot which looked a very fairyland in surroundings of reproductive green, we all sat down to rest. The air was cool and the path was damp, and water tumbling everywhere down from the rocks formed pretty cascades and rivulets. We heard the clang of the hatchets, and soon came upon men felling timber and sawing up trees into coffin boards. We were in the Valley of the Shadow, and it was the finest coffin center of the district. I took my boots off to wade through water which overran the pathway, and just beyond my men, exhausted with their awful toil, lay flat on their backs to rest; they were dead beat. One pointed up to the perpendicular cliff, momentarily closed his eyes and looked at me in disgust. I gently remonstrated. It was not my country, I told him; it was the "Emperor's." And after a time we reached the top.

Shadows were lengthening. In the distance we saw the mountains upon which we had spent the previous night, whose tops were gilded by the setting sun. Down below all was already dark. A cold wind blew the trees bending wearily towards the Valley.

And still we plodded on.

We had come to Siao-p'ing-ho, 115 li instead of the 140 I had been led to believe my men would cover. Every room in the hut was full, we were told, but the next place (with some unpronounceable name), fifteen li farther down, would give us good housing for the night. Lao Chang and I resolved to go on, tired though we were. Before I resolved on this plan I stopped to take a careful survey of the exact situation of the sheltering hollow in which we meant to pass the night. The sun was fast sinking; the dust of the road lay grey and thick about my feet; above me the heavens were reddening in sunset glory; the landscape had no touch of human life about it save our own two solitary figures; and the place, fifteen li away, lay before me as a dream of a good night rather than a reality.

Then on again we plodded, and yelled our intentions to the men behind.

From the brow of the hill we descended with extreme rapidity—down, down into a valley which sent up a damp, oppressive atmosphere. Through the trees I could see one lovely ball of deep, rich red, painting the earth as it sank in a beauty exquisite beyond all else. Four men met us, stared suspiciously, thought we were deaf, and yelled that the place was twenty li away, and that we had better return to the brow of the hill. But we left them, and went still farther down. In the hush that prevailed I was unaccountably startled to see the form of a woman gliding towards me in the twilight. She came out of the valley carrying firewood. She spoke kindly to my man, and invited me to spend the night in her house near by.

I was for the moment vaguely awed by her very quiescence, and gazed wondering, doubting, bewildered. What was the little trick? Could I not from such things get free, even in Inland China? The red light of the sunken sun playing round her comely figure dazzled me, it is admitted, and I followed her with a sigh of mingled dread and desire for rest. Shall I say the shadow of the smile upon her lips deepened and softened with an infinite compassion?

Dogs rounded upon me as I entered the bamboo hut stuck on the side of the hill—they knew I had no right there. Inside a man was nursing a squalling baby; our escort was its mother, the man her husband. So I was safe. The place was swept up, unnecessary gear was taken away, fire was kindled, tea was brewed, rice was prepared; and whilst in shaving (for we were to reach Tengyueh on the morrow) I dodged here and there to escape the smoke and get the most light, giving my hospitable host a good deal of fun in so doing; every possible preparation was made for my comfort and convenience by the untiring woman at whose invitation I was there. Their attentions embarrassed me; every movement, every look, every gesture, every wish was anticipated, so that I had no more discomfort than a roaring wind and a low temperature about the region which no one could help. It was bitterly cold. In front of the fire I sat in an overcoat among the crowd drinking tea, whilst the soldiers drank wine—they bought five cash worth. Had my lamp oil run out, I should have bought liquor and tried to burn it instead. Soon the spirit began to talk, and these braves of the Chinese army got on terms of freest familiarity, telling me what an all-round excellent fellow I was, and how pleased they were that I had to suffer as well as they. But they never forgot themselves, and I allowed them to wander on uncontradicted and unrestrained. After a weary night of tossing in my p'ukai, with a roaring gale blowing through the latticed bamboo, behind which I lay so poorly sheltered, we started in good spirits.

Twenty-five li farther we reached Kan-lan-chai (4,800 feet), February 9th, 1910, New Year's morning. Nothing could be bought. Everywhere the people said, "Puh mai, puh mai," and although we had traveled the twenty-five li over a terrible road, with a fearful gradient at the end, we could not get anyone to make tea for us. It is distinctly against the Chinese custom to sell anything at New Year time, of course. We had to boil our own water and make our own tea. A larger crowd than usual gathered around me because of the general holiday; and as I write now I am seated in my folding-chair with all the reprobates near to me—men gazing emptily, women who have rushed from their houses combing their hair and nursing their babies, the beggars with their poles and bowls, numberless urchins, all open-mouthed and curious. These are kept from crowding over me by the two soldiers, who the day before had come on ahead to book rooms in the place. I stayed at Kan-lan-chai on another occasion. Then I found a good room, but later learned that it was a horse inn, the yard of which was taken up by fifty-nine pack animals with their loads. Pegs were as usual driven into the ground in parallel rows, a pair of ponies being tied to each—not by the head, but by the feet, a nine-inch length of rope being attached to the off foreleg of one and the near foreleg of the other, the animals facing each other in rows, and eating from a common supply in the center. Everyone in the small town was busy doing and driving, very anxious that I should be made comfortable, which might have been the case but for some untiring musician who was traveling with the caravan, and seemed to be one of that species of humankind who never sleeps. His notes, however, were fairly in harmony, but when it runs on to 3:00 a.m., and one knows that he has to be again on the move by five, even first-rate Chinese music is apt to be somewhat disturbing.

From the Salwen-Shweli watershed I got a fine view of the mountains I had crossed yesterday. Some ten miles or so to the north was the highest peak in the range—Kao-li-kung I think it is called—conical-shaped and clear against the sky, and some 13,000 feet high, so far as I could judge.

An easy stage brought me to Tengyueh. I stayed here a day only, Mr. Embery, of the China Inland Mission, a countryman of my own, kindly putting me up. But Tengyueh, as one of the quartet of open ports in the province, is well known. It is only a small town, however, and one was surprised to find it as conservative a town as could be found anywhere in the province, despite the fact that foreigners have been here for many years, and at the present time there are no less than seven Europeans here.

I was glad of a rest here. From Tali-fu had been most fatiguing.

# CHAPTER XXIV

## *The Li-Su Tribe of The Salwen Valley*

*Travel up the Salwen Valley. My motive for travelling and how I travel. Valley not a death-trap. Meet the Li-su. Buddhistic beliefs. Late Mr. G. Litton as a traveler. Resemblance in religion to Kachins. Ghost of ancestral spirits. Li-su graves. Description of the people. Racial differences. John the Baptist's hardship. The cross-bow and author's previous experience. Plans for subsequent travel fall through. Mission work among the Li-su.*

*O*n my return journey into Yuen-nan, I stopped at Lu-chiang-pa,[63] and left my men at the inn there while I traveled for two days along the Salwen Valley. My journey was taken with no other motive than that of seeing the country, and also to test the accuracy of the reports respecting the general unhealthy nature of this valley of the Shadow of Death. The people here were friendly, despite the fact that my route was always far away from the main road; and although my entire kit was a single traveling-rug for the nights, I was able to get all I wanted. Lao Chang accompanied me, and together we had an excellent time.

I might as well say first of all that the idea of this part of the Salwen Valley being what people say it is in the matter of a death-trap is absolutely false. With the exception of the early morning mist common in every low-lying region in hot countries, there was, so far as I could see, nothing to fear.

---

63    The town by the double suspension bridge over the Salwen.

During the second day, through beautiful country in beautiful weather, I came across some people who I presumed were Li-su, and I regretted that my films had all been exposed. The Li-su tribe is undoubtedly an offshoot from the people who inhabit south-eastern Tibet, although none of them anywhere in Yuen-nan—and they are found in many places in central and eastern Yuen-nan—bear any traces of Buddhistic belief, which is universal, of course, in Tibet. The late Mr. G. Litton, who at the time he was acting as British Consul at Tengyueh traveled somewhat extensively among them, says that their religious practices closely resemble those of the Kachins, who believe in numerous "nats" or spirits which cause various calamities, such as failure of crops and physical ailments, unless propitiated in a suitable manner. According to him, the most important spirit is the ancestral ghost. Li-su graves are generally in the fields near the villages, and over them is put the cross-bow, rice-bags and other articles used by the deceased. "It is probably from foundations such as these," writes Mr. George Forrest, who accompanied Mr. Litton on an excursion to the Upper Salwen, and who wrote up the journey after the death of his companion, "that the fabric of Chinese ancestor worship was constructed," a view which I doubt very much indeed.

I am of the opinion that the Li-su may be closely allied to the Lolo or the Nou Su, of whom I have spoken in the chapters in Book I dealing with the tribes around Chao-t'ong. And even the Miao bear a distinct racial resemblance. They are of bony physique, high cheek bones, and their skin is nearly of the same almost sepia color. The Li-su form practically the whole of the population of the Upper Salwen Valley from about lat. 25 deg. 30' to 27 deg. 30', and they have spread in considerable numbers along the mountains between the Shweli and the Irawadi, and are found also in the Shan States. Those on the Upper Salwen in the extreme north are utter savages, but where they have become more or less civilized have shown themselves to be an enterprising race in the way of emigration. Of the savages, the villages are almost always at war with one another, and many have never been farther from their huts than a day's march will take them, the chief object of their lives being apparently to keep their neighbors at a distance. They are exceedingly lazy. They spend their lives doing as little in the way of work as they must, eating, drinking, squatting about round the hearth telling stories of their valor with the cross-bow, and their excitement is provided by an occasional expedition to get wood for their cross-bows and poison for their arrows, or a stock of salt and wild honey.

Mr. Forrest, in his paper which was read before the Royal Geographical Society in June, 1908, speaks of this wild honey as an agreeable sweetmeat as a change, but that after a few days' constant partaking of it the European palate rejects it as nauseous and almost disgusting, and adds that it has escaped the Biblical commentators that one of the principal hardships which John the Baptist must have undergone was his diet of wild honey. In another part of his paper the writer says, speaking of the cross-bow to which I have referred: "Every Li-su with any pretensions to *chic* possesses at least one of these weapons—one for everyday use in hunting, the other for war. The children play with miniature cross-bows. The men never leave their huts for any purpose without their cross-bows, when they go to sleep the 'na-kung' is hung over their heads, and when they die it is hung over their graves. The largest cross-bows have a span of fully five feet, and require a pull of thirty-five pounds to string them. The bow is made of a species of wild mulberry, of great toughness and flexibility. The stock, some four feet long in the war-bows, is usually of wild plum wood, the string is of plaited hemp, and the trigger of bone. The arrow, of sixteen to eighteen inches, is of split bamboo, about four times the thickness of an ordinary knitting needle, hardened and pointed. The actual point is bare for a quarter to one-third of an inch, then for fully an inch the arrow is stripped to half its thickness, and on this portion the poison is placed. The poison used is invariably a decoction expressed from the tubers of a species of *aconitum*, which grows on those ranges at an altitude of 8,000 to 10,000 feet ... The reduction in thickness of the arrow where the poison is placed causes the point to break off in the body of anyone whom it strikes, and as each carries enough poison to kill a cart horse a wound is invariably fatal. Free and immediate incision is the usual remedy when wounded on a limb or fleshy part of the body."[64]

Some time after I was traveling in these regions I made arrangements to visit the mission station of the China Inland Mission, some days from Yuen-nan-fu, where a special work has recently been formed among the Li-su tribe. Owing to a later arrival at the capital than I had expected, however, I could not keep my appointment, and as there were reports of trouble in that area the British Consul-General did not wish me to travel off the main road. It is highly encouraging to learn that a magnificent missionary work is being done among the Li-su, all the more gratifying because of the enormous difficulties which have already been overcome by the pioneering workers. At least one European, if not more, has mastered the language, and the China Inland Mission are expecting great things to eventuate. It is only by long and continued residence among these peoples, throwing in one's lot with them and living their life, that any absolutely reliable data regarding them will be forthcoming. And this so few, of course, are able to do.

---

64    The poisoned arrows and the cross-bow are used also by the Miao, and the author has seen very much the same thing among the Sakai of the Malay Peninsula.

# Fifth Journey: Tengyueh (Momien) to Bhamo in Upper Burma

## Chapter XXV

*Last stages of long journey. Characteristics of the country. Shan and Kachins. Author's dream of civilization. British pride. End of paved roads. Mountains cease. A confession of foiled plans. Nantien as a questionable fort. About the Shans. Village squabble, and how it ended. Absence of disagreement in Shan language. Charming people, but lazy. Experience with Shan servant. At Chiu-Ch'eng. New Year festivities. After-dinner diversions. Author as a medico. Ingratitude of the Chinese: some instances.*

The Shan, the Kachin and the abominable betel quid! That quid which makes the mouth look bloody, broadens the lips, lays bare and blackens the teeth, and makes the women hideous. Such are the unfailing characteristics of the country upon which we are now entering.

By the following stages I worked my way wearily to the end of my long walking journey:—

|  | LENGTH OF STAGE | HEIGHT ABOVE SEA LEVEL |
|---|---|---|
| 1st day—Nantien | 90 li. | 5,300 ft. |
| 2nd day—Chiu-Ch'eng (Kang-gnai) | 80 li. | —- |
| 4th day—Hsiao Singai | 60 li. | —- [65] |
| 5th day—Manyueen | 60 li. | 2,750 ft. |
| 6th day—Pa-chiao-chai } | Approx. | 1,200 ft. |
| 7th day—Mao-tsao-ti } | 55 English | 650 ft. |
| 8th day—Bhamo (Singai) } | Miles. | 350 ft. |

---

65   The 3rd day is missing in the original book. —*publishers*

Shans here monopolize all things. Chinese, although of late years drawn to this low-lying area, do not abound in these parts, and the Shan is therefore left pretty much to himself. And the pleasant eight-day march from Tengyueh to Bhamo, the metropolis of Upper Burma, probably offers to the traveler objects and scenes of more varying interest than any other stage of the tramp from far-away Chung-king. To the Englishman, daily getting nearer to the end of his long, wearying walk, and going for the first time into Upper Burma, incidentally to realize again the dream of civilization and comfort and contact with his own kind, leaving Old China in the rear, there instinctively came that inexpressible patriotic pride every Britisher must feel when he emerges from the Middle Kingdom and sets his foot again on British territory. The benefits are too numerous to cite; you must have come through China, and have had for companionship only your own unsympathetic coolies, and accommodation only such as the Chinese wayside hostelry has offered, to be able fully to realize what the luxurious dak-bungalows, with their excellent appointments, mean to the returning exile.

Paved roads, the bane of man and beast, end a little out of Tengyueh. Mountains are left behind. There is no need now for struggle and constant physical exertion in climbing to get over the country. With no hills to climb, no stones to cut my feet or slip upon, with wide sweeps of magnificent country leading three days later into dense, tropical jungle, entrancing to the merest tyro of a nature student, and with the knowledge that my walking was almost at an end, all would have gone well had I been able to tear from my mind the fact that at this juncture I should have to make to the reader a great confession of foiled plans. For two days I was accompanied by the Rev. W.J. Embery, of the China Inland Mission, who was making an itinerary among the tribes on the opposite side of the Taping, which we followed most of the time. He rode a mule; and am I not justified in believing that you, too, reader, with such an excellent companion, one who had such a perfect command of the language, and who could make the journey so much more interesting, you would have ridden your pony? I rode mine! I abandoned pedestrianism and rode to Chiu-Ch'eng—two full days, and when, after a pleasant rest under a sheltering banyan, we went our different ways, I was sorry indeed to have to fall back upon my men for companionship.

But it was not to be for long.

Nantien is, or was, to be a fort, but the little place bears no outward military evidences whatever which would lead one to believe it. It is populated chiefly by Shans. The bulk of these interesting people now live split up into a great number of semi-independent states, some tributary to Burma, some to China, and some to Siam; and yet the man-in-the-street knows little about them. One cannot mistake them, especially the women, with their peculiar Mongolian features and sallow complexions and characteristic head-dress. The men are less distinguishable, probably, generally speaking, but the rough cotton turban instead of the round cap with the knob on the top alone enables one more readily to pick them out from the Chinese. Short, well-built and strongly made, the women strike one particularly as being a hardy, healthy set of people.

Shans are recognized to be a peaceful people, but a village squabble outside Chin-ch'eng, in which I took part, is one of the exceptions to prove the rule.

It did not take the eye of a hawk or the ear of a pointer to recognize that a big row was in full progress. Shan women roundly abused the men, and Shan men, standing afar off, abused their women. A few Chinese who looked on had a few words to say to these "Pai Yi"[66] on the futility of these everyday squabbles, whilst a few Shans, mistaking me again for a foreign official, came vigorously to me pouring out their souls over the whole affair. We were all visibly at cross purposes. I chimed in with my infallible "Puh tong, you stupid ass, puh tong" (I don't understand, I don't understand); and what with the noise of the disputants, the Chinese bystanders, my own men (they were all acutely disgusted with every Shan in the district, and plainly showed it, because they could not be understood in speech) and myself all talking at once, and the dogs who mistook me for a beggar, and tried to get at close grips with me for being one of that fraternity, it was a veritable Bedlam and Tower of Babel in awfullest combination. At length I raised my hand, mounted a boulder in the middle of the road, and endeavored to pacify the infuriated mob. I shouted harshly, I brandished by bamboo in the air, I gesticulated, I whacked two men who came near me. At last they stopped, expecting me to speak. Only a look of stupidest unintelligibility could I return, however, and had to roar with laughter at the very foolishness of my position up on that stone. Soon the multitude calmed down and laughed, too. I yelled "Ts'eo," and we proceeded, leaving the Shans again at peace with all the world.

Shans have been found in many other parts, even as far north as the borders of Tibet. But a Shan, owing to the similarity of his language in all parts of Asia, differs from the Chinese or the Yuen-nan tribesman in that he can get on anywhere. It is said that from the sources of the Irawadi down to the borders of Siamese territory, and from Assam to Tonkin, a region measuring six hundred miles each way, and including the whole of the for-

---

66    The Chinese name for the Shan.

mer Nan-chao Empire, the language is practically the same. Dialects exist
as they do in every country in the world, but a Shan born anywhere within
these bounds will find himself able to carry on a conversation in parts of the
country he has never heard of, hundreds of miles from his own home. And
this is more than six hundred years after the fall of the Nan-chao dynasty,
and among Shans who have had no real political or commercial relation
with each other.[67]

I found them a charming people, peaceful and obliging, treating strangers with kindness and frank cordiality. For the most part, they are Buddhists. The dress of the Chinese Shans, which, however, I found varied
in different localities, leads one to believe that they are an exceptionally
clean race, but I can testify that this is not the case. In many ways they are
dirtier than the Chinese—notably in the preparation of their food. And I
feel compelled to say a word here for the general benefit of future travelers.
*Never expect a Shan to work hard!* He *can* work hard, and he will—when he
likes, but I do not believe that even the Malay, that Nature's gentleman of
the farther south, is lazier.

As servants they are failures. A European in this district, whose Chinese
servant had left him, thought he would try a Shan, and invited a man to
come. "Be your servant? Of course I will. I am honored." And the European thought at last he was in clover. He explained that he should want his
breakfast at 6:00 a.m., and that the servant's duties would be to cut grass
for the horse, go to the market to buy provisions, feed on the premises, and
leave for home to sleep at 7:00 p.m. The Shan opened a large mouth; then
he spoke. He would be pleased, he said, to come to work about nine o'clock;
that he had several marriageable daughters still on his hands and could not
therefore, and would not, cut grass; he objected going to the market in the
extreme heat of the day; he could not think of eating the foreigner's food;
and would go home to feed at 1:00 p.m. and leave again finally at 5:00 p.m.
for the same purpose. He left before five p.m. Another man was called in.
He was quite cheery, and came in and out and did what he pleased. On being asked what he would require as salary, he replied, "Oh, give me a rupee
every market day, and that'll do me." The person was not in service when
market day rolled round, and I hear that this European, who loves experi-
ments of this kind, has gone back to the Chinese.

Chiu-Ch'eng (Kang-gnai) was going through a sort of New Year ca-
rousal as I entered the town, and everybody was garmented for the festival.

---

67　Vide Yuen-nan, the Link between India and the Yangtze, by Major H.R. Davies.—Cambridge University Press.

I had great difficulty in getting a place to stay. People allowed me to career about in search of a room, treating me with courteous indifference, but none offered to house me. At last the headman of the village appeared, and with many kindly expressions of unintelligibility led me to his house. A crowd had gathered in the street, and several women were taking from the front room the general stock-in-trade of the village ironmonger. Scores of huge iron cooking pans were being passed through the window, tables were pushed noisily through the doorway, primitive cooking appliances were being hurled about in the air, bamboo baskets came out by the dozen, and there was much else. Bags of paddy, old chairs (the low stool of the Shan, with a thirty-inch back), drawers of copper cash, brooms, a few old spears, pots of pork fat, barrels of wine (the same as I had blistered the foot of a pony with), two or three old p'u-kai, worn-out clothes, disused ladies' shoes, babies' gear, and last of all the man himself appeared. Men and women set to to clean up, an old woman clasped me to her bosom, and I was bidden to enter. New Year festivities were for the nonce neglected for the novel delight of gazing upon the inner domesticity of this traveling wonder, into his very holy of holies. I received nine invitations to dinner. I dined with mine host and his six sons.

Through the heavy evening murk a dull clangor stirred the air—the tolling of shrill bells and the beating of dull gongs, and all the hideous paraphernalia of Eastern celebrations. The populace—Shan almost to a man—were bent on seeing me, a task rendered difficult by the gathering darkness of night. Soldiers guarded the way, and there were several broken heads. They came, stared and wondered, and then passed away for others to come in shoals, laughingly, and seeming no longer to harbor the hostile feelings apparent as I entered the town.

My shaving magnifier amused them wonderfully.

There was an outcry as I entered the room after we had dined, followed by a scream of women in almost hysterical laughter. When they caught sight of me, however, a brief pause ensued, and the solemn hush, that even in a callous crowd invariably attends the actual presence of a long-awaited personage, reigned unbroken for a while; then one spoke, then another ventured to address me, and the spell of silence gave way to noise and general excitability, and the people began speedily to close upon me, anxious to get a glimpse of such a peculiar white man. Later on, when the shutters were up and the public thus kept off, the family foregathered unasked into my room, bringing with them their own tea and nuts, and laying themselves out to be entertained. My whole gear, now reduced to most meager proportions, was scrutinized by all. There were four men and five women, the usual offshoots, and the aged couple who held proprietary rights over the place. They sat on my bed, on my boxes; one of the children sat on my knee, and the ladies, seemingly of the easiest virtue, overhauled my bedclothes unblushingly. The murmuring noise of the vast expectant New Year multitude died off gradually, like the retreating surge of a distant sea, and the hot motionless atmosphere in my room, with eleven people stepping on one another's toes in the cramped area, became more and more weightily intensified. The husband of one of the women—a miserable, emaciated specimen for a Shan—came forward, asking whether I could cure his disease. I fear he will never be cured. His arm and one side of his body was one mass of sores. Before it could be seen four layers of Chinese paper had to be removed, one huge plantain leaf, and a thick layer of black stuff resembling tar. I was busy for some thirty minutes dressing it with new bandages. I then gave him ointment for subsequent dressings, whereupon he put on his coat and walked out of the room (leaving the door open as he went) without even a word of gratitude.

The Chinese pride themselves upon their gratitude. It is vigorous towards the dead and perhaps towards the emperor (although this may be doubted), but as a grace of daily life it is almost absent. I have known cases where missionaries have got up in the middle of the night to attend to poisoning cases and accidents requiring urgent treatment, have known them to attend to people at great distances from their own homes and make them better; but never a word of thanks—not even the mere pittance charged for the actual cost of medicine.

# CHAPTER XXVI

*Two days from Burma. Tropical wildness induces ennui. The River Taping. At Hsiao Singai. Possibility of West China as a holiday resort from Burma. Fascination of the country. Manyueen reached with difficulty. The Kachins. Good work of the American Baptist Mission. Mr. Roberts. Arrival at borderland of Burma. Last dealings with Chinese officials. British territory. Thoughts on the trend of progress in China. Beautiful Burma. End of long journey.*

*I* was now two days' march from the British Burma border. The landscape in this district was solemn and imposing as I trudged on again, very tired indeed, after a day's rest at Chiu-ch'eng. In the morning heavy tropical vapors of milky whiteness stretched over the sky and the earth. Nature seemed sleeping, as if wrapped in a light veil. It attracted me and absorbed me, dreaming, in spite of myself; ennui invaded me at first, and under the all-powerful constraint of influences so fatal to human personality thought died away by degrees like a flame in a vacuum; for I was again in the East, the real, luxurious, indolent East, the true land of Pantheism, and one must go there to realize the indefinable sensations which almost make the Nirvana of the Buddhist comprehensible.

The river Taping farther down, so different from its aspect a couple of days ago, where it rushed at a tremendous speed over its rocky bed, was now broad and calm and placid, and extremely picturesque. The banks were covered with trees beyond Manyueen. Near the water the undergrowth was of a fine green, but on a higher level the yellow and red leaves, hardly holding on to the withered trees, were carried away with the slightest breath of wind.

At Hsiao Singai, on February 15th, I again had difficulty in getting a room; so I waited, and whilst my men searched about for a place where I could sleep, an extremely tall fellow came up to me, and having felt with his finger and thumb the texture of my tweeds and expressed satisfaction thereof, said—

"Come, elder brother, I have my dwelling in this hostelry, and my upper chamber is at your disposal." And then he added with a twinkle in his eye, "Ko nien, ko nien,"[68] whereat I became wary.

Lao Chang, however, was more cute. Whilst I was assuring this well-dressed holiday-maker that he must not think the stranger churlish in not accepting at once the proffered services, but that I would go to look at the room, he sprang past us and went on ahead. In a few moments I was slowly going hence with the multitude. Lao Chang nodded carelessly to the strange company there assembled, and passing through the room with a soft, cat-like tread, began to ascend a dark flight of narrow stairs leading to the second floor of the inn. And I, down below startled and bewildered by mysterious words from everyone, watched his blue garments vanishing upwards, and like a man driven by irresistible necessity, muttered incoherent excuses to my amazed companions, and in a blind, unreasoning, unconquerable impulse rushed after him. But I wish I had not. There were several ladies, who, all more or less *en deshabille*, scampered around with their bundles of gear—sewing, babies' clothes, tin pots, hair ornaments, boxes of powder and scented soap of that finest quality imported from Burma, selling for less than you can buy the genuine article for in London!—and then we took possession.

If once there is a railway to Tengyueh from Burma, a visit to West China, even on to Tali-fu, for those who are prepared to rough it a little, will become quite a common trip. A few days up the Irawadi to Bhamo, through scenery of a peculiar kind of beauty eclipsed on none other of the world's great rivers, would be succeeded by a day or two over some of the best country which Upper Burma anywhere affords, and then, when once past Tengyueh, the grandeur of the mountains is amply compensating to those who love Nature in her beautiful isolation and peace. From a recuperating standpoint, perhaps, it would not quite answer—the rains would be a drawback to road travel, and it would at best mean roughing it; but for the many in Burma who wish to take a holiday and have not the time to go to Europe, I see no reason why Tengyueh should not develop into what Darjeeling is to Calcutta and what Japan is to the British ports farther East. Expense would not be heavy. To

---

68    i.e. New Year, New Year.

Bhamo would be easy. As things now stand, with no railway, one would need to take a few provisions and cooking utensils, and a camp bed and tent, unless one would be prepared to do as the author did, and patronize Chinese inns, such as they are. The rest would be easy to get on the road. For three days from Bhamo dak bungalows are available, and to a man knowing the country it would be an easy matter to arrange his comforts. To one who knows the conditions, there is in the trip a good deal to fascinate; for in the lives and customs of the people, in the nature of the country, in the free-and-easy life the traveler would himself develop—having a peep at things as they were back in the ancient days of the Bible—to the brain-fagged professional or commercial there is nothing better in the whole of the East.

He would get some excellent shooting, especially in the Salwen Valley, not exactly a health resort, however; and had he inclinations towards botanical, ethnological, craniological, or philological studies, he would be at a loss to find anywhere in the world a more interesting area.

But a man should never leave the "ta lu" (the main road) in China if he would experience the minimum of discomfort and annoyance, which under best conditions is considerable to an irritable man. As I sit down now, on the very spot where Margary, of the British Consulate Service was murdered in 1875, I regret that I have sacrificed a great deal to secure most of the photographs[69] which decorate this section of my book. No one, not even my military escort, knows the way, and is being sworn at by my men therefor. How I am to reach Man Hsien, across the river at Taping, I do not quite know. Manyueen, so interesting in history, is a native Shan-Kachino-Chinese town untouched by the years—slovenly, dirty, undisciplined, immoral, where law and order and civilization have gained at best but a precarious foothold, the most characteristic feature of the people being the gambler's instinct. But I remember that I am coming into Burma, into the real East, where the tangle and the topsy-turvydom, the crooked vision and the distorted travesty of the truth, which result from judging the Oriental from the standpoint of the Europeans and looking at the East through the eyes of the West, impress themselves upon one's mind in bewildering fashion as a hopeless problem. Everything is all at cross purposes.

However, although I lost my way from Manyueen to Man Hsien, I got my photographs of Kachins, those people whose appearance is that they have no one to care for them body or soul. Their thick, uncombed locks, so long and lank as to resemble deck swabs, overlapped roofwise the ugliest aboriginal

---

69    The photographs were included in the original hardcover edition of the book but are not included in this edition —publisher

faces I ever saw in Asia or America, and their eyes under shaggy brows looked out with diabolical fire.

So much information is to be obtained from the *Upper Burma Gazetteer* about the Kachins that it is needless for me to write much here, especially as I can add nothing. But I feel I should like to say just a word of praise of the remarkable work of the American Baptist Mission, which has its headquarters at Bhamo, among this tribe in Burma. At the time I arrived in the city the annual festival was being conducted at the Baptist Church, and hundreds of Kachins were assembled in the splendid premises of this mission. They had come from many miles around; and to one who at previous times in his residence in the Far East had written disparagingly about missionaries and their work, there came some little personal shame as he looked upon the extremely creditable work of the American missionaries in this district. Kachins are a somewhat uncivilized and quarrelsome race, unspeakably immoral, and steeped in every vice against which the Christian missionary has to set his face—a most difficult people to work among. But there I saw scores and scores of baptized Christians living a life clean and ennobling, endeavoring honestly to break away from their degrading customs of centuries, some of them exceedingly intelligent people.

I speak of this because I feel that in the face of untruthful and malicious descriptions which in former years have got into print respecting this very mission and the very missionaries on this field, it is only fair that people in the homeland interested in the work should know what their American brethren are doing here. I cannot praise too highly this mission and the enthusiastic band of workers whom it was my pleasure to meet. In Mr. Roberts, the superintendent of the field, the American Baptist Board have a man of wonderful resource, who is not only an ardent Christian evangelist and capable administrator, but a gentleman of considerable business ability and a remarkable organizer. A writer who, passing through in 1894, was indebted to Mr. Roberts for many kindnesses, found that the only adverse criticism he could make of the missionary was in respect to his knowledge of horses. My experience is that in the whole of the Far East there can be found no more capable pioneer missionary, and his friends in America should pray that Mr. Roberts may be spared many years still to control the work on the successful mission field in which he has spent so much of his labor of love for the Kachins.

Kachins form the bulk of the population in the extreme north of Burma. To the west they extend to Assam, and to the south into the Shan States, as far even as latitude 20 deg. 30'. By far the largest proportion of them live in

Burmese territory, but they also extend into Western Yuen-nan, though no-where are they found farther east than longitude 99 deg..

Man Hsien is the last yamen place before reaching the British border. I crossed the river Taping from Manyueen, being shown the road by a Bur-mese member of the Buddhistic yellow cloth, who was most pressing that I should stay with him for a few days. Again did I get a fright that my manu-script would never get into print, for my pony, Rusty, probably cognizant of the fact that he, too, was finishing his long tramp, nearly stamped the bottom of the boat out, and threatened to send us down by river past Bhamo quicker than our arrival was scheduled.

The large official paper given to one's military escort from point to point was here produced for the last time, and great ado was made about me. Read-ing this document aloud from the top of the steps, when he came to my name the mandarin bowed very low, called me Ding Daren[70] (a sign of highest respect), asked if I would exchange cards, and then lapsed unconsciously into profuse congratulation to myself that I should have been born an English-man. So far as he knew, I could be assured that the existing relations be-tween the administrative bodies of his contemptible country and my own royal land were of a nature so felicitously mutual and peaceful—in fact, both Governments saw eye to eye in regard to international affairs in Far Western China—that he felt sure that I should arrive at the bridge leading into Burma without personal harm. He then, with a colossal bow to myself and a gentle wave of his three-inch finger-nail, handed me over with pungent emphasis of speech to the keeping of a Chinese and a Shan, who with a keen sense of favors to come were to form my escort to Burma's border.

A low grunt of unrestrained approval came from the multitude. The un-derlings—Chino-Kachino-Burmo-Shan people—who ran about in a little of each of the clothing characteristic of the four said races, were all busy in their endeavors to extricate from me a few cash apiece by doing all and more than was necessary.

Then the great man rose. He condescended to depart. He passed from the threshold, turned, paused, bowed, turned again, went down the steps, bowed again—a long curving bow, which nearly sent him to the ground—and then continued with a light heart towards that loveliest land of the East. My men exhibited no emotion. That they were coming into British territory was of no concern to them; they had come from far away in the interior, and were the greenest of the green, the rawest of the raw.

But soon I passed over a small bridge, a spot where two great empires meet. I was in Burma.

---

70    i.e. Great Man. "Ding" is my Chinese name.

So I have crossed from one end of China to the other. I entered China on March 4th, 1909; I came out on February 14th, 1910.

I had come to see how far the modern spirit had penetrated into the hidden recesses of the Chinese Empire. One may be little given to philosophizing, and possess but scanty skill in putting into words the conclusions which form themselves in one's mind, but it is impossible to cross China entirely unobservant. One must begin, no matter how dimly, to perceive something of the causes which are at work. By the incoming of the European to inland China a transformation is being wrought, not the natural growth of a gradual evolution, itself the result of propulsion from within, but produced, on the contrary, by artificial means, in bitter conflict with inherent instincts, inherited traditions, innate tendencies, characteristics, and genius, racial and individual. In the eyes of the Chinese of the old school these changes in the habit of life infinitely old are improving nothing and ruining much—all is empty, vapid, useless to God and man. The tawdry shell, the valueless husk, of ancient Chinese life is here still, remains untouched in many places, as will have been seen in previous chapters; but the soul within is steadily and surely, if slowly, undergoing a process of final atrophy. But yet the proper opening-up of the country by internal reform and not by external pressure has as yet hardly commenced in immense areas of the Empire far removed from the imperial city of Peking. And the mere fact that the Chinese propose such an absurd program as that which plans the building of all their railways without the aid of foreign capital is sufficient to react in an unwholesome manner economically.[71] [72]

I cannot but admit that, whilst in most parts of my journey there are distinct traces of reform—I speak, of course, of the outlying parts of China—and some very striking traces, too, and a real longing on the part of far-seeing officials to escape from a humiliating international position, it is distinctly apparent that in everything which concerns Europe and the Western world the people and the officials as a whole are of one mind in the methods of procrastination which are so dear to the heart of the Celestial, and that peculiar opposition to Europeanism which has marked the real East since the beginning of modern history.

---

[71]    I believe personally that the main object of the Yuen-nan provincial government in employing two American engineers, who at the present moment (August, 1910) are surveying a route from Yuen-nan-fu to the Yangtze, is merely official bluff. It is preferable to pay two men a monthly stipend if the official "face" can be preserved and the Chinese dogged official procrastination be maintained, rather than to allow foreigners to come in still farther.

[72]    This was of course written long before the Four Nations Loan was signed, and Tuan Fang appointed Director General of the Railways in May, 1911. We should now see a speedy reformation of Railway matters in China if Tuan is given an absolutely free hand.— E.J.D.

And now lovely, lovely Burma!

I had not been in Burma two minutes before the very box containing the clothes into which I must change before I could enter into the social life of Bhamo swung from the broken pole of one of my coolies, and rolled rapidly towards the river. It was recovered after great trouble.

Thick jungle land lay out before me, fleecy clouds in the dense blue sky hung lazily over the green hills, the heavy air was pregnant with that delicious ease known only in the tropics—all was still and sweet. The river flowed grandly from the interior through magnificent forest country, receiving on either shore the frequent tribute of other minor streams, and its banks were marvelous cliffs of jungle—tangles of giant trees on crowding underwood, clinging vine and festooning parasite—rising sheer from the water's brink. Now long clusters of villages, deep in the shade of palm and fruit trees; now wide expanses of grass-grown meadow, where the grazing grounds dip to the river, and where the only echoes of China are the resting pack-horse caravans—the banks cut into huge trampled clefts by the passage of the kine trooping down to drink. Occasional wooded islands broke the monotony of the river, and were just discernible from the magnificent English roads which skirted the hills high up from the river, and yellow sandspits and big wedges of granite and rock ran far out into its uneven course. By day the joyous Burma sun smiled upon all, and at midday poured its merciless heat down upon all mankind, unheeding the weary wanderer whose tramp was now near done. At night the tropical moon turned all this riverine world to the likeness of a very fairyland. Lying in a long chair in the dak bungalows one drank in the scenes which succeeded one another in bewildering succession, and felt himself thrilled by an almost fierce appreciation of eastern beauty. It was good to meet again an Englishman, a sturdy, firm-featured Englishman, whose love of the East, like mine own, was a veritable obsession. The sun glare of the tropics had parched the color out of our white skin, and despite the fact that malaria came back again here to taunt me, yet I was again in the East that I loved, that had scarred and marked me ere my time mayhap. And yet I, with many such of my own countrymen, despite her rough handling, worship her.

In three days I was in Bhamo.

www.ingramcontent.com/pod-product-compliance
Lightning Source LLC
LaVergne TN
LVHW022340080426
835508LV00012BA/1287